Nika Standen Hazelton

The Continental Flavour

Illustrations by Juliet Renny

Penguin Books

Penguin Books Ltd, Harmondsworth,
Middlesex, England
Penguin Books Australia Ltd, Ringwood,
Victoria, Australia

First published by Doubleday 1961
Published in Penguin Handbooks 1969
Copyright © Nika Standen Hazelton, 1961

Made and printed in Great Britain by
Hazell Watson & Viney Ltd
Aylesbury, Bucks
Set in Intertype Juliana

For Jill Norman, with love

Contents

Introduction

The recipes in this book were chosen because, to my mind and that of the people I've cooked for, they are excellent eating as well as representative of their countries of origin.

They are the best of continental cooking, whether they stem from the *haute cuisine*, family, restaurant, or peasant kitchens, or from the ingenuity of one cook. Some of the recipes are easy, some are inexpensive, and others are neither. All assume a certain amount of cooking knowledge on the part of the cook. They aim for reasonable elegance, which is not synonymous with fussiness.

The recipes in this book are for the home cook and the home kitchen. There are many great dishes which simply cannot be made at home because they involve complicated ingredients and special skills, and have to be made in larger quantities than those needed at home.

All the dishes in this book are correctly seasoned and should need no more ingredients than specified. But taste is a personal affair, and the most correctly cooked dish is pointless if it does not meet your taste. You may dislike the taste of one herb or of one liqueur; in this case, substitute for the offender one you like better. Cooking is for eating, and for eating with pleasure.

Cooking is also a chemical process – some of it, such as baking, more so than others. In all of the recipes I have tried to give the most accurate amounts of ingredients. But ingredients may vary amazingly as to size, weight, and moisture content. How big is an egg or an onion, how juicy a lemon? In case of doubt, start with less rather than more, and let your nose, eyes, and taste be your guide.

The Continental Flavour makes no claim to all-inclusiveness. It is not a guidebook to the various national cuisines, but rather an anthology, and an anthology of lesser known dishes. Apart from attempting to describe each dish as well as I could for cooks who might not be familiar with it, I have tried to keep things simple. Kitchen utensils, for instance – it is really quite surprising how few you need to turn out a first-class meal.

Finally, I have done my best to keep away from the mystique which seems to surround so much cooking nowadays. Much high-flown twaddle is written about herbs, wines, gourmets, epicures, and the like, when some of the best cooks who ever lived were and are quite illiterate and unsophisticated.

There is no mystery to food. It should be delicious wherever possible, but not a fetish. We eat to live, and there are other pleasures in life besides eating. But well-prepared food is one of the greatest, and one within the reach of anybody who can read and who cares enough to take a little trouble to do things well.

A cookbook like this one, which is not a standard cookbook or an all-inclusive one, reflects of necessity the taste of the author. Food tastes, like other tastes, are very definite, and it is possible, and indeed probable, that I have not included many dishes that are favourites of some people who will pick up this book. To these readers I apologize, asking for their leniency. I can only para-phrase Montaigne's remark: 'I have gathered a posie of other men's flowers and nothing but the thread that binds them is my own', by saying that I have gathered a 'posie' of other countries' recipes, and nothing but the taste that chose them is my own, in the hope that the food that gives me pleasure will also please others.

NIKA STANDEN HAZELTON

British Editor's Note

As far as possible British weights in pounds and ounces have been substituted in every recipe. These equivalents are accurate enough to cook from.

A few recipes may need some adapting – a little more flour to thicken, or a few drops of liquid to dilute to the right consistency, or a seasoning is increased or decreased to suit personal taste. Adapting in this way makes no difference to most dishes, but it is likely to affect baking. It may therefore be necessary to do a little experimenting to achieve perfect results from the cake and biscuit recipes.

JILLIAN NORMAN

Metric Measures

One pint=approximately ½ litre
One oz.=approximately 28 grammes
One lb.=16 oz.=approximately 450 grammes

Oven Temperatures

	electricity	gas
very slow	250°–275°	½–1
slow	300°–325°	2–3
moderate	350°–375°	4–5
hot	400°–425°	6–7
very hot	450°–475°	8–9
extremely hot	475°–525°	9–10

Hors-d'Œuvres, Appetizers, and Salads

It may seem odd to lump these three categories together, but these dishes can and do overlap in usage. A salad may be served in lieu of other vegetables, or it may be served as an hors-d'œuvre. And where does the appetizer end and the hors-d'œuvre begin, or vice versa?

I, for one, have never been able to arrive at a clear-cut solution but, generally speaking, I would say that appetizers are goodies that are eaten standing up, whereas hors-d'œuvres are eaten at the table, as the beginning of a meal. The Latins follow this latter practice, the Scandinavians and Russians the former – again, very generally speaking.

Russian appetizers are called *zakuski*, and in old Russia a table holding sometimes as many as a hundred varieties was set up in a room next to the dining-room. The galaxy of hot and cold dishes of caviar, fish, eggs, salads, pâtés, vegetables, aspics, and small savoury pies was washed down with vodka in before-dinner sessions that often went on for hours.

At their more elaborate dinners the ancient Romans served *gustatio* (hors-d'œuvres), which consisted of raw and cooked vegetables, salt fish, oysters, pickles, and snails cooked in different ways. With *gustatio* they drank *mulsum*, a wine sweetened with honey. There were as many opinions about how to make *mulsum* as there are about martinis.

Escoffier and the classic French cuisine reserve hors-d'œuvres for luncheon and soup for dinner, though oysters or caviar may take the place of soup.

Thus the choice of how to start a dinner rests squarely with the hostess. She must observe one rule only – that the appetizers or hors-d'œuvres, wherever served, be light and teasing to the palate, and never filling.

To come back to salads. Vegetables lend themselves admirably to salads in raw or cooked form. Cauliflower, broccoli, string beans, carrots, artichokes make excellent salads (and hors-d'œuvres). If they are cooked, the dressing should go on while the vegetables are still hot, so that it can be properly absorbed.

Neither hors-d'œuvres nor salads should be served pell-mell, but should be kept neat and orderly in separate dishes, from which each person is served or helps himself. However simple, they should tempt the palate, and look like a still life.

The number of excellent hors-d'œuvres, appetizers, and salads is legion. Therefore I demand the reader's pardon if I have failed to include his own favourites, for lack of space.

French Hors-d'Œuvres
[Hors-d'Œuvre Variés]

In France hors-d'œuvres are always eaten at lunch, and few are the families that do not serve one or two kinds, choosing from meat, fish, and vegetables served as salads. In France as in Italy, every town has a *charcuterie* which makes delicious sausages of many kinds, pâtés, brawn, galantines, and other foods of the kind; these are bought in small quantities fresh for each meal.

French hors-d'œuvres are strictly for eating at table. They are served either in individual dishes, called *raviers*, or in a single dish with a number of divisions to hold the separate varieties.

French Tuna [*Thon*]

Chop together the contents of 1 can of tuna (drained of oil) and 2 hard-boiled eggs. Blend together with 2 tablespoons (1 oz.) soft butter and 1 teaspoon chopped or dried herbs (parsley, chives, and tarragon). Shape into a small pyramid. Cover with a thin layer of mayonnaise and decorate with capers and parsley sprigs.

Radishes [*Radis*]

The French always serve radishes with butter, a very pleasant habit. The radishes are washed and cut into roses. They are placed on a silver or glass dish. Butter curls are served separately. The butter is spread on the radishes – the way butter is spread on bread.

Celeriac Salad [*Céleri-rave vinaigrette*]

Peel the celeriac and cut into julienne strips. Do not use woody core. Cover with boiling water and cook for 1 minute. Drain, and rinse with cold water. Cover with Sauce Vinaigrette (page 254) with mustard. Chill. Serve with a sprinkle of chopped parsley.

Mussels Rémoulade [*Moules rémoulade*]

One of the more popular hors-d'œuvres.

Allow 4 to 6 mussels for each serving. Clean mussels by brushing them with a stiff brush under running cold water. Place in large saucepan. For each quart of mussels, add 2 sprigs parsley, a pinch of thyme, 1 bay leaf, a few peppercorns, and ½ glass dry white wine. Cover and cook over medium heat 8 minutes. Drain. Force half-open shells open. Remove hairy beard from mussels but keep mussels in shells. Chill. Before serving, cover with Sauce Rémoulade (page 255).

French Eggs in Aspic [*Œufs en gelée*]

This is an extremely popular hors-d'œuvre in France, where it is served by itself. The proper eggs to use are cooked *au mollet* – that is, semi-soft and still runny – and the French take great pride in producing a perfect *œuf mollet*, which must be carefully timed. However, if the cooking time given below is too short for your taste, simply cook the eggs longer or use hard-boiled eggs.

The following recipe is the classic one, as it appears in thousands of French restaurants and homes almost daily. *Œufs en gelée* also make a good luncheon or buffet dish.

6 eggs	2 tablespoons Madeira or port
1 tablespoon gelatine soaked in	6 thin ham slices
2 fl. oz. cold water	Fresh tarragon leaves or tiny
12 fl. oz. clear chicken consommé	parsley sprigs

Boil eggs for 6 minutes and cool under running water. Shell eggs very carefully, since they are still soft. Heat chicken consommé, add gelatine soaked in water, and stir until gelatine is completely dissolved. Add Madeira or port. Cool aspic but do not jell.

Use small moulds, ramekins, or cups that are just large enough to hold 1 egg each and 1 slice of ham. Trim ham the size of the top of the moulds. Pour about ¼-inch deep layer of aspic into each mould. Chill aspic until almost but not quite firm. Place two crossed leaves of tarragon or a tiny sprig of parsley on aspic. Gently place an egg in each mould. Spoon aspic over eggs until mould is almost filled. Cover each egg with a slice of ham. Spoon a little more aspic over ham. Chill eggs until aspic is set. Dip moulds for one *short instant* in hot water and unmould on a bed of lettuce. Decorate with slices of tomato topped with 3 capers.

French Anchovy Eggs with Garlic
[*Œufs aux anchois et à l'ail*]

A sight familiar to the patron of inexpensive French restaurants is a half of a hard-boiled egg decorated with two crossed fillets of anchovies and reposing on a leaf of lettuce.

Here is a more interesting way of making this simple hors-d'œuvre, which combines anchovies and garlic, both so beloved by the French of Provence.

2 cloves garlic	1 teaspoon wine vinegar
4 anchovy fillets, drained	Salt
8 capers	Pepper
3 tablespoons olive oil	6 hard-boiled eggs

Chop and crush garlic. Add anchovies and capers, and mash with a fork into a smooth paste. Blend in oil, vinegar, and salt and pepper to taste. Peel hard-boiled eggs and cut into quarters. Cover with the sauce. Serve on lettuce leaves and decorate with parsley.

Italian Hors-d'Œuvres Plate
[Antipasti Variati]

On a large platter, arrange attractively the foods below, grouping them around a small glass dish containing butter curls.

Thin salami slices

Finger-length slices of thin prosciutto or ham slices, which have been fastened with a toothpick

Anchovy fillets, drained of oil (the rolled kind is best)

Sardines, drained of oil

Tuna fish, drained

Artichoke hearts in oil or vinegar, drained

Black and pimento-stuffed olives

Strips of red and green peppers, marinated in oil and drained

Pickled red peppers

Crisp spring onions

Halves of stuffed eggs

Stalks of white celery

The Italians are also very partial to all sorts of pickled antipasti, which are bought in Italian delicatessen stores or – in cans or jars with Italian labels – in supermarkets. They are seldom, if ever, made at home. Here are a few suggestions:

Pickled cauliflower in jars (cavolfiore marinato)

Pickled garbanzos or chick-peas (ceci)

Small mustard pickles (cetriolini alla senape)

A formal antipasto also calls for various meats in aspic, sliced thin. These are almost invariably bought in the salumeria. In every Italian city there are several salumerie that have risen to fame on their cold dishes, which they display in artistic tableaux, worthy of the brush of a Bellini or Tintoretto. The citizens flock from all over town to buy them, and it is common to see substantial businessmen on their way home, a flat parcel of delicatessen dangling from one finger. The Italians say that you can see at once whether or not a man is married. The bachelor carries flowers or bonbons, the spouse a parcel of antipasti or cakes.

Caponata Alla Siciliana

There is no English word for this pickled vegetable concoction, and it is sold in cans or jars under this name or its diminutive – *caponatina*. Since it is one of the best, it is worth making it up at home and storing it either in sterilized jars or in the refrigerator.

4 medium-size aubergines	12 black olives, pitted and
12 fl. oz. olive oil	coarsely chopped
4 onions, sliced	1 tablespoon pine nuts (optional)
1 14-oz. tin Italian tomatoes,	8 tablespoons wine vinegar
forced through a sieve	2 oz. sugar
4 stalks celery, diced	½ teaspoon salt
4 tablespoons capers	½ teaspoon pepper
1–1½ oz. chopped parsley	

Peel and dice the aubergines. Heat two thirds of the olive oil and fry the aubergine in it until it is soft and brown. Remove aubergine, add remaining oil, and sauté onions in it. Add tomatoes and celery and cook until celery is tender. To prevent scorching, add a little water, if necessary. Add capers, parsley, olives, pine nuts, and fried aubergine. Heat vinegar in small saucepan. Dissolve sugar in vinegar and pour over aubergine mixture. Add salt and pepper and simmer gently over very low heat for about 20 minutes. Stir frequently. Cool before serving.

Melons or Figs with Ham
[*Melone o fichi con prosciutto*]

The only fruits Italians admit as hors-d'œuvres are melons or fresh figs, served with prosciutto. Though this dish can be served with English ham, it is worth while to use Italian ham, which is saltier and therefore presents a better contrast to the sweetness of the melon or fig. This is a knife-and-fork dish.

1 medium-sized melon	½ lb. prosciutto, thinly sliced
(honeydew, cantaloupe,	Freshly ground black pepper
Persian, or Cranshaw)	

Peel melon and cut in small wedges (about 2 for each serving). Wrap each wedge in prosciutto. Serve with pepper.

Or use 2 ripe figs for each serving. Cut figs open diagonally to form 4 petals. Arrange prosciutto slices on the side of the open figs.

English Appetizers or Savouries

Savouries are usually hot, and made from fish, cheese, eggs and other well-seasoned ingredients, served on toast, in most cases. They are served at the end of a dinner, after the dessert, ostensibly to clear the palate for the port and other choice spirits that are partaken of by the gentlemen of the party, after the lady of the house has taken the female guests to the drawing-room. The savoury habit goes back to the eighteenth century, when the 'sweets' consisted of well-boiled or baked puddings that could only be called most substantial. The savoury is still served, in a touching manner, in the dim hotels of Victorian London, where it might be a lone sardine, and also in the posh restaurants, where it can be a wonderful morsel indeed.

Savouries also make excellent cocktail appetizers. The ones that follow here are among the best known.

Toasted Prunes in Bacon

This sounds strange but is rather good.

Large prunes   Bacon
Salted almonds

Soak prunes in cold water until soft. Remove the stones. Fill each prune with a salted almond. Roll each prune in a slice of lean bacon and secure with toothpick. Grill or bake in hot (425° F., gas 7) oven until bacon is crisp. Serve hot.

Note: The almonds may be omitted, but they do add a nice touch.

Madras Anchovy Toast

Anchovies, either whole, minced, or as a paste or sauce, are a most popular ingredient of savoury appetizers. This recipe goes back to 1860, and it is ideal for a chafing dish.

2 tablespoons (1 oz.) butter	1 tablespoon dry sherry or beer
2 egg yolks	Cayenne pepper
2 teaspoons anchovy paste or sauce	Hot toast fingers

Melt butter in a double boiler or in a chafing dish. Add egg yolks and beat well with a fork. Add sherry or beer, anchovy, and cayenne pepper to taste and mix thoroughly. Serve hot as a dip or spread on hot toast fingers.

Devilled Almonds

| Almonds | Salt |
| Butter or salad oil | Cayenne pepper |

Pour boiling water over almonds. Let stand for a few minutes. Pinch off brown skins. Dry almonds on clean kitchen towel. Heat a little butter or oil in skillet – there should be just enough to keep the almonds from burning. Fry almonds golden brown, stirring constantly. Drain on absorbent paper and, while hot, sprinkle with salt and cayenne pepper. Serve very hot, in heated wooden bowls.

Angels on Horseback

Bacon
Fresh or canned oysters or clams, shelled

Trim the rind from thin slices of lean bacon. Wrap an oyster or clam in each slice of bacon. Secure with a toothpick or thread several on a skewer. Grill or bake in a hot (425° F., gas 7) oven until bacon is crisp. Serve as it is or remove toothpick or skewer and serve on a round of hot toast.

Scandinavian Hors-d'Œuvres

In Swedish they're called smörgåsbord, in Danish smørrebrød, in Norwegian koldt bord, and in Finnish voileipäpöptä – all appetizers, sandwiches, aspics, salads, and hot dishes with which the Nordics begin their meals.

The origin of this spread, which has become symbolic of Scandinavian cooking, is said to go back to the days when guests used to bring food contributions for their host's table. These contributions were laid out on one long table, for the guests to help themselves. Nowadays, except for special occasions, a family will have no more than four or five dishes. There is fish, such as herring, salmon, eel, and shrimp, pickled or smoked, in aspic or au gratin or in one or other of the many ways the Scandinavians cook their fish; a liver pâté; an egg or macaroni dish; small meatballs or sausages; pickled beets; and a cheese. The accompaniment is akvavit, a clear, potent spirit which is sometimes flavoured with caraway and which is served iced in small glasses and should be tossed down in one swallow.

Since the number of excellent smorgasbord dishes (to use the most familiar name) is almost legion, and since there are many excellent Scandinavian cookbooks which list them for the home cook who wants to specialize in these Nordic delights, I have limited myself to the dishes that have been favourites in my house.

Smorgasbord is heavy on preserved fish, dating undoubtedly from the times when refrigeration was unknown and all fish had to be pickled in some way to keep it edible. Excellent pickled herring, sprats, eels, and whitefish, with many different sauces, are sold in Scandinavian shops, delicatessens, and supermarkets throughout the United States, so that it is unnecessary to prepare these fish at home. It is socially perfectly acceptable, for those who may be concerned, to open the cans or jars, remove the covers, and place them on trays with caviar and other fish specialities.

Whatever the components of one's own smorgasbord, it is well to remember that the Scandinavians excel at presenting their foods in a handsome manner. Each dish is attractively laid out and presented with a garnish of hard-boiled eggs, sliced, quartered, or sieved, with sprigs of dill, the favourite herb of Scandinavia, sprigs of parsley, onion rings, and ornaments carved from beetroot. There is no reason why we can't do the same.

Here is a specific suggestion for Swedish – and generally Scandinavian – smorgasbord, as it might be served to guests in one's home:

Pickled herring
Smoked eel
Sardines
Omelet with creamed mushrooms
Meatballs

Sliced tongue
Cucumber salad
Radishes
Cheese

Herring Salad [Sillisalaatti]

This is a Finnish version of a combination salad of fish, vegetables, and meat which is extremely popular in Scandinavia, Holland, and northern Germany. It should be tart in taste and contain red beets. This salad is said to have great restorative effects on the morning after.

1 salt herring
2–3 medium beets, cooked and diced
1–2 medium potatoes, cooked and diced
2 carrots, cooked and diced

5–6 oz. diced leftover cold meat or fowl
2 dill pickles, thinly sliced
2 tart apples, unpeeled and diced
2 hard-boiled eggs, chopped
Pepper

Soak herring in cold water to remove excess salt; change water frequently. (Herring varies in saltiness, so it is impossible to give soaking time.) Drain; cut off head and tail. Skin and bone the herring. Cut into small pieces and combine with all other ingredients. Chill thoroughly. Serve piled high on a bed of lettuce. Before serving, mix with the following dressing:

DRESSING
6 oz. double cream
1 tablespoon sugar
2 tablespoons wine vinegar

1 teaspoon dry mustard
Salt

Whip cream, not too stiffly. Blend in other ingredients and mix thoroughly. Add salt to taste.

Pickled Oysters (all Scandinavian countries)

1 pint oysters
4 fl. oz. oyster liquid
½ medium-sized onion, thinly sliced
4 tablespoons wine vinegar
Salt

1 bay leaf
⅛ teaspoon allspice
3 whole peppercorns
⅛ teaspoon mustard
½ lemon, sliced thin

tied in a muslin bag

Heat oysters in their own liquid until the edges curl. Drain and
set aside. Add other ingredients to oyster liquid and bring to the
boil. Pour over oysters. Chill for several hours. Remove the muslin
bag. Serve oysters in their liquid in a small glass dish.

Anchovies and Potatoes (Jansson's Temptation)
[*Janssons frestelse*]

This is an immensely popular Swedish dish which is served not
only as an hors-d'œuvre but also for late suppers. Every cook has
her own version of this specific Temptation, which is really a
very good potato pudding affair, pepped up by the anchovies. As
for the unknown Jansson, it is left to the individual imagination
to speculate about the consequences of his fall.

6 medium-sized potatoes, peeled	1¾ pints single cream
12 anchovies, drained	Butter
1 onion, finely chopped	Crumbs
Pepper	

Cut potatoes into paper-thin slices. Cut the anchovies into pieces.
Put alternate layers of potato slices and anchovies into a buttered
and crumbed baking dish – the top layer should be potatoes.
Sprinkle each layer with onion and a little pepper. Pour cream
over mixture and bake in moderate (375° F., gas 5) oven until
potatoes are done and the top is delicately browned. About 10
smorgasbord servings or 4 to 6 ordinary servings.

Danish Open Sandwiches

Open sandwiches are typical of Denmark, and there are literally
hundreds of them in the Danish restaurants which specialize in
them. Indeed, these sandwiches can be superb creations, piled
high with almost every flesh, fish, and fowl known to man, not
to mention combinations thereof, and vegetables and salads as
well, garnished to the last inch. The open-sandwich craze started
in Denmark in the early years of the nineteenth century and has
become an art in itself. A harmony of flavours and colours is

sought, and these in their turn must harmonize with the bread upon which they rest.

Perhaps the most popular Danish open sandwich is made with the tiny shrimps which abound in Denmark. They are piled high on the bread or laid in orderly rows.

Danish open sandwiches, though devoured by foreign travellers in their native habitat, have never really caught on abroad. But a patient cook might have fun preparing a platterful for a summer luncheon. Cold roast pork slices might be topped with cucumber salad and a few capers. Alternate rows of minced herring, minced white of egg, and minced egg yolk – hard-boiled, of course – can be arranged on dark rye bread. Pâté, pickles, meat aspic, fish in every version – they all go on endless varieties of bread that has been not too heavily buttered.

Hans Christian Andersen Sandwich

This is said to have been the favourite of the author of 'The Little Match Girl' and 'The Emperor's New Clothes'.

Butter a piece of dark or light rye bread. Cover it with 2 rows of crisp bacon. Place a slice of liver pâté across one of the rows, and, diagonally, tomato slices on the other row of bacon. Sprinkle the tomato slices with grated horseradish and put strips of aspic on the pâté.

Steak Tartar Sandwich

A Nordic favourite. Success depends entirely on using the finest, freshest beef, and mincing or scraping it just before serving time. Some people are mad for it, others aren't.

½ lb. raw sirloin, free of all fat	Pepper
1½ tablespoons minced onion	2 raw egg yolks
Salt	Capers

Mince meat as finely as possible, or scrape with a knife, removing all membranes and tendons. Mix with onion and add salt and pepper to taste. Spread the meat in a thick layer on 2 slices of buttered bread, making a well in the middle. Place 1 egg yolk in each well and circle with capers. Makes 2 open sandwiches.

Variation: In lieu of egg yolks, arrange a large raw oyster on the meat and surround it with tiny cooked, shelled shrimps. Sprinkle with caviar. Omit capers.

Russian and Polish Hors-d'Œuvres
[*Zakuski*]

In old Russia, and Poland too, among the few who could afford the full glory of the voluptuous Slav cuisine with its floods of sweet and sour cream, *zakuski* used to be a great production. One reads of noble houses where a room adjacent to the dining-room was set aside for the *zakuski*, dozens and dozens of them. There the guests lingered, eating their fill of appetizers and washing them down with little glasses of vodka.

To this day the Slavs like *zakuski*, even though, in daily living, their number may be trimmed down to one or two or three. In the words of a Moscow housewife, recently quoted in the *New York Times*: 'You need *zakuski* and vodka to get the appetite going.' Incidentally, *zakuski* are not served only at the beginning of a meal. They appear whenever vodka is drunk, since few Russians drink unless an appetizer accompanies the vodka.

In Moscow today, in an ordinary household, *zakuski* might consist of sliced salami or herring sprinkled with chives and boiled potatoes, the Russians being as fond as the Scandinavians of the combination of fish and potatoes. Like smorgasbord, *zakuski* consist of both hot and cold dishes. Caviar, of course, is the most elegant of all. But cured fish, such as herring, smoked salmon, and sturgeon, dominate the *zakuski* table. Salads, especially those made from cucumbers and mushrooms, which can be called the national vegetables, are well liked, and so are various cold cuts, aspics, and mayonnaise dishes, the more decorated the better, since the Russians much admire the art of garnishing foods.

Among the hot *zakuski* are *blini*, which have become known in England. Russians are fond of pancakes in general, and serve them filled with any possible combination of meats, fish, and vegetables. But the typical Russian pancakes are quite different from a French pancake. They are made with yeast and buckwheat flour, and eaten with sour cream and caviar or with any kind of cured fish.

The hot dishes include puff-paste patties, Coulibiaci (pies filled with meat or fish or mushrooms) (page 222), and hot casseroles.

Dragomirovsky Hors-d'Œuvre Casserole
[*Dragomirovsky vorschmack*]

To the unknown Dragomirovsky, this may have been but a favourite hors-d'œuvre (*vorschmack* means a before-taste). To me, it is a very adequate way of using leftovers for a rather nice luncheon or supper main dish.

1½ tablespoons minced onion	5–6 oz. olives, stoned and diced (either green or black)
2 tablespoons (1 oz.) butter	
2–4 oz. chopped mushrooms	Salt
5–6 oz. any leftover cooked meat, diced	Pepper
5–6 oz. diced ham	8–12 fl. oz. sour cream
5–6 oz. diced cooked chicken	2 hard-boiled eggs, chopped
5–6 oz. diced boiled potatoes	2 to 3 tomatoes, sliced
1 dill pickle, diced	Grated cheese

Sauté onion in butter. Add mushrooms and cook until just tender. Combine with meat, ham, chicken, potatoes, dill pickle, and olives. Add salt and pepper to taste. Mix with sour cream.

Turn mixture into buttered baking dish and cover with hard-boiled eggs. Surround with tomato slices. Sprinkle grated cheese over top and bake in a moderate (350° F., gas 4) oven until thoroughly heated and brown.

Little Russian Meat Pies [*Piroshki*]

Traditionally, *piroshki* (little individual pies) are served with soup in Russian cooking. They may have a meat filling, or a mixture of sautéed mushrooms, egg, and onions, or one of browned onions and chopped cabbage. They can be made with any kind of dough, from puff paste to yeast dough. They are also eaten, in my house, as hot hors-d'œuvres, since they can be made beforehand and popped into the oven as needed. I use a sour-cream dough, since it's faster to make than either puff paste or yeast dough, and richer than ordinary pie crust. But there is no reason why anybody's favourite pastry dough could not be used for *piroshki*.

As for the filling, anything that tastes good in combination and can be minced is suitable. Russian fillings somehow always seem to include chopped hard-boiled eggs, and since I think this a splendid idea, here is my own favourite filling.

PIROSHKI DOUGH

6 oz. plain flour	About 4 to 6 tablespoons sour
1 teaspoon salt	cream
2 oz. butter	Beaten egg or milk

Sift flour and salt together. Cut in butter with pastry cutter or two knives, leaving the mixture in coarse lumps. Add sour cream, a little at a time, and just enough to hold dough together. Roll out dough. Fold in three thicknesses. Chill for about 1 hour or more. Roll out as thinly as possible. With cutter or bottom of glass, cut out rounds about 3 to 4 inches in diameter. Put 1 to 2 teaspoonfuls of filling on each round. Fold over and pinch edges together carefully, so that the filling won't ooze out during baking. Paint with beaten egg or milk. Place on greased baking sheet. Bake in hot (425° F., gas 7) oven 15 to 20 minutes, or until golden brown. Serve hot or cold.

FILLING

1 tablespoon (½ oz.) minced onion	1 hard-boiled egg, minced
1 tablespoon (½ oz.) butter	¼ teaspoon Worcester sauce
8 oz. minced cold meat or chicken	1 teaspoon chopped dill, parsley, or dill seed
2 oz. mushrooms, minced	Salt
	Pepper

Sauté onion in butter until soft. Add remaining ingredients and salt and pepper to taste. Cook for 5 to 10 minutes over low heat. If too dry, add 1 or 2 tablespoons bouillon. Cool before using. Enough for about 15 3-inch *piroshki*.

Russian Mushroom Caviar

1 medium-sized onion, minced	1 tablespoon lemon juice
2 tablespoons olive oil	Chives
½ lb. mushrooms, chopped	1 tablespoon sour cream
Salt	(optional)
Pepper	

Sauté onion in hot olive oil until soft. Add mushrooms and cook until just soft. Add salt and pepper to taste and lemon juice. Add chopped chives and sour cream. Chill before serving garnished with tomato slices.

Russian Pancakes [Blini]

Traditionally, blini are eaten the week before Lent. But since they are among the few dishes that are well known outside Russia, it is thoroughly worth while to adopt them as hors-d'œuvres to serve at any time.

Real blini are made with buckwheat flour, which can be bought easily in health stores. To make drier blini, half buckwheat, half plain flour can be used. As with all pancakes, there are many recipes. I like the following one, which seems to be a kind of synthesis of all the blini recipes I have seen.

1 envelope dry yeast or 1 yeast cake (about ¼ oz.)	3 eggs, separated
1 pint lukewarm milk	¼ lb. butter
¾ lb. buckwheat flour	½ teaspoon salt

Dissolve yeast in a little milk and add sufficient flour to make a thick sponge. Set to rise in a warm place for about 3 hours. Cream egg yolks, butter, and salt. Add yeast sponge and remaining flour and milk. Beat until smooth and let stand, covered, for about 30 minutes. Beat egg whites until stiff and fold into batter.

Heat griddle and butter very lightly. Bake the pancakes until golden on both sides. They should be about 3 inches in diameter. Serve very hot, with caviar and sour cream or any smoked or salted fish, preferably salmon or sturgeon.

Note: Blini can also be made very small and very thin, like

crêpes Suzette, and eaten with sugar and jam, or filled with cottage cheese. In short, the Russians love pancakes, and they make them any convenient way, though, traditionally, buckwheat and yeast are what make a pancake typically Russian.

Pâtés

You can always tell a good French restaurant by the kind of pâté served there. Pâtés do not have to be made from such expensive ingredients as goose liver and truffles, but they have to be made carefully, with a certain amount of love. Pâté de foie gras (goose-liver pâté), with truffles, is and always will be the king of pâtés: it is imported – preferably from Strasbourg, the home town of the finest pâté de foie gras.

Following are the recipes for 3 different kinds of pâté, of which I am very fond and which my guests seem to like year in, year out. One is made in a blender; it is very smooth and can be used as a sandwich spread. The second one is the favourite of my friend Fernande Garvin, the only woman I know of who is in charge of a Wine Information Bureau, and an absolutely wonderful cook. The third is a simple shrimp pâté, good for starting a rather heavy meal.

There is nothing very difficult about making pâté. Of course, as with all cooking, complicated – and most delicious – combinations of meats and spices are made in fine restaurants. But a good pâté maison is within reach of any home cook, and if he or she is creative, new combinations of meats, liver, sausage – in fact, anything that can be minced and cooked – can form the cornerstone of a cook's fame.

Pâté can be made either by cooking the meats first and mincing them afterward, or by baking the minced or chopped meats in the oven. It can be encased in a rich dough – in that case, it is called pâté en croûte. I don't advocate making pâté en croûte at home, because I have noticed that guests, thinking pâté is already fattening enough, simply leave the tender, lovingly made crust on the plate. So why bother?

All pâtés, to my mind, benefit from the addition of a little *good* brandy or dry Madeira. As an hors-d'œuvre, pâté is served sliced, on a bed of lettuce, with crusty bread or toast.

Pâté Fernande

1½ lb. pork liver
1½ lb. lean pork
¾ lb. salt pork
2 eggs
1 teaspoon salt
½ teaspoon pepper
1 bay leaf, crumbled fine

⅛ teaspoon thyme, chopped very finely
2 tablespoons finely chopped onion
1 to 2 tablespoons brandy
½ lb. sliced bacon

Chop pork liver, lean pork and salt pork as fine as possible, or pass through the finest blade of the mincer. (If the salt pork is very salty, soak first in cold water for 30 minutes. Dry carefully before using.) Combine meats with eggs. Work together until eggs are well blended. Add salt, pepper, thyme, bay leaf, onion, and brandy and combine thoroughly. Line a 9-inch loaf tin with bacon strips. Fill with pork mixture. Cover with bacon strips. Place tin in dish with water (water should be about ½ inch up the sides of loaf tin) and bake in moderate (350° F., gas 4) oven for 2 hours. Cool before unmoulding. Chill and serve sliced on a bed of lettuce.

Chicken Liver Pâté Maison [*Pâté maison*]

This is a very finely textured pâté and a very rich one. For a cocktail party, a splendid effect can be created by moulding the pâté into the shape of a pineapple, covering it with slices of pimento-stuffed olives, and topping it with a fresh pineapple frond.

1 lb. butter
2 lb. chicken livers
2 medium-sized onions, quartered
1 teaspoon curry powder
1 teaspoon paprika

¼ teaspoon salt
¼ teaspoon pepper
3 tablespoons cognac
½–¾ lb. sliced pimento-stuffed olives

Melt 4 oz. of the butter. Add chicken livers, onions, curry powder, paprika, salt, and pepper. Cover and cook over low heat 8 to 10 minutes. Force through fine sieve or, better, blend in electric blender until smooth. Add cognac and remaining butter and blend again. Chill until firm. Shape into pineapple and cover with olive slices. Top with fresh pineapple frond.

Fresh Shrimp Pâté [Pâté de crevettes]

½ lb. cooked shrimps
3 tablespoons lemon juice
Grated rind of 1 lemon

1 teaspoon pepper
4 fl. oz. olive oil

Put the shrimps twice through the finest blade of a mincer, or blend in electric blender. Add lemon juice, lemon rind, pepper, and a little salt, if necessary. Gradually blend in olive oil, making a smooth, creamy paste. Place in covered jar and chill. To serve, place pâté by the spoonful on lettuce. It should be eaten with toast or any crisp crackers or Melba toast.

Hot Hors-d'Œuvres

Only one of these hors-d'œuvres is needed to start a meal.

Artichoke with Goose-liver Pâté
[Le mariage de l'artichaut]

Prepare artichoke hearts as described on page 227. Parboil until half cooked – no longer. In separate saucepan heat about 1 inch of dry Madeira (it must be Madeira). Place artichoke hearts in wine. Simmer over low heat until tender. Drain, and keep very hot. Prepare as many slices of pâté de foie gras as there are artichoke hearts. Place artichoke hearts on heated platter and cover each heart with a slice of pâté. Serve immediately. The contrast in flavour brought out by the hot artichoke and the cold pâté is absolutely delicious.

Using frozen artichokes: Cook as directed on package, but substitute Madeira for half of the cooking liquid specified. Proceed as above.

Using canned artichoke hearts: Heat artichokes in Madeira, taking care to keep whole. Proceed as above.

French Anchovies, Fried [*Anchois frits*]

Excellent with drinks.

Anchovy fillets, drained	Flour
Beaten egg	Fat for frying

Dip anchovy fillets into beaten egg. Roll in flour. Heat fat to 350° F. Fry anchovies in fat for 2 minutes. Sprinkle with chopped parsley and serve very hot.

French Cheese Puffs [*Beignets au fromage*]

These are made from choux paste – the same kind of paste that goes into cream puffs. The cream-puff mix which is now commercially available is, however, not suited to this dish, because it is sweetened, whereas *beignets* are hors-d'œuvres.

8 fl. oz. water	1 oz. grated Parmesan cheese
2 oz. butter	Salt
4 oz. sifted flour	Pepper
3 eggs	

Boil together water and butter until butter is dissolved. Remove from heat. Add flour all at once. Beat until glossy and dough comes off sides of the pan in a ball. Beat in eggs one at a time. Add cheese, and salt and pepper to taste. According to the size of the *beignets* desired, drop dough from teaspoon or soup spoon on ungreased baking sheet. Place *beignets* about 2 inches apart to allow for spreading. Bake in very hot (425–50° F., gas 7–8) oven for 15 minutes (less if *beignets* are small), then reduce heat to moderate (350–75° F., gas 4–5) and bake about 20 minutes longer or until *beignets* are golden. Cut slit in side of *beignet* and fill with Mornay Sauce (page 255) to which sliced truffles have been added.

*

Hungarian Cheese Spread [Körözött liptói]

In Central Europe this spread, eaten on very dark bread as an accompaniment for beer, is very well known under the name of Liptauer.

8 oz. cream or cottage cheese	1 teaspoon chopped chives or
6 oz. butter	minced onion
1 teaspoon paprika	Salt
½ teaspoon French mustard	Pepper
1 teaspoon caraway seeds	About 3 tablespoons sour cream
2 teaspoons capers	

Cream cheese and butter. Add remaining ingredients and salt and pepper to taste. Mix thoroughly. Chill.

Little Swiss Cheese Pies [Ramequins]

Ramequins are a fond memory of my student days in Geneva. We used to dance all night, eat *ramequins* in a shop that kept open all night in the Rue du Rhône, and then go mountain climbing after a quick change. Sleep never seemed necessary in those happy days.

Ramequins can be made as small as one likes. For a cocktail party, I suggest tiny ones that can be eaten in one bite. If you wish to serve it as a luncheon dish, the amount of filling given below will be sufficient for a 9-inch pie.

Pie crust	8 fl. oz. single cream
½ lb. Swiss cheese, grated	Salt
1 tablespoon flour	Pepper
3 eggs, well beaten	

Line muffin tins or other moulds with pie crust. Chill. Dredge cheese with flour. Place cheese in moulds. Combine eggs with cream and add salt and pepper to taste. Pour over cheese – moulds should not be more than three-quarters full. Bake in hot (425° F., gas 7) oven for 20 to 25 minutes. Serve hot or warmed up, never cold.

Normandy Cheese Mixture [*Malaxé*]

Malaxé means mixture, and since it is Norman, it should be made with an apple brandy, such as Calvados or applejack. At a pinch, cognac will do.

2 oz. Roquefort or blue cheese	2 tablespoons Calvados
4 oz. butter	

Mash cheese until free from lumps. Cream together with butter. Blend in Calvados and beat until smooth and creamy. Serve on dark bread or dry crackers.

Bohemian Pickled Hard-boiled Eggs

Flavourful and interesting-looking eggs which are a speciality of Bohemia, one of the provinces of Czechoslovakia. They are good eaten out of hand at cocktail parties or used as a garnish instead of stuffed eggs.

1 dozen eggs	2 tablespoons caraway seeds
2½ tablespoons salt	1½ pints water
4 oz. dry yellow onion skins	

Hard-boil eggs in the usual manner. Cool them under cold water. Crack the shells all over but do not peel.

Boil together salt, onion skins, caraway seeds, and water for 5 minutes. Place eggs in deep heatproof bowl and pour boiling brine over them. Cool eggs in brine for 1 hour. Remove eggs from brine and chill for several hours. Peel and serve eggs cut in halves or quarters on a bed of lettuce or on tomato slices.

Caviar-stuffed Eggs [*Œufs au caviar*]

Hard-boiled eggs	Lemon juice
Caviar	

Cut eggs into halves lengthways. Scoop out the yolk carefully so that egg white remains neat. Fill whites with caviar and sprinkle with a very little lemon juice. Garnish each egg-caviar shell with about ½ teaspoon sieved egg yolk. Serve on lettuce leaves.

Creamed Camembert Cheese [Crème de Camembert]

Marcel Boulestin invented this one – he is one of the great French chefs who lived in England to promote the cause of French cooking as eaten in France. I think this is about the best cheese-wine spread I've ever had.

Dry white wine – Rhine, Moselle, Riesling, or Chablis	1 ripe Camembert cheese Unsalted butter

The Camembert for this spread must be really ripe. Keep it at room temperature until the cheese is soft and runny. Scrape cheese and place it in a deep non-metal dish. Pour just enough wine to cover cheese – no more. Steep cheese in wine for 12 hours. Drain if necessary. Take about half as much soft, unsalted butter as you have cheese. Blend cheese and butter into a smooth paste. Reshape into a round and let the mixture harden somewhat, but do not chill. Serve on crackers for cocktails or with fresh pears or apples for dessert.

German Fried Cheese Appetizer [Gebackener Käse]

This is an excellent appetizer, provided it can be made fresh for each handing around. However, the cheese can be prepared beforehand for frying and kept in the refrigerator. Any semi-hard cheese, such as Münster, Port Salut, Edam, etc., can be used, cut into triangles or diamonds or any desired shape. I like to use the triangular portions of Gruyère cheese, which can be cut in halves without any trouble.

6 1-oz. portions of Gruyère, cut in halves	⅛ teaspoon pepper
1 egg	⅛ teaspoon curry powder or turmeric
4 fl. oz. milk	3 oz. fine dry bread crumbs
1 teaspoon salt	Butter

Combine egg, milk, salt, pepper, and curry powder or turmeric. Dip cheese pieces in egg mixture, then in bread crumbs. Dip again in egg and crumbs. Chill. Fry in butter until brown on both sides. Serve on toothpicks, very hot.

Italian Parmesan Crisps [*Salatini al Parmigiano*]

4 oz. butter	½ teaspoon baking powder
2 oz. grated Parmesan cheese	½ teaspoon salt
4 oz. flour	

Cream butter until soft. Add Parmesan cheese. Blend thoroughly. Add flour which has been sifted with baking powder and salt. Roll out thin on lightly floured board. Cut into rounds about 1 inch in diameter. Place on ungreased baking sheet. Bake in hot (400–25° F., gas 6–7) oven for 8 to 10 minutes, or until lightly brown. Serve hot, or cold with the following filling:

2 tablespoons (1 oz.) butter	2 tablespoons double cream
1 oz. grated Parmesan cheese	

Cream butter until soft. Beat in Parmesan cheese and cream, and mix until well blended.

Salads

Rice Salad

Rice salad turns up in France, Italy, Spain, and even Austria, though it is most popular in France. The following recipe is a basic one, which lends itself to the addition of cooked shrimps, lobster, or any of the meats that go into a chef's salad. Fortified this way, rice salad can become the main dish for a summer luncheon. Served in small helpings, it is an excellent hors-d'œuvre.

½ lb. rice	½ teaspoon dried tarragon
6 tablespoons olive oil	2½ tablespoons chopped parsley
3 tablespoons wine vinegar	1½ tablespoons finely chopped
Salt	onion
Pepper	3 oz. cooked green peas
4 tablespoons chopped green pepper or red pimento	2½ tablespoons chopped chives (optional)

Boil the rice until just tender. Long-grain rice is best, since it keeps its shape. Drain. While still hot, add oil, vinegar, salt and

pepper to taste, and tarragon. Cool. Add remaining vegetables
and mix well. Chill. At serving time, pile rice salad on platter in
the shape of a pyramid. Surround with slices of tomato and with
black and pimento-stuffed green olives.

Rice Salad with Shrimps. ½ lb. cooked, shelled shrimps can
be mixed into the rice salad. Or the shrimps can be placed in
orderly rows on the rice salad pyramid.

Rice Salad with Lobster. Mix about ½ lb. diced cooked lobster
meat into the rice salad.

Chef's Rice Salad. Mix into rice salad 2–3 oz. each of cooked
ham, chicken, tongue, and Swiss cheese cut into julienne strips.

Cheese Salad from Switzerland [*Salade au fromage*]

½ lb. Swiss cheese, cubed	Salt
1 teaspoon grated horseradish	Pepper
1 small onion, minced	Radishes
8 tablespoons French dressing	Parsley sprigs

Combine Swiss cheese with horseradish, onion, and French dressing and mix thoroughly. Add salt and pepper to taste. Place in
salad bowl and decorate with a ring of radish slices and parsley
sprigs.

Vegetable Salads

Broccoli, cauliflower, carrots, courgettes, string beans, to name
just a few vegetables, are excellent as salads. The vegetables are
cooked until just tender. While still warm (so that the dressing
can be properly absorbed) they are dressed with White Wine
Salad Dressing (page 49) to which fresh or dried herbs, such as
tarragon, thyme, marjoram, chives or chervil, as well as salt and
pepper, have been added to taste.

White Bean Salad [*Haricots blancs en salade*]

Dried beans of any kind are good for a salad or hors-d'œuvre. They
are boiled in the usual manner, but care must be taken not to
overcook them. While *warm* – and that is essential – they are

dressed with White Wine Salad Dressing (page 49) and sprinkled with parsley. Beans thus prepared should be marinated at least 4 hours and served cold but not chilled. Drain, if necessary, before serving, and add salt and pepper to taste.

Lentil Salad [*Insalata di lenticchie*]

This is a classic of the French and Italian hors-d'œuvre table, and is prepared in the same manner as White Bean Salad above.

Potato and Combination Salads

Potato salad can be added to any of the vegetable salads above or to a combination of bean and vegetable salads.

German or Austrian Lobster Salad [*Hummernsalat*]

¾ lb. diced cooked cold lobster
6 oz. diced cooked cold chicken (white meat only)
3 oz. diced heart of celery
1 tablespoon capers, drained

Mild French dressing made with tarragon vinegar
Lettuce
Sauce Rémoulade (page 255)

Combine lobster, chicken, celery, and capers. Cover with French dressing and chill. Marinate for 1 to 2 hours. Drain. Pile salad on shredded lettuce. Cover with Sauce Rémoulade.

Russian Salad [*Salade à la russe – Insalata alla russa*]

When I was young, 'boughten' mayonnaise did not exist. It was freshly made whenever it was to be used, and it was considered no mean achievement to produce a good mayonnaise. Consequently, all mayonnaised dishes were most festive and elegant, and none more so than Russian salad, which in German, for reasons unknown, is called *Italienischer Salat*, or Italian salad.

Russian salad graced all hotel and restaurant tables, made as the chef's own – and often changeable – ideas dictated. Some Russian salads were more famous than others. Horcher's, the best restaurant in pre-Second-World-War Berlin, excelled at it, serving it with cold lobster. My father, not a sentimental man when it came to criticizing food, used to eat this combination at Horcher's with his colleagues from the old Auswärtiges Amt, the German Foreign Office, at their stag luncheon, called *Herrenfrühstück* (gentlemen's breakfast). I had it there once, and I have reason to remember the occasion very well.

In those days Berlin maidens indulged in the horrible fashion of wearing a black ribbon tied over their foreheads and hair, in what they hoped was a classical Greek fashion. I had come to Berlin for a vacation from my strict Roman convent school, where we wore white aprons over our uniforms, and our hair tied at the neck with no nonsense about it. The Berlin maidens impressed me with their international savoir-faire, and I promptly tied a black ribbon around my forehead and hair. Unfortunately this was the day I chose to call on my father at his office. He was in a small meeting but asked that I should be shown in to meet the other members of his staff. When I came into the room he gave me one anguished look, and with a strangled cry he seized me by the hand and yanked me out of the room. In a back passage, he tore the ribbon off my head and bade me comb my hair in a less artistic fashion. Then he asked me to wait, since, so he said, he did not have the courage to show his only daughter again that day. Later, to teach me reasonable manners, he took me to Horcher's for lunch, and there I had what still seems to me the most glorious of all Russian salads.

It is a salad of cubed vegetables bound together with mayonnaise. Sometimes cubed meats or lobster are added. The success of this salad depends on the absolute freshness of the vegetables, which should first be marinated in a mild French dressing – separately, of course – before being bound with mayonnaise. Use any combination of the following vegetables.

Cooked green beans, cut in
   pieces
Cooked beets, cubed (use a small
   amount, or salad will discolour)
Cooked carrots, diced
Raw celery, cubed
Raw cucumber, cubed

Spring onion, chopped
Small amount of white onion,
   chopped
Cooked green peas
Cooked cauliflowerets
Cooked cold potatoes, cubed

Marinate vegetables separately in a mild French dressing for
1 hour. Drain. Combine with small amounts of cubed cold cooked
chicken, cubed ham and cubed cold veal. To every 4 cups salad
add 2 pickled cucumbers, cubed, and 4 chopped anchovy fillets.
Bind with a good home-made mayonnaise and add salt and pepper
to taste. Pile the salad high on a crystal or china platter. Cover it
with a smooth, thin layer of mayonnaise. Garnish with capers,
pimento strips and black olives, tastefully arranged on the
mayonnaise. Stand meat from cooked lobster claws against salad
pyramid, or arrange in a circle at the bottom.

Mixed Salad Niçoise with Ravigote Sauce
[*Salade niçoise ravigote*]

Salade niçoise is a perfect main dish for luncheon on a hot
summer day. The olives in it must be black, never green.

Cut into thin julienne strips:

6 oz. cooked cold chicken	Whites of 3 hard-boiled eggs
2 slices lean ham	1 can anchovy fillets, drained
4 to 6 slices Italian salami	1 medium-sized boiled beet

Dice:

2 medium-sized cold boiled potatoes	2 stalks celery
1 unpeeled small tart apple	1 green or red pepper

Also needed:

1 head crisp lettuce, shredded Ravigote Sauce	About 15 black olives (the Italian or Greek are best)

Rub a wooden salad bowl with a cut clove of garlic. (This is not
a garlicky salad, though garlic may be added to taste.) Toss
together all ingredients and pile up in a pyramid. Chill until
serving time. Then pour about ½ pint Ravigote Sauce over the
salad. Decorate with thin slices of lemon and more black olives.
Serves 4 as a salad or 8 as an hors-d'œuvre.

RAVIGOTE SAUCE

The true, classic French *sauce Ravigote* is a hot one, and quite
different from the cold one. The French, apparently, have never

made up their minds as to the exact specifications of the cold Ravigote, which therefore turns up in various versions, all of them spicy. I therefore choose the kind I like best for my favourite *salade niçoise*.

8 fresh or 1½ teaspoons dry tarragon leaves	½ teaspoon prepared mustard (preferably French)
3 tablespoons watercress leaves (stems must be removed)	2 tablespoons wine vinegar
1 tablespoon chopped chives	6 fl. oz. olive oil
1 small clove garlic, minced	Salt
1 tablespoon chopped parsley	Pepper

Pound together to a smooth paste tarragon, watercress, chives, garlic, and parsley. This is most easily done in a mortar, a blender, or with the back of a heavy knife on a cutting board. In a small bowl, blend mustard, vinegar, and olive oil. Add herb paste and stir until smooth. Season with salt and pepper. Stir again before using.

Vegetables Cooked Greek Style [*Légumes à la grecque*]

This is one of the best ways of cooking vegetables that are to be served cold. Celery, asparagus, leeks, cauliflower, cucumbers, mushrooms, celeriac, courgettes, lima beans, flageolets, and almost any vegetable can be prepared this way. Artichokes, especially the frozen kind, are particularly suited to the *à la grecque* method of cooking, and they do not have to be defrosted first.

HOW TO PREPARE THE VEGETABLES FOR À LA GRECQUE COOKING

Cut vegetables into bite-sized pieces that are not too small. Some vegetables, such as cauliflowerets, little white onions, celery, peppers or, in short, any vegetables that are not tender, should be blanched first. To do this, pour boiling water over the vegetable and drain it off after 1 or 2 minutes. If the vegetable is rather tough, boil it for a couple of minutes, then drain and cook *à la grecque*.

GREEK MARINADE (MARINADE À LA GRECQUE)

Make a small bag from a triple layer of muslin and fill it with:

1 teaspoon dry fennel seeds or 3 fresh 2-inch pieces of fennel	12 coriander seeds
½ teaspoon dried thyme or 1 sprig fresh thyme	1 bay leaf
	2 peppercorns

Combine:

12 fl. oz. water	½ teaspoon salt
4 fl. oz. dry white wine	Juice of 3 lemons
4 fl. oz. olive oil	

Place the bag of mixed herbs (bouquet garni) into liquid in a saucepan. Bring slowly to a boil. Pour boiling marinade over vegetable that is to be cooked. Cook until just tender. Let cool in marinade. Drain, and chill before serving.

À *la grecque* vegetables may be served separately or combined in a mixed salad. But it is essential to cook each vegetable by itself, since cooking time differs. It is also essential that the vegetables should remain very crisp.

Note: The reason for making a bouquet garni bag is that the herbs and spices are kept together and can be easily removed. Otherwise they float in the liquid and cling to the vegetables, spoiling the appearance and taste – since it is not pleasant to bite into a peppercorn.

Marinated Mushrooms 1

One of the simplest and best salads.

French dressing made from oil and lemon juice	Salt and pepper
Mushrooms	Herbs – such as thyme or basil

Have French dressing ready in a bowl. Trim stem ends of firm white mushrooms and slice them very fine. As mushrooms are sliced, drop the pieces immediately into the French dressing to prevent darkening. Season with salt and pepper. Add fresh chopped or dried herbs to taste. Marinate for a few hours in refrigerator. Before serving, drain off excess liquid.

Marinated Mushrooms 2

½ lb. mushrooms	Pepper
1 onion, minced	1 tablespoon lemon juice
2 tablespoons olive oil	Chopped chives or spring onions
Salt	

Trim stem ends of mushrooms and chop coarsely. Sauté onion in 1 tablespoon of the oil until soft. Add mushroom pieces and sauté 2 to 3 minutes. Season with salt, pepper, remaining oil, and lemon juice. Sprinkle with chives or spring onions. Chill.

Fennel Salad [Insalata di finocchi]

An outstanding way of serving fennel as an hors-d'œuvre.

Remove tough outer leaves and green tops from fennel. Slice in wafer-thin slices. Cover with olive oil and a sprinkle of lemon juice. Season with salt and pepper to taste. Let stand 1 to 2 hours before serving.

Courgette Salad [Insalata di zucchine]

Parboil the courgettes until just tender. Slice into ½-inch slices. Drain for about 30 minutes. Dress with White Wine Salad Dressing (page 49) or any other French dressing. Chill and serve sprinkled with chopped parsley. This is a very refreshing salad, but the courgettes, which are watery, must be drained thoroughly.

Finnish Cucumber Salad with Dill [Kurkkusalaatti]

4 cucumbers	½ teaspoon sugar
Salt	2 tablespoons chopped dill
8 fl. oz. sour cream	Salt
1½ tablespoons wine vinegar	Pepper
6 tablespoons salad oil	

Cut ends off cucumbers. Do not peel, but score with tines of fork. Sprinkle with salt and let stand 1 hour. Drain and rinse several times in cold water to remove excess salt. Combine all other ingredients except salt and pepper, and blend thoroughly. Pour over cucumbers. Add salt and pepper. Chill thoroughly. Serve in glass dish and decorate with dill sprigs.

Salad of Red, Green and/or Yellow Sweet Peppers

This salad turns up wherever peppers are eaten. It is extremely simple to make and equally good to eat, though its success does depend on the trick of peeling off the bitter, coarse outer skin of the peppers. This is done by placing the peppers on the open flame of a gas burner until the outer skin is black and blistery. The peppers should be rotated to obtain an even effect. Then the hot peppers are whisked under running cold water and peeled until not a shred of black skin remains. They are then cleaned of seeds and membrane, and cut into julienne strips. (It is easiest to do this with a pair of scissors.) Finally, the pepper strips are marinated in olive oil to cover, with or without the addition of salt and pepper or herbs. They should marinate several hours before serving time, and are served cold but not chilled.

In France the peppers are marinated in a regular French dressing, whereas the Italians use only oil. I prefer the latter way.

Italian Pickled Vegetables [*Verdure marinate*]

4 tablespoons wine vinegar	4 oz. diced cauliflower
6 fl. oz. olive oil	1 tablespoon capers
1 tablespoon sugar	1 carrot, diced
1 large clove garlic, mashed	2 oz. diced turnip
1 teaspoon salt	3 oz. small white onions
¼ teaspoon pepper	1 courgette, diced
1 teaspoon paprika	4 tablespoons diced green pepper
5 oz. pimento-stuffed or plain green stoned olives	4 tablespoons chopped canned pimento
2 stalks celery, chopped	

Combine vinegar, oil, sugar, garlic, salt, pepper, and paprika; blend thoroughly. Add remaining ingredients and toss thoroughly. Chill at least 48 hours. This pickle will keep in the refrigerator for at least 1 week.

Cucumber Hors-d'Œuvre Salad from the Balkans [Terituar]

Though the Balkan countries are very different from one another, there is a similarity in their cooking. This dish turns up, in one form or another, in several Balkan countries. The combination of ingredients may seem odd, but it tastes good and is very refreshing on a hot day – well worth trying as an appetizer or a salad.

2 cloves garlic	1 tablespoon wine vinegar
3 oz. shelled walnuts	Salt
2 medium-sized cucumbers	Pepper
4 tablespoons olive oil	Chopped mint (optional)

Mince garlic and chop or grind walnuts finely. (The walnuts should be dry – not pasty as they are if ground in a blender.) Peel cucumbers and chop coarsely. Combine garlic, walnuts, cucumbers, olive oil, and vinegar and mix thoroughly. Add salt and pepper to taste. Chill. Serve on lettuce, with chopped mint sprinkled over salad.

German Celeriac and Potato Salad [Adlon Salat]

This salad used to be one of the many specialities of the Hotel Adlon in Berlin, one of the great European hotels in the days of the Kaiser. International royalty and aristocracy, as well as the international *haut monde* of finance, business, the theatre and arts, made the Adlon their headquarters, and the hotel's comfort, service, and cuisine were unparalleled until it was destroyed in the Second World War. In tune with North German eating habits, which, even in the home, favour hams, sausages, and other cold cuts of a wide variety, the Adlon set a most elaborate cold table and excelled in salads. These were created by a series of lady salad cooks who enjoyed great fame in Berlin. According to local custom they were called 'Kalte Mamsells' (cold misses,

in a literal translation), *Mamsell* being the North German name
for the cook of a big private house or a restaurant. By the same
token, a restaurant would have a '*Warme Mamsell*' (a warm
miss), portly, decisive and extremely well-paid ladies all, who
took great pride in their work (and no nonsense from anybody). I
remember one intimate dinner at the Adlon which my father
gave in honour of his lifelong friend Friedrich Ebert, the first
President of the Weimar Republic, and which I attended, though
still in pigtails. The President had remained faithful to the Berlin
habit of eating a supper of cold cuts and salads, and the *Kalte
Mamsell* had outdone herself. Summoned to receive his congratu-
lations, she blushed and curtsied in her starched white apron
while Herr Ebert shook her by the hand and wished more women
were like her, then devoted himself further to her beautifully
dished-up creations, which might well have included this salad.

3 large or 5 small celeriac roots	5–6 fl. oz. mayonnaise thinned
6 fl. oz. wine vinegar	with lemon juice to the
3 large or 5 small potatoes	consistency of thin pancake
3 red apples	batter
Watercress	Salt
Black truffles or black olives	Pepper

Cook celeriac in salted water to cover for about 15 to 25 minutes,
or until just tender. Peel while hot. Remove woody core, if any,
and cut into 1-inch julienne strips. Marinate immediately in half
of the vinegar, or the celeriac will darken. Cook potatoes at the
same time, but separately. Peel while hot, cut into 1-inch julienne
strips, and marinate in remaining vinegar while hot. (If marinated
cold, the vegetables will not be so tasty.) Keep celeriac and potatoes
in marinade for about 30 minutes. Combine vegetables. Quarter
and core apples, but do not peel. Cut into 1-inch julienne strips
and add immediately to vegetables, or apples will darken. Drain
surplus vinegar from salad, taking care not to break the julienne
strips. Add mayonnaise and salt and pepper and blend thoroughly.
Line a salad bowl (in Germany, glass bowls are used) with a bed
of washed watercress that has been shaken dry. Pile salad in the
middle to form a dome. Smooth down and garnish with slices of
truffles or black olives.

German Asparagus Salad [*Spargel Salat*]

Lettuce
Cooked asparagus spears
Slices of hard-boiled egg
Red pimento strips
Capers

Simple French dressing made
with lemon juice instead of
vinegar, or thin Herb
Mayonnaise (page 256)

Line a salad bowl with big lettuce leaves so that they reach
above the rim of the bowl. Arrange bunches of asparagus spears
on them, separated by the slices of hard-boiled egg. Cut the red
pimento into neat, even strips. Arrange 2 strips crosswise on
each side of egg. Top each egg slice with 3 capers. Serve French
dressing or Herb Mayonnaise separately.

German Bon Vivant Salad [*Schlemmer Salat*]

All salads can be made without truffles. But truffles add such
flavour to a dish that, at least for festive occasions, it is well
worth investing in a can of imported truffles. There should be
equal parts of artichokes and mushrooms in this salad.

Artichoke hearts
Equal parts of dry white wine
and water
Mild French dressing made
with lemon juice instead of
vinegar
Mushrooms
Truffles

Salt
Pepper
Madeira
Watercress
Very thin tomato wedges
Mayonnaise thinned with
lemon (optional)

Prepare artichoke hearts and cook until just tender in equal parts
of wine and water. (Frozen artichokes are excellent for the
purpose.) Drain, slice or cut in ½-inch cubes, and marinate in
French dressing. Wash mushrooms and trim bottoms of stems.
Slice very thinly lengthwise, and marinate immediately in French
dressing or the pieces will discolour. Marinate vegetables for 30
minutes. Peel 3 or 4 truffles and simmer covered in 8 tablespoons
Madeira. Cool in Madeira. Reserve 1 truffle and slice others fine.

Drain vegetables and combine carefully with truffles. Add salt
and pepper. Line a salad bowl with watercress. Pile vegetables in
middle to form a dome. Cut remaining truffle into rounds and
decorate salad with it. Arrange tomato wedges around salad.
Serve mayonnaise separately, if wanted.

Continental Radish Salad [Radieschen Salat]

Red radishes
French dressing with a pinch of
    mustard

Salt
Pepper
Chopped parsley

Wash and trim radishes. Slice fine. Marinate in French dressing.
Add salt and pepper. Before serving, drain, and sprinkle thickly
with chopped parsley. (This radish salad can be added to any
bland potato or green vegetable or tossed salad to give colour and
texture, as well as flavour.)

Poor Man's Caviar (Aubergine caviar)

This recipe came originally from Russia and the Balkans though
now it is found in France, Spain, and wherever aubergines grow
in profusion. It is another of those either/or salad/hors-d'œuvre
dishes, and a very refreshing one.

It is also one of the more-or-less dishes that can be adapted to
different tastes, as long as the basic combination is kept.

1 large aubergine
2 onions
4 skinned and seeded tomatoes
6 fl. oz. olive oil

4 cloves garlic (can be more or
    less)
Salt
Pepper

Prick aubergine with a fork (to let steam escape during baking)
and bake on baking sheet in moderate (350° F., gas 4) oven until
tender. Chop onions, tomatoes, and garlic very fine. When the
aubergine is soft, peel and remove excess seeds. Chop fine and
combine with onions, tomatoes, and garlic. Blend in olive oil and
salt and pepper to taste. Chill before serving on a bed of lettuce.

White Wine Salad Dressing

To my mind, this dressing is far better for cooked vegetable, meat, and sea-food salads than the ordinary French dressing.

12 tablespoons dry white wine
8 tablespoons olive oil
4 tablespoons tarragon vinegar
1½ tablespoons onion, chopped fine

½ garlic clove, minced (can be left out or increased to taste)
Salt
Pepper

Combine all ingredients and blend thoroughly. Use while foods to be dressed are still hot.

Soups

Formerly soup almost invariably started the dinner. It is a pity this is no longer the case, since a well-chosen soup does pleasant service in warming the stomach before the arrival of more solid food. But the point is to warm it, not to surfeit it.

Soup preceding a substantial dinner should be neither too rich nor served in too large a quantity. A cup of good strong bouillon meets these requirements admirably, especially if served with perhaps a dash of sherry and a simple little garnish . . . a sprinkling of cheese, a few sprigs of watercress, or a slice of cooked carrot or string bean. How well the genuine *haute cuisine* thinks of this treatment can be seen by turning to the *Concise Encyclopaedia of Gastronomy* by André Simon, probably the world's greatest living authority on food and wine. Simon lists 43 ways of garnishing consommé. Escoffier in his cookbook lists 84!

The mystique so often associated with soup runs rampant in many people when they come to the making of soup stock or bouillon. In this the Italians are leaders since they firmly believe in what can only be called the Grail-like qualities of *il brodo* (bouillon) as the healer of all bodily and mental distress. In times past there were few Italian homes that were not constantly permeated by the smell of simmering soup meat – not a strong but a most insinuating smell, very much like that of wet blotting paper. Canned bouillons and bouillon cubes are now clearing up the atmosphere. This is all to the good, I think, especially since many (notably Swiss) brands are really excellent.

For the purists among my readers I give the basic bouillon recipes, for them to make from scratch for soups and sauces. However, I must warn these enterprising souls that making basic stocks is neither a quick nor an inexpensive process, because, if they are to taste and look right, they must be made in the classic, slow way and with the correct ingredients. And the clarifying of bouillon, to make it into clear consommé, is scarcely a diverting operation.

Far be it from me to dampen these readers' cooking enthusiasm – yet I must state my own opinion, namely, that today's canned clear soups are about as good as, when not better than, most made at home. I suggest using them without dilution.

For the reader still determined to make consommé in the grand manner, I can only recommend that he be guided by the old Duke of Bedford. His grandson, the present Duke of Bedford, in his delightful autobiography* tells how this noble old party invariably had, for his first course, one cup of beef consommé. But what consommé! Precisely 9½ lb. of the best shin of beef were required to make 1 cupful. It was made exactly the same way every day, and only one special kitchenmaid was entrusted with the making of it. Even after she married, this kitchenmaid was induced to return to the house to perform this single duty.

The selection of soup recipes in this chapter ignores soups that are easily available canned. Like all the recipes in this book, they reflect my own and my friends' preferences in the choice of soups we feel are characteristic of the various European countries. Unless stated otherwise, each recipe makes 4 to 6 servings.

A Few Explanatory Notes on Soup Making

Consommé is clear broth, or bouillon that has been clarified. In the following recipes, they can be interchanged.

---

*John, Duke of Bedford, A Silver-plated Spoon (1959).

The bones for bouillon should be in small pieces and cracked. The meat of the cooked bouillon is not worth eating, though it can be used chopped or sliced.

It is possible to make all of the following soups with either beef, chicken, or veal bouillon or consommé, or with vegetable broth if a meatless soup is desired. Naturally, the flavour of the soup will vary, depending on the liquid used. The kind of bouillon specified in the recipes is what makes the soup authentic.

Skimming. Meticulous skimming is essential in all soup making (and in other slow cooking), since it affects the flavour and the aspect of the bouillon, especially if this has to be clarified later for consommé. Skimming is done with a slotted spoon. When the impurities rise to the surface as the soup is boiling, producing scum, they are lifted off with the spoon. During the skimming, a tablespoonful of cold water is added to the soup from time to time, since it brings more scum to the surface to be lifted off. Skimming also includes wiping the inside of the soup pot with a damp, clean cloth down to the high-water mark, since the clearness of the soup depends on the total removal of scum. Broadly speaking, a soup should be skimmed at least three or four times before being allowed to boil or simmer.

De-greasing bouillon. To remove a good deal of the grease, strain the stock through a triple layer of muslin or a piece of flannel that has been wet and wrung out. More can be removed by blotting the surface of the stock with unglazed brown paper or kitchen paper towels. However, the simplest way is to chill the stock in the coldest part, or the freezing compartment, of the refrigerator. The grease then rises to the top and can be lifted off easily in one slab, after loosening the edges from the container with a knife. Remaining particles are removed with slotted spoon.

To clarify bouillon for consommé. Clarified bouillon becomes consommé. The *haute cuisine* knows various ways of doing this, but the simplified method that follows is sufficient for the purposes of the recipes in this book.

The bouillon should be cold and clear, since a muddy bouillon will not clarify well. It is better to use a pan other than aluminium, because aluminium tends to cloud the bouillon further. For each quart of bouillon, use the white and shell of 1 egg. Beat the white lightly, add the crushed shell and 2 teaspoons cold water. Add this mixture to the cold bouillon. Bring to the boil, over moderate heat, and let boil for 3 minutes, stirring constantly. Remove from heat and let stand undisturbed for 20 to 30 minutes. Strain through a fine sieve lined with a triple thickness of muslin. Cool, and store in refrigerator.

*

Beef Bouillon

For soups, sauces, and other dishes.

1 veal knuckle, cracked
1 lb. beef brisket or shin
1 beef knuckle, cracked
4 chicken feet, cleaned and skinned
2 whole leeks, sliced (when in season)

1 large onion, stuck with 2 cloves
2 celery stalks with tops, sliced
1 carrot, sliced
3 sprigs parsley
5 pints cold water
2 teaspoons salt

Place all ingredients except salt in soup kettle. Cover and bring slowly to the boil. Skim as needed. Simmer for 2 hours, add salt, and simmer for 3 more hours. Strain broth through a fine sieve lined with a triple layer of muslin. Chill, remove fat. Store in refrigerator, where it will keep from 4 to 5 days.

White Veal Stock or Bouillon

Use in sauce recipes that call for veal stock and in other dishes. Since it is delicate in flavour, it can serve also in place of chicken bouillon. I think veal stock is worth making because it cannot be bought canned, as far as I know.

5 lb. veal bones, including knuckle, cracked
1 lb. veal, cut in pieces
4 chicken feet, cleaned and skinned
5 pints cold water

2 celery stalks, with tops, sliced
1 onion
1 carrot, sliced
3 sprigs parsley
2 teaspoons salt

Cover bones, veal, and chicken feet with water and parboil until the scum rises. Skim and drain. Place bones, veal, and chicken feet in a soup kettle with 5 pints water and remaining ingredients. Bring to the boil, and simmer for 5 hours, skimming as needed. Strain broth through a fine sieve lined with a triple layer of muslin. Chill, remove fat. Store in refrigerator, where it will keep from 4 to 5 days.

Chicken Bouillon

1 3- to 5-lb. boiling fowl	1 celery stalk with top, sliced
1 veal knuckle, cracked	1 carrot, sliced
2 lb. chicken backs and wings	1 bay leaf
5 pints cold water	2 teaspoons salt
1 onion, stuck with 2 cloves	

Place all ingredients in soup kettle. Cover and bring slowly to the boil. Skim as needed. Simmer for 3 hours. Strain broth through a fine sieve lined with a triple layer of muslin. Chill, remove fat. Store in refrigerator, where it will keep from 4 to 5 days. (Remove fowl from broth when the breast is tender. Cut the entire breast off the carcass and return the carcass to the broth and continue simmering. The breast can be used in any dish that calls for cooked chicken.)

Vegetable Broth

Sometimes a vegetable broth is needed for soups or for cooking vegetables or making gravies. The one below will serve the purpose.

1 large onion, sliced	2 to 3 leeks (when in season), sliced
2 carrots, sliced	
2 stalks celery (including tops), chopped	2 fresh, ripe tomatoes
8 sprigs parsley	1 quart water
	1 tablespoon salt

Combine vegetables with water and salt, and simmer about 1½ hours. Strain through triple layer of muslin. Clarify, if needed, with 1 egg white and the crushed shell of 1 egg.

Scotch Broth

The vegetables in this soup should be diced as uniformly as possible.

First step:

3 lb. lamb bones	1 boiling fowl, cut in pieces
1 lb. beef bones	6 pints cold water

Add the lamb and beef bones and the fowl to water in deep pan. Bring to the boil, skim as needed, and simmer for 3 hours. Strain broth through triple layer of muslin.

Second step:

4 oz. pearl barley	1 lb. boneless shoulder of lamb,
Half a small parsnip, diced	trimmed of all fat, and diced
2 carrots, diced	Salt
1 onion, diced	Pepper
1–2 leeks, sliced	⅛ teaspoon thyme
1–2 stalks celery, diced	Chopped parsley
Hot broth	

Reheat broth and combine it in deep pan with barley, parsnip, carrots, onion, leeks, celery, and lamb. Bring to the boil, skim as needed, and simmer, covered, for 2 hours. Add salt, pepper and thyme. Serve in bowls with a sprinkling of parsley. Serves 8 to 10.

Swiss Mushroom Bouillon
[Consommé aux champignons]

This soup, a light and invigorating curtain raiser for a meal, is typical of the fine cooking in Swiss hotels. Serve it in cups rather than plates, accompanied with Cheese Biscuits.

2½ pints hot strong beef bouillon	8 fl. oz. good dry sherry
	Salt
½ lb. mushrooms, finely chopped	Pepper

Simmer mushrooms in consommé in covered pan until tender. Add salt and pepper to taste. Just before serving, stir in sherry.

CHEESE BISCUITS

2 oz. grated very sharp Cheddar cheese	¼ teaspoon Worcester sauce
4 oz. butter	4 oz. flour, about

Cream cheese and butter together until soft. Blend in Worcester sauce. Gradually add flour, mixing until a soft dough is formed. Chill for ½ to 1 hour. Roll dough into small balls. Place on lightly greased baking sheet. Bake in hot (425° F., gas 7) oven for 10 minutes, or until golden. Serve hot in a napkin.

Spanish Saffron Bouillon [Consommé de Cadiz]

This bouillon should be served in cups, with a sprig of watercress in each serving. The saffron gives the bouillon a charming flavour as well as colour. I had it in Cadiz, the whitest of all white Spanish cities.

2½ pints hot strong chicken or beef bouillon	1 teaspoon onion juice or ½ teaspoon instant onion powder
Salt	
White pepper	¾ teaspoon saffron

Blend onion juice or dissolve onion powder in ¼ pint of the broth and add salt and pepper to taste. Dissolve saffron in another ¼ pint of the broth. Stir both mixtures into remaining broth. Serve very hot with French Beignets au Fromage (page 32).

French Onion Soup [Soupe à l'oignon]

Another version of the classic French soup, made with white wine or champagne.

4 oz. butter	2½ pints hot beef bouillon
2 tablespoons salad oil	¾ pint dry white wine or champagne
1 to 2 lb. onions, sliced, depending on whether a thicker or thinner soup is desired	Salt
	Pepper
	French bread, sliced
1 to 2 tablespoons flour	4 oz. grated Parmesan cheese

Melt butter and oil in casserole. Sauté onions in it until soft and
dark brown, stirring frequently. Do not allow to burn. Sprinkle
flour over onions and stir until smooth. Avoid lumps. Add
bouillon and wine or champagne, and salt and pepper. Simmer,
covered, over low heat for about 1 hour. Place slices of French
bread in a tureen or individual bowls. Pour soup over them.
They will rise to the surface. Sprinkle bread with Parmesan
cheese. Heat in hot (425° F., gas 7) oven until cheese is melted.

German Potato Soup [Kartoffel Suppe]

A butter-flour thickening, added to the cooked soup, is a typical
German way of binding soups.

1 lb. potatoes, cubed	Salt
1 carrot, diced	Pepper
1 stalk celery, minced	2 tablespoons (1 oz.) butter
2½ pints any cold bouillon, or	3 tablespoons flour
water	1 tablespoon chopped parsley
⅛ teaspoon marjoram	

Put potatoes, carrot, and celery into a soup kettle. Add bouillon
or water, marjoram, and salt and pepper. Bring to the boil, skim
as needed, and simmer until vegetables are tender. Strain, and
reserve stock. Rub vegetables through sieve, or purée in an electric blender. Return to stock. Reheat soup. Heat butter to a light
brown, stir in flour, and cook until golden brown. Do not allow
to scorch. Add to soup and simmer 10 minutes longer. Serve
with sprinkled parsley. (Some may prefer to leave the vegetables
whole.)

Austrian Barley Soup [Gersten Suppe]

Austrians, Czechs, Poles, and Russians are all very fond of barley
soup. Depending on the cook's taste, they make it in varying
degrees of heftiness, purée it or not, add sweet or sour cream. I
like this lighter version, and make my barley soup with vegetable
bouillon, though of course meat bouillons can be used.

This soup comes from Frau Richard Strauss, the wife of the
composer, whom my mother entertained in Milan while the

maestro was conducting some of his own works at La Scala. My mother did not like barley soup, but Frau Strauss did, as I remember from a spirited discussion, which yielded this recipe.

4 oz. medium barley	2½ pints hot vegetable or veal
1 stalk celery, minced	bouillon
1 medium-sized onion, minced	Salt
3 tablespoons (1½ oz.) unsalted	Pepper
butter	4 fl. oz. double cream, or more,
1 tablespoon flour	according to taste

In a soup kettle sauté the barley, celery, and onion in the melted butter. Stir in flour. Add hot bouillon. Cover and simmer for about 1 hour, or until barley is tender. Add salt and pepper. Just before serving, add cream. Do not reheat. (This soup may be made in advance and reheated with perfect success. The cream, however, must not be cooked, but added at the last moment.)

Hungarian Cream of Mushroom Soup [*Gombaleves*]

Excellent cream of mushroom soups turn up in almost every European country, and they are usually made with butter, a white sauce, or sweet cream. The Hungarian version below not only tastes very good, but is unusual since it uses lard and sour cream, which give the soup its typical flavour. If you have no lard, use dry salt pork drippings or, as a last resort, bacon drippings.

1 lb. mushrooms, sliced	2½ pints veal or beef bouillon
2 tablespoons (1 oz.) lard	2 tablespoons double cream
2 teaspoons paprika	2 egg yolks
2 tablespoons flour	12 fl. oz. sour cream
1 tablespoon chopped parsley	

Sauté mushrooms in hot lard in soup kettle and stir in paprika. When soft, sprinkle with flour and parsley. Add bouillon and cream. Cover and simmer for 1 hour. Blend egg yolks with sour cream. Remove soup from heat and stir egg-sour cream-mixture into it carefully, a little at a time. Serve with pancake strips, made from any standard egg pancake recipe. The cooked pancakes are rolled individually and cut into finger-size strips which are put in the soup.

Portuguese Almond Soup [Sopa de amendoa]

Non-sweet almond soups are popular in Portugal and in Spain. Some are made with garlic, peppers, and saffron. I do not care for these versions, as those ingredients overshadow the almond flavour. I prefer this soup, which is delicate. The coriander, an essential ingredient, adds a lemony taste. An electric blender helps immensely in grinding the almonds.

¾–1 lb. blanched almonds, depending on how thick a soup is wanted	2½ pints hot chicken bouillon
	Salt
	Pepper
1 small onion, grated	6 fl. oz. double cream
1 teaspoon ground coriander seed	3 egg yolks
	Grated rind of ½ lemon

Chop almonds and grind them to a paste in mortar or electric blender. Blend with onion and coriander. Add to bouillon with salt and pepper. Cover and simmer for 15 minutes. Remove from heat. Blend together cream, egg yolks, and lemon rind. Carefully stir this mixture into the hot soup. Serve immediately.

Swiss Leek Soup with Wine [Potage aux poireaux]

I had this soup in Neufchâtel, a very pretty, non-touristy Swiss town in a region that produces a superior white wine of the same name.

6 leeks, both green and white parts, sliced	Salt
	Pepper
5 tablespoons rice	6 oz. grated Swiss cheese
1½–2 pints hot beef bouillon	12 fl. oz. dry white wine

Simmer leeks and rice in just enough water to cover for about 20 minutes, or until rice is tender. Add bouillon and salt and pepper. Simmer 10 minutes. In top of double boiler, over boiling water, melt cheese with wine. Blend thoroughly. Put a generous spoonful of the cheese sauce in each soup plate and pour soup over it.

Watercress Soup [*Potage cressonnière*]

Watercress soup is usually made with potatoes, but here is an excellent recipe without them. The simplest way to handle the watercress is to wash the whole bunch, keeping it tied, under the cold-water tap, then shake it dry and snip the leaves with kitchen scissors.

1 medium-sized onion, minced	1 tablespoon flour
2 tablespoons (1 oz.) butter	Salt
2 bunches watercress, chopped	Pepper
1¼ pints hot chicken bouillon and ¾ pint hot milk, mixed together	1 egg yolk
	4-6 fl. oz. double cream

Sauté onion in melted butter over low heat until golden but not brown. Add watercress, cover pan, and cook 5 minutes. Stir in flour and chicken bouillon and milk. Simmer for 15 minutes. Rub through a fine sieve or purée in electric blender. Add salt and pepper. Return to pan and heat again. Blend together egg yolk and cream. Remove soup from heat and carefully stir in egg–cream mixture. Serve in cups and garnish with a sprig of fresh watercress. (This soup does not have to be puréed but many people prefer it that way.)

Parsley Soup [*Potage au persil*]

This soup is made like Watercress Soup, above, substituting for watercress a handful of parsley, and garnishing with a sprig of fresh parsley. (Use Italian parsley, since it has more flavour than curly parsley.)

Norwegian Spinach Soup

2 lb. spinach, chopped, or 2 packets frozen chopped spinach	2 tablespoons flour
	Salt
	Pepper
2½ pints hot beef bouillon	2 teaspoons sugar
3 tablespoons (1½ oz.) butter	

Cook spinach in bouillon for 5 to 10 minutes, or until just tender. Drain, reserving liquid. Keep spinach hot. Melt butter and stir in flour, avoiding lumps. Blend into spinach liquid and bring to the boil. Add spinach, salt and pepper, and sugar. Simmer about 5 minutes. Serve with thin slices of buttered rye bread.

Greek Lemon Soup [Soupa avgolemono]

One of the best light soups ever invented.

3 oz. rice	Juice of 1 large lemon
2½ pints hot chicken bouillon	Salt and pepper
2 egg yolks	

Wash rice in several waters to remove all excess starch, and drain. Add to bouillon and simmer, covered, for 20 minutes or until light and fluffy. Beat yolks together gently and add lemon juice gradually, stirring all the time to avoid curdling. Add gradually 6–8 tablespoons hot broth to egg–lemon mixture, stirring constantly. Add to remaining broth in saucepan and heat for 2 to 3 minutes, stirring constantly. Be very careful not to boil, or the soup will curdle. Add salt and pepper and serve immediately.

Turkish Yoghurt Soup [Yoğurt Çorbasi]

A thin, pale, and rather tart soup that does well with a dinner featuring roast meats. Men like it very much. The soup must be kept thin and served very hot.

16 fl. oz. plain yoghurt	1 tablespoon flour
2½ pints hot beef bouillon	2 tablespoons chopped fresh or
1 tablespoon (½ oz.) butter	dry mint

Stir yoghurt into bouillon. Keep hot but do not boil, or soup will curdle. In another saucepan, melt butter and stir in flour, blending thoroughly. Cook 3 to 4 minutes. Do not allow to brown. Carefully pour the yoghurt–bouillon mixture into the blended flour and butter, stirring constantly. Bring to the boil quickly once, and no more – stirring constantly. Just before serving, sprinkle with mint.

Italian Fish Soup [*Zuppa di pesce*]

There are as many fish soups as there are Mediterranean countries, and they are generally made with whatever fish is handy. Since these soups are not too different from one another, and since no authentic Mediterranean fish soup can be made in England because our fish is different, I give a modified version of the famous *zuppa di pesce* from the Danieli in Venice. The luxurious Danieli, on the Riva degli Schiavoni, is surely one of the world's most romantic hotels, with a melting view of the city and lagoon.

1½ lb. lobster, cut up
½ lb. prawns
2 pints water
1 onion, sliced
1 stalk celery with leaves, sliced
2 tablespoons vinegar
2 tablespoons salt
2½ lb. mixed whole fish, such as haddock, trout, cod
4 tablespoons oil
2 garlic cloves, minced

2 bay leaves, crumbled
½ teaspoon thyme
1 teaspoon basil
2 tablespoons chopped parsley
2 pints fish broth
4 fl. oz. dry white wine
½ lb. chopped peeled tomatoes
Pinch of saffron (optional)
Salt
Pepper

Boil lobster and prawns for 5 minutes in water with onion, celery, vinegar, and salt. Remove, reserve broth, and shell lobster and prawns. Save shells. Cut heads and tails off fish, and, with lobster and prawn shells, add to broth. Simmer for 20 minutes. Strain, and set broth aside. Cut up lobster and fish into bite-size chunks and cut prawns in half. Heat oil, and sauté fish with garlic, bay leaves, thyme, basil, and parsley for 5 minutes, stirring constantly. Add fish broth, wine, tomatoes, saffron, salt and pepper. Bring to the boil, cover and simmer for 20 minutes. Serves 8 to 10. Serve with slices of bread or Polenta (page 143) fried in oil.

Note: To make this soup more authentic, ½ lb. squid may be added and cooked with the lobster and prawns.

Borshch

Eastern Europeans are great on soups, and there are endless recipes for them, from Frenchified cream soups to sturdy vegetable soups, with and without meat, which are meals in themselves. What makes these interesting is that the correct versions usually have a sour base, either in the stock used or added to the soup as a souring agent. In Rumania, for example, it is the fermented juice of wheat bran, and in Russia, Kvass, the fermented juice of rye and beetroot. Other souring agents are also used, such as yoghurt, sour cream, sauerkraut, pickled cucumbers, sour apples or plums or unripe grapes. Lemons are not used, since they are not a native fruit. These sour bases give the soups their typical flavour. It is possible to omit them – to make borshch with water or bouillon – but the results will not be as good. Fresh dill or dill seeds are the characteristic flavourings.

The best known of these soups is borshch, which originated in Poland where it has been common fare for centuries. To be authentic, it must contain beetroot. There are several varieties of borshch, and cooks generally have their own special versions, diddling with the proportions and ingredients, as all cooks do when they make this kind of soup. Here are two of the best-known recipes.

Ukrainian Borshch

1 lb. chuck beef, cut in slices
3 pints beef bouillon or Kvass
Salt
Pepper
1 bay leaf
2 tablespoons (1 oz.) butter
1 onion, chopped
3 medium-sized raw beetroots, shredded
2 carrots, sliced
½ medium cabbage, shredded
1 tablespoon minced parsley
1 8-oz. can tomato paste
1 tablespoon vinegar (omit if Kvass is used)
2 medium-sized potatoes, cubed
Sour cream

Put beef into a soup kettle with cold beef bouillon or Kvass. Add salt, pepper, and bay leaf. Bring to the boil, skim, and simmer, covered, for about ½ hour. In another pan melt butter and in it sauté onion, carrots, beetroot, cabbage, and parsley for 3 to 4 minutes. Add tomato paste and vinegar and simmer over low heat for about 10 minutes. Add to stock with potatoes, and simmer, covered, for about 1 hour, or until the meat is tender. Skim when needed. Add salt and pepper. If Kvass is not used, colour the soup with 2–3 tablespoons grated raw beetroot.

Remove the beef to separate platter, slice, and serve separately. Serve soup in bowls with a sprinkling of fresh minced dill over each serving. Pass sour cream separately and accompany with Kasha (page 141) or Piroshki (page 26).

Serves 6 to 8.

KVASS

This is soup kvass, but kvass is also a beverage, made differently from the kvass below, and quite potent. Most non-Russians feel that drinking kvass is an acquired habit, like drinking mead and sake.

1 lb. rye bread, the darkest kind available	6 large raw beetroot, peeled, and thinly sliced
5 pints lukewarm boiled water	

Place slices of bread in large earthenware or china bowl. Add water and beetroot. Cover and stand in warm place 2 to 3 days. Strain through a triple layer of muslin before using. The kvass should have a pleasant, acid taste. If it is too strong, dilute with water.

Clear Borshch

A quick version of the original recipe.

1 lb. beetroot	½ fresh or pickled cucumber, thinly sliced
1 pint water	
1 pint hot beef bouillon	Fresh dill, minced
Salt and pepper	Sour cream

Cover beetroot with water and simmer for 45 minutes, or until it is pale. Remove beetroot but save stock. Add bouillon to stock. Cover and simmer for about 10 minutes. Add salt and pepper. Serve hot, or iced, in cups. Garnish each serving with cucumber slices and a sprinkling of dill. Pass sour cream separately.

*

Russian Sauerkraut Soup [Shchi]

1 medium-sized onion, chopped	2½ pints hot beef bouillon or
2 tablespoons (1 oz.) butter	Mushroom Stock
1½ lb. sauerkraut	Salt
2 tablespoons flour	Pepper
Sour cream	2 bay leaves

Sauté onion in butter until golden. Drain sauerkraut but reserve the juice. Add to butter and onion, and sauté over medium heat for about 5–10 minutes. Be careful not to scorch. Stir in flour. Add bouillon or Mushroom Stock, salt, pepper, and bay leaves. Simmer, covered, for about 30 minutes to 1 hour. (Longer simmering improves the taste.) Shchi should have a sharp flavour, and if it is not nippy enough, add the reserved sauerkraut juice. Pass sour cream separately.

MUSHROOM STOCK

Since our mushrooms are too bland in taste, the mushrooms for this stock must be dried, imported mushrooms, which have a pronounced flavour.

2 oz. dried mushrooms, or more, if a stronger stock is desired	1½ pints water
	Salt
1 medium-sized onion, peeled and cut in half	Pepper

Wash mushrooms, put in saucepan with water and onion. Simmer, covered, over low heat for 2 to 3 hours. Strain. The mushrooms can either be used in other dishes which call for mushrooms or be chopped and added to the stock.

Cold Soups

There are few worth-while cold soups. In fact, I know of none except the ones printed here. The German and Scandinavian fruit soups are delicious, but since they are sweet, they're hard to think of as soups – unless one was raised on them.

Cream soups are the most popular summer soups, but almost all of them suffer from three grave defects: they are either cooked with potatoes or thickened with flour or with double cream. Cold potatoes do not taste good except in potato salad, and somehow the very coldness of the soups accentuates their flavour, so that they overshadow the other ingredients, such as cucumbers, leeks, or watercress. A flour thickening makes iced soups taste pasty. Double cream is just too heavy for soups that should be thin and a trifle pungent. All in all, few summer iced soups are light enough for the purpose.

Iced Cream Soups

When you make iced cream soups, bear in mind that they should be drunk from cups rather than spooned. The best are made of a good clear meat or chicken consommé, heated, to which a few tablespoons of single cream are added and then chilled. The proportions are 3 tablespoons of single cream to each cup of broth. These soups can be flavoured delightfully and fancifully: with a small amount of whatever herbs are handy, such as tarragon, a leaf of lemon verbena, or grated lemon peel; such spices as a little ground ginger, mace, coriander, cumin; or with a dash of sherry or brandy. One's ingenuity can go very far in a most pleasing manner. Never cool iced cream soups in metal containers, or they may discolour.

Spanish Cold Vegetable Soup [Gazpacho]

One of the many versions of a very refreshing cold soup from Spain.

1 lb. tomatoes, peeled and very finely chopped	3 to 4 tablespoons olive oil
½ cucumber, finely diced	1 tablespoon wine vinegar
2 cloves garlic, finely chopped	Salt
2 spring onions, finely sliced, or 1 small onion, diced, or 1 red or green pepper, seeded and cut in strips	Pepper
	⅛ teaspoon cayenne pepper
	Chopped parsley
	Sprigs of fresh marjoram
1½ dozen black olives, stoned	Iced water

Combine all ingredients except iced water and chill. Just before serving, dilute soup with iced water to taste, depending on how thick or thin a soup is desired. Serve with an ice cube floating in each bowl.

Iced Chicken and Curry Soup [Potage Sénégalaise]

3 sour apples, peeled, cored, and sliced
1 large onion, sliced
1 tablespoon (½ oz.) butter
2 teaspoons curry powder
Salt
Pepper

⅛ teaspoon cayenne pepper
1 pint chicken broth
8 fl. oz. dry white wine
8 fl. oz. single cream, chilled
2–3 oz. finely diced cooked chicken

Sauté apples and onion in butter over low heat until soft. Do not brown. Add curry powder and cook 5 minutes, stirring constantly. Add salt, pepper, and cayenne pepper. Add chicken broth and wine. Cook over low heat for 10 minutes, stirring constantly. Rub through fine sieve, or purée in an electric blender. Chill thoroughly. Just before serving, stir in cream and add chicken. Serve very cold.

Bulgarian Cold Cucumber Soup [Tarator]

This soup is very popular throughout the yoghurt-loving countries of the Balkans and the Middle East. But since yoghurt is so typical of Bulgaria, whose inhabitants attribute their extraordinary longevity and fertility to it, I'll attribute it to this country.

1½ pints yoghurt
3 oz. chopped walnuts
1 cucumber, diced

Salt
White pepper
2 cloves garlic, crushed

Beat yoghurt until smooth. Combine walnuts, cucumber, salt, pepper, and garlic. Add to yoghurt and blend. Chill thoroughly. At serving time, you may add 1 ice cube to each serving.

Fish and Shellfish

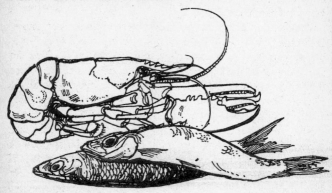

I have often speculated on the nature of the person who first thought of eating a lobster. How would it occur to one that any animal so clad in armour would be edible at all? And did this pioneer progress from lobster to shellfish or vice versa? Who knows, indeed?

All fish has been considered food since antiquity and, like grains, is interwoven with religious significance. The Christians adopted the sign of the fish, and there were fish gods before them. The ancient Romans were inordinately fond of fish, and so were the Greeks. Many of the Greeks' cooks came from the then Greek province of Sicily, and the cook Trimalchio was said to be so clever that when he could not provide a scarce and much-desired fish he could counterfeit its shape and flavour so well that even Neptune might be deceived.

Ancient literature abounds in descriptions of Roman fishponds, which were to the rich of that time what ocean-going yachts are to the rich of our times, and of fish cookery. Fabulous prices were paid for fish, notably the famed red mullet, which was eaten with a seasoning of pepper, rue, onions, dates, and mustard, to which was added the flesh of the sea hedgehog reduced to a pulp and seasoned with oil. The liver was considered an even greater delicacy, fit for emperors and senators. Apicius, the Fanny

Farmer of two thousand years ago, gives in his books an endless number of recipes for fish and sea-food cookery, including several very good marinades.

The passion for fish during and since the Middle Ages is well understandable in view of the rigorous fasting laws that governed life. Perhaps it is more accurate to say non-meat-eating laws, for fish cookery in the monasteries could hardly be called a fast. Fishponds were as essential to the clerics as they were to the Romans, and ecclesiastic fish cookery shows a delicacy and palatability to our present-day tastes not often found in other dishes.

Fish cookery, spiced and caparisoned beyond belief, continued to flourish in Elizabethan England, in Renaissance Europe, among the rich and the poor. For fish is cheap to raise, and a great deal is to be had free for the catching. In our age of plenty it is almost impossible to imagine how poor the populations of Europe have been during most of their history. Everything that could be eaten, and was free, made the difference between life and death from starvation.

All good European cookbooks abound in excellent fish recipes, some of which are incredibly complicated and of the highest of the *haute cuisine*. Whatever purists say, these recipes can be adapted to various kinds of fish, though of course the flavour will be different, depending on the fish used.

As to what to serve with fish, I personally agree with the classic opinion that plain boiled potatoes are the only fit accompaniment, at least for most fish dishes.

For those among my readers who like to speak correctly, I offer the following fish language: to tusk barbels and breams; to fin chevins or chubs; to tame crabs; to transsene eels; to side haddocks; to string lampreys; to barb lobsters; to splat pikes; to sauce a plaice or tench; to undertraunch a porpoise; to chine a salmon; to straunch a sturgeon; to culpon a trout.

How Much Fish to Buy

½ lb. of fillets or steaks per person; or 1 lb. if the fish is whole with the head and tail left on.

The Mediterranean Way of Cooking Fish

The Mediterranean is rich in fish, and since the countries that border it are poor and fish are free for the catching, it is a most important item in the people's diet. Fish is brushed with oil and grilled whole or in parts; it is dipped in flour and fried in deep or shallow oil; and it is stewed with tomatoes, vegetables, potatoes and whatever is handy. Lack of space prevents me from describing all the various Mediterranean ways of preparing fish, but there is rarely a great difference between them. The seasoning, of course, varies, depending on the country. In the Iberian Peninsula, saffron, coriander, cumin are used; at the other end of the Mediterranean we find pine nuts and currants. Olive oil, garlic, and onions are almost always used, and lemon juice is also a frequent ingredient.

Unlike the poor of many other countries, the poor people of the Mediterranean care greatly whether their food is nicely prepared and of the freshest ingredients. Thus, the fish eaten in the Mediterranean countries (where until recently refrigeration was unknown) had to be of the freshest quality, and therefore excellent. We must also remember that such care is lavished on fish in these southern countries because they are Catholic countries, where Lenten and other fasts used to be prolonged and frequent. 'If you want good fish, go to the monks and priests,' they say in Italy, and from the old books and manuscripts that I have seen, a book on ecclesiastical fish cookery in Europe would be a delightful enterprise.

Some of the best Mediterranean fish are not served in the elegant restaurants, which do not consider them classy enough for an international clientele. Fresh anchovies and sardines and salt cod turn up in regional dishes in the local taverns, the small restaurants frequented by neighbourhood people. It's worth finding them out, as the food is good, the wine cheap, and the company jolly.

*

Spanish Sherry-baked Brook Trout [*Truchas al Jerez*]

An excellent way of baking trout and other small fish.

4 small brook trout	4 tablespoons bread crumbs
½ lemon	1 clove garlic, crushed
Salt	2 tablespoons chopped parsley
Pepper	Juice of ½ lemon
2 tablespoons olive oil	3 fl. oz. dry sherry

Rub trout lightly with lemon. Season with salt and pepper. Heat oil. Remove from heat and stir in bread crumbs, garlic, and parsley. Spread half of this mixture on the bottom of a shallow greased baking dish. Place trout on top. Cover with remaining bread crumbs. Sprinkle with lemon juice. Bake in moderate (350° F., gas 4) oven 10 minutes. Add sherry and bake 10 more minutes, basting occasionally.

Spanish Soused Anchovies or Other Fish
[*Escabeche de boquerones*]

The sousing (pickling) of fish goes back into antiquity, since it is a good method of preserving it in an unusually flavourful way. The Romans knew it, and the medieval clerics soused their fish in many different ways. Elizabethan, German, Scandinavian, Balkan cooking – soused fish appears in them all. All fish can be soused, but I prefer the Spanish and Portuguese way of treating fresh anchovies, sardines, whiting, and mullet. Smelts and herrings, too, are excellent prepared in the *escabeche* manner, with the Iberian spicing.

The Spaniards do their anchovies rather prettily, crossing the tails of 3 or 4 fish before frying them.

2 lb. anchovies or other small fish	1 teaspoon ground ginger
Flour	8 fl. oz. wine vinegar
8 fl. oz. olive oil	8 fl. oz. water
6 cloves garlic	Salt
½ teaspoon saffron	Pepper
1 teaspoon cumin seeds	1 lemon, sliced
	2 bay leaves

Roll the fish in flour and shake off surplus. Heat oil as hot as
possible and fry fish for about 5–10 minutes, depending on size.
Drain on absorbent paper and place in a crock or deep china
dish. (Do not use a metal container.) Reserve oil and heat again.
Fry garlic in oil until golden. Add saffron, cumin, ginger and
gradually stir in vinegar. Add water and salt and pepper to taste.
Bring to the boil, cover, and simmer over low heat 5 minutes.
Pour over fish. Top fish with lemon slices and bay leaves. Cover,
and marinate 24 hours in a cool place before using. Serve from
the same dish with a little marinade for each helping. Fried aubergine is a good accompaniment for soused fish.

Greek Baked Fish [Psaria plaki]

This is not a very dainty dish, but it's a savoury one. It is made
from any white fish. If the fish is large, like cod or haddock, it
should be cut into thick slices. Smaller fish can be used whole.
Plaki is also good cold, but not chilled. It's a standard Greek way
of cooking fish. The recipe serves 4 to 6.

2 lb. white fish	2 cloves garlic, crushed or minced
4 tablespoons lemon juice	6 tablespoons chopped parsley
Salt	3 tomatoes, peeled and sliced
Pepper	2 fl. oz. water or dry white wine
4 fl. oz. olive oil	4 large tomatoes, sliced
6 medium-sized onions, sliced	2 lemons, sliced

Sprinkle fish with lemon juice, salt, and pepper. Heat olive oil
and cook onions, garlic, and parsley in it for 5 minutes, or until
onions are soft. Add 3 tomatoes and simmer for 5 minutes. Add
water or wine and cook 5 minutes longer. Grease a large shallow
baking dish and put half of the onion and tomato sauce in it.
Place fish on this and cover with remaining onion and tomato
sauce. Arrange 4 sliced tomatoes on top in overlapping rows
with the lemon slices. Bake uncovered in moderate (350° F.,
gas 4) oven about 30 to 45 minutes, or until fish is tender. Do not
overbake. If the plaki looks dried out while baking, add a little
hot water or white wine. Serve hot with a Rice Pilaff (page 128)
or cold with a Rice Salad (page 36).

Grilled Swordfish Steaks from the Balkans

Excellent swordfish is caught in the eastern Mediterranean; they are big fish, weighing anything up to 200–300 lb. They are brought to market swiftly and sold to the housewives almost alive. The fish markets in any Greek, Yugoslav, Italian, or Turkish town are worth seeing for the incredible and colourful variety of fish and shellfish displayed on the open stalls and for the spirited bargaining of the housewives. Tourists should really get up early for the sight.

Fish in the Balkans is usually cooked simply, with a lemon and oil dressing, and preferably grilled over charcoal. When fish is good, there is no better way of cooking it.

2 lb. swordfish	Salt
¾ pint olive oil	Pepper
Juice of 2 large lemons	½ teaspoon cayenne pepper
1 tablespoon onion juice	

Trim thick skin off swordfish and cut into steaks. Marinate 6 hours in half the olive oil, the juice of 1 lemon, onion juice, salt and pepper to taste. Line grill pan with aluminium foil for easier cleaning. Preheat grill for 10 minutes. Arrange swordfish steaks on pan. Grill 10 to 15 minutes, depending on the thickness of the steaks. Baste with marinade frequently. If steaks are more than 1 inch thick, turn after 5 minutes, using a spatula or pancake turner. Test for doneness with a toothpick – the fish should flake easily but not fall apart.

Make a sauce by combining remaining oil, lemon juice, and cayenne pepper. Place swordfish steaks on hot platter and pour sauce over them. Decorate with parsley and serve with a cooked vegetable salad.

Ischia Anchovies or Other Fish [Alici all'Ischiana]

Ischia, an island off Naples, is like its neighbour Capri, only better, though it must be admitted that there is no Blue Grotto. But in Ischia, where I used to spend childhood summers, there are hot springs beneficial to almost any human ills, so the natives say, an extinct volcano with the biggest and most heavenly peaches growing on its sides, a church (in the town of Lacco Ameno) where the holy-water container is upheld by a little statue of Hercules, and an eerie, eroded landscape of rocks and stones like a banshee's dream of the moon. And in Ischia there also was a young fisherman, whom at the age of ten I wanted to marry. When I came back many years later we both were married, but his mother cooked fish as well as ever. She made the following dish with fresh anchovies, but it is good with any kind of small, whole fish, especially smelts.

Split, bone, and wash small fish. Oil a round baking dish and arrange fish in several circles, heads all facing the same way. Pour about ¼ inch of French dressing (made from two thirds oil and one third lemon juice – do not use vinegar) over fish. Sprinkle a little fresh or dried herbs, such as thyme, basil, or oregano, over fish. Cover and bake in hot (425° F., gas 7) oven about 10 minutes, depending on size of fish. Test with toothpick for doneness. Do not overbake.

Fresh Tuna Provençale

Fresh tuna is virtually unknown in this country, but it is possible to get it by speaking to the fishmonger in advance, and I wish more people would, since it is a wonderful fish, and one that is easy to eat. The best and tenderest cut is from the stomach.

Off Sicily, they catch tuna at night. From my childhood, I remember the flickering lights of the boats on an opalescent, dense-skinned sea that was streaked with phosphorescent patches, under a moonless sky thick with stars.

1½–2 lb. fresh tuna
Salt
Pepper
2 tablespoons olive oil
1 large onion, chopped
4 tomatoes, peeled, seeded, and
    chopped, or 1 small tin
    tomatoes
1 clove garlic, minced
8 fl. oz. white wine (or lemon
    juice and water mixed)

8 fl. oz. hot water
1 tablespoon chopped parsley
1 bay leaf
1 tablespoon chopped fresh
    fennel or 1 teaspoon dry
    fennel seeds
⅛ teaspoon thyme
1 tablespoon flour
1 tablespoon (½ oz.) butter
1 tablespoon capers

Sprinkle fish with salt and pepper. Heat olive oil until very hot, and sauté fish in it until golden on all sides. Add onion, tomatoes, garlic, and wine. Cover, and simmer 10 minutes. Add water, parsley, bay leaf, fennel, and thyme. Cover, and simmer over very low heat about 20 to 30 minutes, or until done. Test fish for tenderness with toothpick; it should be flaky. Remove fish to deep hot serving dish. Blend together flour and butter and stir into sauce. Bring to the boil, stirring constantly. Lower heat, and simmer 3 to 5 minutes. Pour sauce over fish and garnish with capers. Serve with firm Polenta (page 143), rice, or plenty of hot French bread.

French Fillets of Sole En Goujons
[Filet de sole en goujons]

Any good French cookbook has more recipes for cooking sole than all other fish put together. Escoffier mentions 54 of them, and there are more, probably. This one is very simple, and so good that it is surprising that it is not better known.

Cut fillets of sole into thin strips. Give a twist in the middle. Dip in seasoned flour and fry in deep fat. It takes but a minute or two on each side. Drain on absorbent paper and serve on a white napkin with Fried Parsley (page 242) in the centre. Mustard Sauce (page 95) is good with these fillet strips.

French Fish Fillets Cardinal [Filet de sole à la Cardinal]

The authentic French dish is made with Dover sole, but this method of cooking fish fillets is a delicious one, and goes well with any delicate white fish fillets that may be at hand, preferably lemon sole, flounder, pike, and the like.

The sauce is made with lobster, and mine is a simplified version. The classic way of making it involves pounded lobster coral and lobster shell to give it a delicious pink colour, but to my mind the taste is not sufficiently superior to justify the effort, at least for the home cook.

8 fish fillets, skinned, washed and dried

Salt and pepper
Good ½ pint dry white wine

Sprinkle fillets with a little salt and pepper. Roll up or fold both
ends under. Place in a buttered shallow baking dish. Cover with
wine. Bake in moderate (350° F., gas 4) oven 10 minutes, basting
occasionally with wine. Remove fish to hot serving platter and
coat with Sauce Cardinal. Top each fillet with tiny shrimps
sautéed in butter and surround with additional shrimps. Serve
with boiled parsleyed potatoes.

SAUCE CARDINAL

2 tablespoons (1 oz.) butter	12 fl. oz. double cream
2 tablespoons flour	2 to 3 leaves fresh tarragon or
Salt and pepper	½ teaspoon dry tarragon
4 tablespoons hot fish stock or	4 oz. cooked lobster meat,
hot milk	minced
Few drops anchovy essence or	2 oz. cooked lobster meat, cut in
½ teaspoon anchovy paste	½-inch pieces

Melt butter. Remove from heat. Blend in flour and salt and pepper.
Cook over low heat, stirring constantly, until just golden.
Gradually add hot fish stock and cream, stirring constantly. Cook
until thickened. Stir in anchovy essence and tarragon. Add lobster
and heat through thoroughly, without boiling. If necessary, keep
hot in double boiler over hot (not boiling) water, stirring occasionally.

French Poached Pike Dumplings [*Quenelles de brochet*]

These are tiny and most delicate dumplings, a French speciality
that is usually served with a lobster or shrimp sauce. It takes a
little time to make *quenelles*, but it is well worth the trouble if
you want an elegant dish. *Quenelles* are used in *haute cuisine*
to decorate other fish dishes, but they can also be served as an
entrée, with Sauce Cardinal (see previous recipe). Real *quenelles*
are made with pike, but other fresh-water fish, such as trout or
perch, can be used. Salt-water fish will not do.

The recipe may seem a laborious one, and one that could be
adapted to a blender. It can, of course, but having made *quenelles*
both by hand and in a blender, I know the first method gives far
superior results, because the *quenelles* are lighter and airier – as

they should be. The basic paste can be prepared beforehand and kept in the refrigerator, leaving the shaping and cooking of the *quenelles* until just before mealtime.

1 cup very fine fresh white
bread crumbs (about 9 slices of
bread, trimmed of crusts)
About ¼ pint hot milk and
single cream mixed
2 teaspoons salt
1 teaspoon white pepper

1 lb. fresh pike, free of skin and
bones
½ lb. unsalted butter
2 whole eggs
2 egg yolks
⅛ teaspoon nutmeg

Work bread crumbs and hot milk and cream to a smooth paste. Season with 1 teaspoon of the salt and ½ teaspoon of the pepper. If paste is too soft, dry out by stirring a minute or two over fire. Strain paste through a food mill or fine sieve. Chill until firm.

Mince pike twice through the meat mincer, or pound it to a paste in a mortar. Blend butter and fish together until absolutely smooth. Work in bread-crumb mixture and beat until smooth. Strain again through food mill or sieve. Add whole eggs and egg yolks one at a time, beating well after each addition. Season with remaining salt, pepper, and nutmeg. Strain mixture again through food mill or sieve. Chill in refrigerator for at least 6 hours.

To *shape quenelles*: Flour a bread board. Keep additional flour handy. Roll about 1 tablespoon of *quenelle* mixture on the board into the shape of a thumb-sized sausage. This is best done by hand. Keep hands floured. Repeat, keeping board floured. Work quickly and keep *quenelle* mixture as cold as possible – if necessary, in a bowl over cracked ice.

To *cook quenelles*: Butter a shallow baking pan or skillet. Line up *quenelles* in pan. Keep well apart, as they swell during cooking and must not touch each other. Add boiling water to cover carefully, not touching *quenelles*. Poach over very low heat about 7 minutes. *The water must not boil again* or *quenelles* will disintegrate. Remove *quenelles* with a slotted spoon and drain on a dry towel. Serve on heated platter lined with a napkin and cover with napkin ends. Serve the Sauce Cardinal separately.

Kedgeree

A dish of Indian origin. Many recipes say that it can be made from any cooked white fish. It can, but the kedgeree will be rather flat. If, however, it is made from cooked smoked finnan haddock, it is absolutely delicious. The smoky flavour of the fish blends particularly well with the rice and egg, and I urge all neophytes to try kedgeree at least once.

3–4 oz. butter	2 hard-boiled eggs, chopped
4 oz. boiled rice	Salt
¾ lb. cooked flaked finnan	Pepper
haddock or other cooked fish	

Heat butter until golden but not brown. Add all other ingredients. Over low heat, heat through thoroughly, since the dish must be very hot. Stir occasionally to prevent scorching. Serve very hot, garnished with parsley.

Note: Another way of making kedgeree is to separate the cooked egg whites from the yolks. The whites are chopped and added to the rice and fish. The yolks are rubbed through a sieve and sprinkled on top of the kedgeree.

To cook smoked finnan haddock, poach in simmering water. Skin and bone before using.

Scottish Herring Fried in Oatmeal

This is a very Scottish dish, combining the two staple foods of the country. Somehow the two flavours combine into an absolutely perfect food. Incidentally, oatmeal gives a delicious flavour to other fried fish when it is used as a coating instead of flour or crumbs.

Clean and bone herring and split in half. Season fine oatmeal with salt and pepper. Dip fish into oatmeal and coat on all sides, shaking off excess oatmeal. Heat any fat (bacon fat is very good) to smoking point. Fry herring for 5 minutes on each side, or longer if fish are large. Drain on absorbent paper and serve very hot, with Gooseberry Sauce (page 256).

Danish or German Fried Herring with Onion Sauce
[Stegt Sild med Løgauce – Gebratener Heering mit Zwiebelsosse]

This dish is very popular in both Denmark and northern Germany. A very old woman I knew in my youth, who in *her* youth had worked in Bismarck's kitchens, told me that the Iron Chancellor had been very fond of this dish, with which he drank champagne, of which he was also very fond. Fond enough, in any case, to have half a bottle of it every morning.

8 medium-sized herrings	Bread crumbs
Flour	Fat for frying
2 eggs, beaten	

Bone herrings, wash, and dry. Dip in flour, beaten eggs, and bread crumbs. Fry in hot fat 5 minutes on each side, longer if large. Drain on absorbent paper and keep hot in serving dish.

SAUCE

2 tablespoons (1 oz.) butter	½ teaspoon sugar
2 onions, thinly sliced	½ teaspoon paprika (or more)
1 tablespoon flour	¼ teaspoon pepper
¾ pint hot milk	

Drain fat from pan in which herrings were fried. Melt butter and heat until light brown. Cook onions in it until soft. Sprinkle flour on onions and blend thoroughly. Slowly add milk, stirring constantly. Blend in sugar, paprika, and pepper. Cook sauce over low heat until thickened, stirring constantly. Pour sauce around the hot herrings. Serve with boiled potatoes sprinkled with dill, and cucumber salad dressed with sour cream.

German Baked Whole Fish à la Hamburg
[Gebackener Fisch Hamburger Art]

Any good-sized fish – 4 to 8 lb. – is delicious cooked this way. In Hamburg they use pike, of which the Germans are extremely fond.

Clean and skin a good-sized fish. Place fish in a baking dish just big enough to hold it. (The fish can also be bent into a U-shape.) Sprinkle with salt and pepper and a little chopped parsley, dill, or tarragon. Fresh herbs are best, but dried ones will do. Heat oven to 400° F., gas 6. Pour sufficient good dry white wine over fish to cover (the Germans use Moselle). Bake uncovered for half of the fish's complete baking time. The wine should have evaporated to half of the original measure. Now add sufficient double cream to reach two thirds up the fish. Cook for remaining time, basting frequently. Do not overcook. Fish takes 10 to 12 minutes a pound. Test for doneness with a toothpick; flesh should be flaky.

Remove fish carefully on to a hot serving plate. If sauce is not the right consistency, either boil gently to reduce or thicken with a little more cream. Finish sauce with a little lemon juice and chopped parsley, or dill, mixed in thoroughly – use the same herb that was sprinkled on the raw fish. Pour sauce over fish and garnish with unpeeled cucumber slices sautéed in butter. Serve with parsleyed boiled potatoes.

Finnish Boiled Pike or Bass [Keitetty Kala]

This is another Scandinavian speciality. When the fish are fresh, it is a most wonderful way of cooking them, especially pike.

2 lb. fresh pike	1 large onion
Water	2 whole allspice

Clean and gut fish. Wash in cold water and dry. Bring water with onion and allspice to the boil. Lower fish into water carefully – the water should reach halfway up the fish (or else use a fish steamer or wrap fish in muslin to avoid breaking). Simmer about 15 minutes over low heat. Do not boil. Place fish on hot platter and serve immediately, with plain boiled potatoes sprinkled with dill, and a sauce of melted butter to which a little horse-radish has been added.

Norwegian Fish Pudding [Fiskepudding]

This is one of the greatest of all fish dishes – a mousse rather than a pudding. Norwegians, like Swedes, Danes, and Finns, are wonderful fish cooks, since fish is a large item of their diet, day in, day out. Other Scandinavians make fish pudding too, but I think the Norwegian version far better than others. I admit that it is troublesome to make, but the results are more than worth it, for a party where utmost elegance and airiness count.

I presume this pudding could be made in a blender, eliminating much work. But since I have never made it in one, I shall limit myself to throwing out the suggestion to an enterprising cook with an urge for modern improvements.

2 lb. fresh cod or haddock fillets, or 1 lb. of each
½ lb. butter
4 eggs, separated
1 oz. sifted flour
2 teaspoons cornflour
2 teaspoons salt
½ teaspoon white pepper
⅛ teaspoon nutmeg
8 fl. oz. single cream
8 fl. oz. double cream
Fine dry white cracker crumbs
Sauce Cardinal (page 76)

Remove all skin and any bones from fish. Pass three times through the mincer, using the finest blade, or pound in mortar until smooth. Add butter, and mince twice more; or pound again until perfectly blended. Beat in egg yolks, one at a time. Sift together flour, cornflour, salt, pepper, and nutmeg. Beat into fish mixture gradually, alternating with single cream, until mixture is absolutely smooth. Beat egg whites until stiff, and whip double cream. Fold into batter alternately, a little at a time. Butter a mould and coat with cracker crumbs. Pour mixture into it – the mould should be three quarters full. Stand in shallow baking pan filled with 1 to 2 inches of boiling water. Bake in slow (325° F., gas 3) oven about 1 hour, or until tester comes out clean. Remove from oven. Let stand about 3 to 4 minutes. Run spatula carefully inside mould to loosen. Bang gently on table and unmould on hot platter. (This is done by placing platter over mould and turning over.) Decorate with tiny shrimps sautéed in butter. Serve with Sauce Cardinal. Don't serve anything else with this dish, because any accompaniment would spoil the rich, delicate flavour of the pudding.

Fish Baked in Sour Cream

This is a way of baking fish dear to people of eastern Europe and the Slavs, where sour cream is triumphant. I think it is particularly suited to the coarse fish, such as carp, eel, or tench, which must be thoroughly washed under running water to rid them of their muddy flavour, and dried before baking. The fish can be used whole or cut in pieces, as well as filleted. Eels should be skinned, since their minute fins are embedded in their smooth skins, and cut into 4-inch pieces.

2 lb. fish	2 oz. butter
Flour	1 oz. grated Parmesan cheese
Salt and pepper	8 fl. oz. sour cream
1 to 2 teaspoons paprika, or more (optional)	Fine dry bread crumbs

Roll fish in flour seasoned with salt and pepper. Shake off excess flour. Heat butter and sauté fish until golden. Arrange in shallow baking dish. Sprinkle paprika over fish. Stir Parmesan cheese into sour cream and pour over fish. Top with bread crumbs and dot with butter. Bake uncovered in hottish (400° F., gas 6) oven until fish is flaky. Serve with lemon slices.

Salt Cod

Salt cod, or ling, as the English call it, has been one of the most important staple foods not only in Europe but in South America ever since the discovery of the Newfoundland fishing banks about four hundred years ago. It may truly be said that salt cod has been the staff of life especially in Catholic countries, where the Lenten fast and countless other fast days, which in the past were very rigorously observed, called for immense quantities of cheap, nutritious meat substitute that could be stored without spoiling and that was within the reach of the impoverished citizen. Thus salt cod became and still is a great staple in Spain, Portugal, Italy, France, and other Catholic countries.

Like herring, salt cod suffers from not being a fashionable fish, and furthermore it is one that needs a little preparation before cooking. Yet it can be prepared in many ways that are worth the attention of gastronomes.

When buying salt cod, one should choose fish that are white, not yellowish. The fish must always be desalted before cooking. But before desalting, it is a good idea to give it a dozen or so good strong whacks against a table to break down the fibres, as they do in Italy. The best way of desalting cod is to leave it in running water overnight. If this is not convenient, soak in cold water for 24 hours, changing water at least 6 times. Desalted cod must *never* be boiled – a fact that is often overlooked, and the result is tough, stringy fish. The liquid in which it cooks must barely simmer. Allow 1 lb. of salt cod for 3 people.

There are many fine recipes for salt cod, but I don't think that any are topped by the classic French Brandade de Morue – a noble dish that appears on the tables of French families but, alas, not in restaurants, perhaps because it is too much trouble to prepare. The Russians also cook their cod in an interesting manner, with sour cherries, a recipe that may seem odd at first but is very good indeed.

Brandade de Morue Provençale

This dish turns up in Venice as *baccalà mantecato*, and also in Spain, showing that the Mediterranean is but one big fraternal sea. The quantities of the ingredients are approximate, something to start with. The end result should be a white, absolutely smooth and creamy mixture, which is brought to the table piled high in a pyramid and garnished with toast triangles fried in oil to a golden crisp, to offset the creaminess of the *brandade*.

1 lb. desalted cod	Pepper
8 tablespoons olive oil (or more)	1 to 2 teaspoons lemon juice
2 fl. oz. single cream (or more)	1 teaspoon grated lemon rind or
1 to 2 cloves garlic, crushed (optional)	⅛ teaspoon nutmeg

Cut soaked, desalted cod into pieces. Put fish in saucepan and cover with cold water. Bring to the boil; lower heat immediately and simmer over low heat 10 to 15 minutes. Do not boil. Drain.

Remove skin and bones, and break fish into small flakes. Pound fish in mortar or blend in blender. It must be absolutely smooth, without the trace of a lump. Heat oil and cream separately until lukewarm – no more. They should both be the same temperature. Add a spoonful of warm oil to the pounded fish, and work it in with a wooden spoon to make the mixture creamy. Add warm cream in the same manner. Continue alternating oil and cream, beating and stirring the mixture until it is white and very smooth. The oil and the cream must be kept warm, and the stirring continuous and vigorous throughout the whole operation. When the *brandade* is the consistency of a thick potato purée, work in garlic, pepper to taste (no salt), lemon juice to taste, lemon rind or nutmeg. Serve tepid. For an elegant touch, decorate with truffle slices or thinly sliced black olives for contrast.

Russian or Polish Cod with Red Wine and Cherries

I once knew a very old Russian lady in Rome, an émigrée even poorer than most of them. She earned her few pennies doing embroidery for one of the tourists' shops and starved most of the time. She had many friends, but she was as proud as Lucifer, and to get her to accept even a luncheon invitation involved Machiavellian skill. The most interesting thing about her was the way she lived, which made a deep impression on me as a child. A Roman princess, a friend of hers, had given her an enormous, high-ceilinged attic rent free in her palace, and here Madame X (she would not like me to use her real name, even though she is dead) camped. Literally, she camped. Since the attic was not heated and had a marble floor, marble being the cheapest flooring at the time the palace was built in the sixteenth century, and since Roman winters can be very cold, Madame X had erected a small army tent in a corner of this gigantic room. There she sat in winter, huddled over a small charcoal brazier, doing her intricate stitches by the light of a small oil lamp, for it was dark in the tent. And there was nothing anybody could do about it. I remember being taken to see her often by my mother, who loved her. Madame X would give us tea in glasses, which we sucked through lumps of sugar, and flat fruit cookies which she called *mazureks*, making the word sound like 'mazurka', which surprised me every time, since I thought mazurkas were dances by Chopin.

To come to the cod with cherries. Madame X could afford only the food of the poorest of the poor, and salt cod was as much part of her diet as of that of the other poor Romans. My mother detested salt cod over all things. But one day Madame X decided to return some of the hospitality shown her, and invited several of her friends, including us, to lunch. The salt cod with cherries was the *pièce de résistance*, and wonder of wonders, my mother liked it and asked for the recipe. I found it among my mother's things many years later, and curiosity prompted me to make it. My mother still liked it, and so did I. It is best made with fresh sour cherries, which are as cheap in Rome as cod, but canned sour cherries will do.

I checked on the recipe and found that cooking cod this way is common practice in Russia and Poland, where they love soured dishes. But there it is made with fresh cod. Poor Madame X could not afford fresh fish, so she made with the salt cod what turned out to be a highly original and excellent dish.

2 lb. desalted cod	Boiling water
¾ pint milk	

Cut soaked, desalted cod into pieces. Put fish in a saucepan and cover with milk. Bring to the boil; lower heat immediately and simmer over low heat 10–15 minutes. Do not boil. Drain, and pour boiling water over cod to wash off milk. Keep hot.

SAUCE

½ lb. sour cherries, stoned and chopped	2 tablespoons (1 oz.) butter
14 fl. oz. water	¼ teaspoon cinnamon
Sugar to taste (the sauce should be tart)	¼ teaspoon cloves
	8 fl. oz. red wine
	1 tablespoon cornflour

Simmer cherries, water, and butter over low heat for 5 minutes. Add sugar, cinnamon, cloves, and red wine. Simmer 5 minutes longer. Dilute cornflour with a little cold water. Bring sauce to the boil and stir in cornflour. Lower heat and simmer until sauce is thickened and shiny, stirring constantly. Put cooked pieces of cod into sauce. Cover, and simmer over low heat 10 minutes. Serve with boiled rice.

Carp

Carp is greatly valued in Europe, and as with all fresh-water fish that patronize the bottom of muddy streams and ponds, the flavour is better when the water is cold – that is, from October to the end of March.

A whole chapter could be written around carp in European history. It is an old, old fish, known to the Romans, who filled it with herbs and spices and baked it in a marinade. The monks stocked the ponds of their convents with carp as an insurance for Lent; and carp was eaten in most Catholic countries on Christmas Eve, which used to be a fast day. Carp grow very old, very fat, and very wily, and more than one fisherman has been outwitted by them. I knew an Austrian who had his eye on a particular and very portly carp and spent a summer trying to catch it in the pond in Styria, the Steiermark, where this evasive old fish lived. He never got him, but the carp used to come to the surface and I would have sworn that he winked as he swam around in the sunshine, opening his large mouth to catch a little fly or two that was skimming on the water.

Carp can be stuffed and baked in wine, in sweet or sour cream, or cooked with vegetables, or fried. In Germany the head is usually served to the most honoured guest at the table, who sucks its cheeks, but though I like carp, I feel that this is too much.

I think that much the best way of cooking carp is with a stuffing or tart sauce. The following recipe is a kind of stew, and it can also be made with other fresh-water fish, such as fresh-water cod and bass.

It is a good idea to soak the carp in cold running water for an hour or so, to remove any possible muddy flavour, and then to wash it in ¾ pint cold water mixed with ¼ pint vinegar, for the same reason.

Czech Carp with Black Sauce

¾ pint wine vinegar or any
   other vinegar
1½ pints water
2 medium-sized onions, sliced
2 stalks celery, diced
1 small carrot, diced

1 clove garlic
2 bay leaves
6 whole cloves
6 whole allspice
1 teaspoon ground cumin
1 4-lb. carp, cut in serving pieces

In deep kettle, combine all ingredients except carp and bring to
the boil. Simmer for 30 minutes. Add carp, cover, and simmer
about 30 minutes, or until the fish separates from the bones.
Drain carp; reserve liquid. Place carp in soup tureen or deep
serving dish and keep hot. While fish is cooking, make Black
Sauce.

BLACK SAUCE
1 lb. cooked prunes, pitted and
   chopped
Juice of 1 lemon
Grated rind of 1 lemon
1 tablespoon (½ oz.) butter

3–4 oz. raisins
3 oz. chopped walnuts or other
   nuts
2 oz. sugar

Combine all ingredients and mix thoroughly. Add to liquid in
which fish was cooked. Simmer for 5 minutes and pour over fish.
Serve with boiled potatoes sprinkled with dill or parsley and with
cucumber salad.

Poached Fish and Shellfish

Poached salmon, sterlet, salmon trout, and other big fish are the
belles or beaux of restaurant and buffet tables, where they repose
on socles of rice or beds of greens, decorated to the last inch
with a coat of mayonnaise or aspic and fanciful, colourful designs
made from cut-up vegetables and surrounded by vegetables carved
into the likes of roses, lilies, and lotus flowers, as well as shrimp
and lobster claws. They look for all the world like eighteenth-
century harem beauties.

   The fact remains that poached fish is wonderful, for no other method of cooking preserves a fish's delicate, fresh taste so well. I think it a shame to prepare really good salmon or trout any other way. But the fish must be poached, *never* boiled, for boiling makes it lose its flavour and renders the texture watery and stringy, as well as disintegrating the fish. Poaching means cooking the fish in water that barely shivers or ripples, and its importance in fish cookery cannot be sufficiently stressed. The fish to be poached must be completely immersed in the liquid or encased in steam in an airtight fish boiler, or the uncovered parts will not be cooked through.

Whole fish, fillets, or centre cuts may be poached. The method is always the same, using salt water or a *court bouillon* (see recipe below). I think *court bouillon* is better for poaching fish and shrimps or prawns, since they will not taste so fishy. Lobster, of course, is cooked in boiling water, and so are crabs.

To poach fish, put enough *court bouillon* in a kettle or saucepan to cover the fish. Bring it to the boil, lower in the fish, turn down the heat immediately, and simmer – do not boil. Fillets are best poached in a skillet. A whole fish, or a centre cut, is best poached in a fish steamer. But since few people have one, here is a way that will preserve the fish intact. Wrap the fish in muslin, leaving long ends at either side that will serve as handles. Lower the fish by the handles into the liquid and leave handles hanging out of the kettle while the fish cooks. The cooked fish is then lifted out by the handles and gently unrolled on to a platter. The skin should come off with the muslin – or else the cooked fish is skinned and then cooled. To test for doneness, use a toothpick or a knitting needle or a thin skewer. If a large fish or a very thick slice of fish is being cooked, it might be necessary to lift out the fish and unwrap it in order to have a look at the cavity and a direct testing at the centre of the backbone.

Wrapping the fish in muslin may seem laborious, but without it, I don't see how it is possible to obtain a fish that is whole and unblurred.

Back to the *court bouillon*. Great fish cooks advocate adding fish bones and trimmings to it for more taste, especially when the strained broth is to be used for sauce or, clarified, for aspic. I prefer not to use them, liking my fish not too fishy.

Another thing that cannot be repeated too often is that fish and shellfish must not be overcooked. They all too often are, whichever way the fish is prepared. Here are the cooking times:

Fillets: 5 to 10 minutes per pound, depending on thickness of fish

Centre slices: 7 to 10 minutes per pound

Whole fish: 8 to 10 minutes per pound, and 5 to 10 minutes more if the fish is very large

These directions may seem on the vague side, but fish are so very different in consistency, fat content, and size that only practice will tell for sure. However, it is important to know the weight of the fish before cooking.

Crabs: must be cooked alive – 8 minutes per pound

Lobster: 5 minutes for the first pound and 3 minutes for each subsequent pound. 1½-lb. lobsters will cook in 8 to 10 minutes, 2-lb. lobsters in 12 to 13 minutes

Scallops: 4 minutes per pound for sea scallops, 2 minutes per pound for bay scallops

Shrimps and prawns: 3 to 5 minutes depending on size. Do not cook longer than 6 minutes. Small shrimps will be cooked through if plunged in boiling *court bouillon*, withdrawn from heat, and let cool in *court bouillon*.

Court Bouillon for Fish and Shellfish

Wine is essential. If necessary, the amounts can be increased or decreased proportionately.

1½ pints water	8 peppercorns
1½ pints dry white wine	1 bay leaf
1 tablespoon wine vinegar	2 sprigs parsley
2 medium-sized onions, sliced	⅛ teaspoon thyme
1 carrot, chopped	⅛ teaspoon mace
Small stalk celery	1 whole clove
1 tablespoon salt	

Combine all ingredients and simmer over low heat for 1 hour. Strain before using.

Note: If a fish is to be served in aspic, use the *court bouillon*

for stock and clarify (see To *clarify bouillon* on page 52). Trout
and salmon are especially good cold and coated with aspic.

Court Bouillon with Dill for Poaching Fish in the Swedish Manner

Nobody knows how good poached fish such as cod, salmon, perch,
mackerel, lobster, crayfish, or shrimps can be unless they've eaten
them flavoured with dill. Here is an excellent *court bouillon* for
fish flavoured with Sweden's favourite herb, dill.

1½ pints water	1 bay leaf
4 tablespoons wine vinegar	1 small onion, chopped
1 tablespoon salt	1 piece carrot, chopped
3 whole allspice	5 to 10 sprigs fresh dill

Combine all ingredients in saucepan. Bring to the boil, cover and
simmer 15 to 20 minutes. Strain, and use liquid for poaching fish.
Garnish cooked fish with additional dill sprigs or chopped dill.

Poached fish is often served with a white sauce enriched with
chopped hard-boiled eggs (½ egg for 1 cup sauce) and chopped
dill.

Shellfish

German Fried Lobster [*Gebratener Hummer*]

This was a popular dish at the Herrenclub in Berlin, a famous
(or infamous, depending on one's political point of view) con-
servative club, where big-time politics used to be hatched. My
father, who told me about it, said that it was served with a rather
thin, ice-cold mayonnaise strongly flavoured with Dijon mustard.
Though there is nothing very original about frying lobster, it is
an excellent way of eating it, and far less laborious than most,
thank heaven (I don't like to work over my food at the table).
As for the sauce, I thin mayonnaise (preferably home-made) with
lemon juice, and flavour it strongly with the superb Grey Poupon
mustard which is one of the glories of the old and beautiful city
of Dijon, famed throughout the world for its fine cooking.

Divide cooked lobster tail meat into quarters and use whole meat from claws. The pieces should not be too small. Sprinkle with salt, pepper, and a little lemon juice. Let stand for 15 minutes. If necessary, dry on absorbent paper. Flame a little good cognac in a warmed spoon and pour over lobster. (This is not absolutely necessary, but it makes a world of difference in the flavour.) Dry again, if necessary. Dip lobster pieces in flour, beaten egg, and fine white bread crumbs. Shake off excess crumbs. Fry in deep fat, heated to 385° F., until golden on all sides. Drain on absorbent paper.

Spanish Shrimp Cocktail [Ensalada de camarones]

Excellent, thanks to the dressing, which can be used on any kind of cold fish or sea food. The recipe comes from a friend in Cadiz, the city that is blindingly white.

8 fl. oz. olive oil
2 fl. oz. white wine vinegar
Juice of 1 large lemon
Grated rind of ½ lemon
1 clove garlic, minced
2 to 3 tablespoons capers
1 teaspoon sugar
⅛ teaspoon Tabasco or hot red pepper sauce
Salt and pepper
1 lb. cooked, shelled shrimps (or prawns)
1 large onion, thinly sliced

Combine all dressing ingredients and blend thoroughly. Place shrimps and onion slices in alternate layers in deep bowl. Pour dressing over layers and chill at least 2 hours. To serve, drain off dressing. Place shrimps and onion on lettuce leaves and decorate with thin slices of lemon and tomato.

Stewed Shrimps

An interesting way of cooking shrimps, which can also be applied to cooking lobster.

3 tablespoons olive oil
36 large shrimps or prawns, shelled
½ clove garlic, minced
3 tablespoons parsley, chopped
1 tablespoon capers
Juice of ½ lemon

Heat the olive oil in a heavy skillet. Add the shrimps and cook about 5 minutes, or until nearly done. Add remaining ingredients and cook 2 to 3 minutes longer, or until done. Serve hot in their own sauce.

Shrimps Cinta

8 fl. oz. lemon juice	1 teaspoon ground red pepper
8 fl. oz. olive oil	(optional)
6 cloves garlic, crushed	24 large shrimps, or prawns or
2 teaspoons chopped parsley	scampi

Combine all ingredients except the shrimps. Pour over the shrimps and marinate overnight in the refrigerator. Remove shrimps from marinade; grill until brown, 5 minutes on each side.

Note : I have treated cooked lobster chunks in the same manner, with very fine results.

Scallops St Jacques [Coquilles St Jacques]

1 lb. fresh scallops	¼ teaspoon white pepper
Juice of 1 lemon	8 fl. oz. single cream
¾ pint water	2 egg yolks
1 bay leaf	2 oz. grated Swiss or Parmesan
3 tablespoons (1½ oz.) butter	cheese
2 tablespoons flour	2 tablespoons dry white wine
1 teaspoon salt	Paprika

Wash and dry scallops. If large, cut into pieces. Sprinkle with lemon juice. Simmer in water with 1 tablespoon butter and bay leaf for 5 minutes. Drain. Melt the rest of the butter, blend in flour, salt, and pepper. Gradually stir in cream, mixing until smooth and well blended. Cook over low heat, stirring constantly, until thick and smooth. Beat in eggs and cheese. Cook 3 minutes longer. Add wine and scallops. Pour into buttered scallop shells. Sprinkle with paprika. Bake in moderate (350° F., gas 4) oven 10 to 15 minutes, or until top is golden brown.

Crab Meat Charentais

Like all recipes depending for their flavour on wine or spirits, this one will be only as good as the liquor employed. The alcohol evaporates in cooking, the flavour remains. The flavour of poor spirits is despicable – better not use any. But a good cognac, armagnac, or Calvados – the kind that is bliss to drink – brings bliss to this essentially simple dish. Incidentally, it makes canned crab meat worth eating.

1 lb. crab meat, free of all bones, cartilage, etc.	4 fl. oz. dry white wine
	Salt and pepper
6 spring onions, sliced fine, green and white parts	1 teaspoon fresh minced tarragon or ½ teaspoon dry tarragon
½ green pepper, minced	6 tablespoons cognac
2 oz. unsalted butter	1 tablespoon chopped parsley

Make absolutely sure the crab meat is carefully picked over. Separate into small lumps. Sauté spring onions and green pepper in hot butter for 5 minutes, or until soft. Do not brown. Add crab meat, wine, salt and pepper to taste, and tarragon. Stir once or twice, taking care not to break crab meat. Heat over medium heat until heated through thoroughly – about 5 minutes. Stir a few times. Warm cognac in spoon or ladle by holding it over direct heat. Blaze and pour over crab meat. Serve on toast.

Turkish Stuffed Mussels [Midye dolmasi]

Mussels stuffed with savoury rice are eaten a great deal in the eastern Mediterranean countries. As with all local recipes of the kind, each housewife has her own version. The following one has met with the greatest success among my own friends. It also works well with clams. Stuffed mussels, eaten cold, are delightful for a summer supper, accompanied by a crisp cucumber salad and a bottle of a light, rather fruity chilled white wine, such as a Neufchâtel.

STUFFING

4 fl. oz. olive oil	2 tablespoons currants
4 medium-sized onions, minced	Pepper
½ lb. uncooked rice	2 tablespoons chopped parsley
2 tablespoons pine nuts, coarsely chopped	¾ pint boiling water or fish stock

Heat olive oil and sauté onions 3 minutes, or until soft. Add rice and sauté over medium heat 5 minutes, stirring constantly. Add pine nuts and sauté 2 minutes longer. Add currants, pepper (no salt), parsley, and boiling water. Stir once, cover, and simmer over lowest possible heat 20 to 25 minutes, or until rice is tender. Liquid should be absorbed. Uncover, and cool.

36 large mussels (about)
1¼ pints boiling water

Brush, scrape, and wash mussels thoroughly. Force open with a blunt knife but do not break the shells completely apart. Remove the beard and the black part of the mussels, and wash carefully under running water. Keep in cold water.

Shake the mussel that is to be stuffed free of water. Push a little stuffing into each shell with a small teaspoon. Close mussel firmly and tie with white thread. Repeat until all mussels are stuffed. Pack mussels tightly into deep kettle so that they cannot float loose. Pour boiling water over them. Press down firmly with inverted plate and keep plate in kettle. Cover kettle tightly and simmer over low heat 30 minutes. Drain mussel liquid from kettle and cool mussels in kettle. Cut thread and remove from mussels. Serve cold with lemon slices.

Mussels Marinière [*Moules marinière*]

Moules marinière is another of the French recipes restaurants have built their fame on. However, the method of cooking mussels is not as exclusively French as they like to think; it turns up in Spain, Italy, and other Mediterranean countries, since it is a rather obvious one. This recipe will serve 2 as a main dish.

24 mussels
2 chopped shallots or 2
    tablespoons chopped scallions
    (white part only) or 1
    tablespoon chopped white
    onion

¼ teaspoon pepper
⅛ teaspoon thyme
8 fl. oz. dry white wine
2 tablespoons chopped parsley
1 tablespoon flour
1 tablespoon (½ oz.) butter

Brush, scrape, and wash mussels thoroughly. Put into deep kettle. Add shallots, pepper (no salt), thyme, wine, and 1 tablespoon chopped parsley. Cover, bring to the boil, and simmer for 6 to 8 minutes, or until the mussel shells open. Stir once or twice. Remove mussels to deep serving dish or individual soup plates and keep warm. Since there is probably some sand from the mussels in the bottom of the kettle, strain kettle juice into another saucepan. Bring to the boil. Knead the flour and butter together into a little ball, and stir into liquid. Cook, stirring constantly, until thickened. Pour over mussels and sprinkle with remaining parsley.

*

Mustard Sauce for Fried or Grilled Fish

Make a white sauce or Béchamel, using half cream, half milk. Flavour with a little grated onion or onion powder. To each cupful of sauce add 1 tablespoon French mustard (Grey Poupon from Dijon is best) and ½ teaspoon dry mustard; 1 tablespoon chopped parsley also greatly improves the flavour and appearance of the sauce.

Eggs, Cheese, and Luncheon Dishes

'To make an omelet, you must break the eggs,' says the French proverb. This saying has different levels of meaning, for the egg has always been not only a food but a symbol of life itself. In the Egyptian *Book of the Dead* a passage speaks 'of that great and glorious god in his egg, who created himself for that which came forth from him'. In India there is the 'cosmic egg' of Brahmanic tradition, and the Buddha uses the symbol of the egg in one of his parables on spiritual rebirth. The egg was held sacred in Greece's Orphic mysteries, and it appears in the myth of Hiawatha. Tiberius Claudius Nero's wife Livia, who wanted to know whether she was carrying a male or a female child, was told by a seeress to place in her breast a newly laid egg until it hatched. If it brought forth a cockerel, the gods would grant Livia a son. This she did and in due time produced Tiberius, who later became an emperor of extremely picturesque habits that cannot be described in a family cookbook.

Eggs are a universal food, and though there are literally thousands of ways of serving them, there are only about 6 methods of cooking them. That is, eggs are either boiled or poached or scrambled or baked or fried or cooked with other foods. All good cookbooks list many wonderful ways of cooking eggs – André Simon, in his *Concise Encyclopaedia of Gastronomy*, has some 240.

In this book I have omitted the national egg dishes that can be found in the different European cookbooks, as well as in cookbooks devoted to eggs and cheese. Instead, I have listed some recipes that lend themselves to luncheons and suppers, because dishes of this kind are a great convenience either as entrées or as pre-entrée courses. All of them, I think, reflect the European art of making much with little.

Basque Scrambled Eggs [*Pipérade*]

A delicious way of cooking eggs with tomatoes and vegetables, and very easy. In the Basque country *pipérade* is served with ham, and a good York ham or Italian prosciutto would go well with it. Be sure to serve plenty of crusty bread. *Pipérade* is never made with butter.

3 oz. lard or bacon fat	3 large or 5 small green or red
4 medium-sized onions, thinly sliced	peppers, sliced
	Salt
4 tomatoes, peeled and coarsely chopped	Pepper
	6 to 8 eggs, beaten
¼ teaspoon thyme or marjoram	

Melt lard in heavy skillet. Cook onions in it over low flame 5 to 10 minutes, or until very soft. They must not brown. Add tomatoes, peppers, salt, pepper, and thyme or marjoram. Cover, and cook over very low heat for about 15 minutes, or until the vegetables are almost a purée. Stir frequently. Pour beaten eggs into vegetables and scramble gently with a fork until eggs are just set. The *pipérade* must be very soft. Serve very hot.

French Poached Eggs in Red Wine [Œufs à la matelote]

It may at first seem strange to poach eggs in wine, but it is a surprisingly good way, and one that gives a little éclat to luncheon.

8 fl. oz. dry red wine	Pepper
8 fl. oz. bouillon	⅛ teaspoon nutmeg
1 onion, sliced	6 eggs
1 clove garlic	1½ tablespoons flour
Salt	1 tablespoon (½ oz.) butter

Combine wine, bouillon, onion, and garlic; season with salt and pepper and add nutmeg. Cover; simmer over low heat 10 minutes. Strain, and bring again to a boiling point. Poach eggs as usual. Remove from liquid and keep hot. Boil liquid until it is reduced by half. Mix flour and butter to a paste and add, a little at a time, to hot liquid, stirring constantly. Serve eggs either on a hot purée of kidney beans or on slices of toast buttered on one side only, placing the eggs on the unbuttered side. Pour sauce over eggs and serve immediately.

French Eggs Baked in Cream [Œufs sur le plat lorraine]

An elegant and easy little luncheon or breakfast dish. The recipe is for 4 people.

Butter 4 ramekins or one large, shallow baking dish. Line dishes or the big dish first with thin slices of ham and top the ham with thin slices of Swiss cheese. Break 2 eggs into each individual dish or 8 eggs into the large dish. Cover with double cream – about 2 to 3 tablespoons for every 2 eggs. Sprinkle with pepper. Usually there is no need for salt, since the ham and the cheese are salty. Bake eggs in moderate (350° F., gas 4) oven 7 to 10 minutes, or until the whites are set, but keep the yolks soft.

Omelette aux Croûtons et Fromage

There is no need here to dwell upon the art of making omelets, since it can be learned from any standard cookbook. As every cook knows, omelets can be combined with hundreds of other foods. The following combination is one of the simplest and best.

For every 2 or 3 eggs that will go into the omelet, cut 2–3 thick slices stale, crustless bread into ¼-inch dice. Fry dice in hot but not browned butter until very crisp. Keep croûtons hot. Pour beaten eggs into hot butter in the omelet pan. Add the croûtons, and 2 tablespoons grated Swiss or Parmesan cheese. Fold the omelet over quickly and slide it on to the hot serving plate.

Omelette du Baron de Barante

According to André Simon's *Concise Encyclopaedia of Gastronomy*, this was Edward VII's favourite omelet, and it does open vistas into Edwardian life, to be interpreted according to one's own temperament. I have not made this stupendous creation, but perhaps some reader will be attracted to this example of voluptuous cooking, which was probably served in a plush-laden *chambre séparée* !

'Peel carefully 1½ lb. of firm, fresh mushrooms. Cut them into thin slices so that they can be cooked easily. Sprinkle with salt and cook in best butter. When they are pale yellow, pour over them a glass of good port. Cover the stewpan and reduce by half. Then add fresh thick cream and 12 slices of the tail of a lobster which has been cooked in a court-bouillon. Place this mixture in an 18-egg omelette, sprinkle liberally with Parmesan cheese, and brown a rich golden colour in a quick oven.'

Spanish Deep-fried Eggs [*Huevos fritos*]

The Spanish people's attitude toward eggs is one that causes foreigners to wonder. It has been my experience that eggs appear at all meals, at home and in restaurants, and regardless of whether they are needed as food. The Spaniards I asked about this merely replied : 'It is our custom.'

The most unusual way I've eaten eggs in Spain is deep-fried. The Spaniards serve eggs in omelets, fried Western style, sometimes even scrambled, all in a very savoury Spanish manner. But I've never come across deep-fried eggs anywhere else. At first the dish seems strange, but it is surprisingly good.

Boil eggs for 4 minutes. Run cold water over them for easier peeling, and peel carefully. Roll eggs in flour, dip in beaten egg, and roll in fine dry bread crumbs which have been seasoned with salt and pepper. Fry them in deep hot olive oil at 375° F. for 1 to 2 minutes. Drain eggs carefully on absorbent paper and serve with a well-seasoned tomato sauce.

Spanish Threaded Eggs [Huevos hilados]

A folly, probably of Moorish origin, at which the nuns of Avila excelled, according to an eighteenth-century chronicle. Oddly enough, these threaded eggs are not a dessert but are eaten now-adays with cold cuts. They are good with ham.

1 pint water	12 egg yolks, slightly beaten
1¾ lb. sugar	

In 12-inch skillet combine water and sugar, and cook until sugar is completely dissolved. Remove from heat. Place egg yolks in double boiler over hot water, and stir until smooth and thinned, 2 to 3 minutes. Pour egg yolks through a fine sieve. Put a small amount of egg yolks into measuring cup. Over low heat, heat syrup to simmering point. Do not boil. Pour egg yolks in very thin stream into syrup, holding the measuring cup about 12 inches from the surface. Use a rotating movement, to keep strands separated and long. Cook 3 minutes. Remove eggs from syrup with slotted spoon and dip in cold water. Drain on absorbent paper. Use remaining egg yolk in the same manner, taking care to keep syrup at the simmering point until all the eggs are cooked.

Note: Instead of pouring the eggs from a cup, you may use a small tin can with the top removed and a hole the size of a pencil punched in the middle of the bottom.

Spanish Eggs Baked à la Flamenco

3 tablespoons (1½ oz.) butter	6 oz. cooked string beans
1 large onion, sliced	1 tablespoon chopped parsley
¼ lb. ham, diced	Salt
1 clove garlic, minced	Pepper
3 tomatoes, peeled, chopped, and diced	4 oz. chopped pimento-stuffed olives
6 oz. cooked peas	4 eggs

Melt butter. Add onion, ham and garlic and cook over medium
heat until onion is tender, stirring occasionally. Add tomatoes
and cook 10 minutes. Add peas, beans, parsley, salt and pepper
to taste, and olives and mix well. Turn into 4 individual baking
dishes. Top with eggs. Bake in moderate (350° F., gas 4) oven
20 minutes, or until eggs are set. Makes 4 servings.

Austrian Parmesan Pudding

This is a substantial main dish, and quite different from a soufflé,
since the pudding is steamed. Steaming is easy provided you
remember these rules. If you don't have a mould with a tight-
fitting cover, use any deep kitchen bowl or baking dish. Cover
the bowl very tightly with several thicknesses of wax paper or
aluminium foil. Tie a string around it as tightly as you can so
that the bowl will remain covered. The water in the pan in which
the pudding is steaming must *never* boil but be kept at no more
than the simmering point. Else the pudding will be watery and
full of holes.

This pudding serves 4 as a main dish, or 4 to 6 as an appetizer.
It should be served with a mushroom or tomato sauce.

6 eggs, separated	Salt
1 oz. flour	Pepper
8 fl. oz. milk	4 oz. grated Parmesan cheese

Beat egg yolks and stir in flour. Add milk and salt and pepper
to taste (go easy on the salt, since the cheese is salty). Cook until
mixture is thick, stirring constantly. Add cheese and cook over
low heat, stirring constantly, until cheese is melted. Grease a
2½-pint mould. Pour mixture into mould. Cover tightly and
steam for 45 minutes in pan of hot water on top of the stove.

Swiss Eggs Lucerne

Very simple and very good.

1 lb. Swiss cheese, sliced	5 fl. oz. double cream
8 eggs	1 oz. grated Swiss cheese
Salt and pepper	

Heavily butter the bottom of a shallow baking dish. Line with sliced cheese. Break eggs over cheese. Season with salt and pepper. Pour cream over eggs. Sprinkle with grated cheese. Bake in moderate (350° F., gas 4) oven for 15 minutes, or until set.

Crème Lorraine

A lovely dish from France, lighter and more delicate than a soufflé. The cheese must be Emmenthal or Gruyère, and Parmesan.

6 slices lean bacon	¾ pint double cream
6 oz. grated Emmenthal or Gruyère cheese	2 eggs, well beaten
	1 teaspoon salt
6 oz. grated Parmesan cheese	¼ teaspoon white pepper

Fry bacon until crisp. Drain, and break into small pieces. Mix with cheese, cream, eggs, salt, and pepper. Pour into buttered 2½-pint baking dish. Bake in moderate (350° F., gas 4) oven 35 to 40 minutes, or until set. Makes 4 servings.

Note: If more than 4 servings are needed, it is better to make up 2 crèmes Lorraine and bake them in 2 dishes, rather than to double the quantities for one large dish.

French Baked Eggs and Onions [Œufs à la tripe]

A country way of cooking eggs that is centuries old, and one more proof of how the French can take a few ingredients that are always at hand and make a delectable dish.

2 large onions	1 teaspoon Dijon or French mustard
2 oz. butter	
6 hard-boiled eggs, sliced	2 tablespoons grated Swiss or Parmesan cheese
Salt	
Cayenne pepper	1 egg yolk
2 tablespoons (1 oz.) butter	2 tablespoons milk
2 tablespoons flour	Butter
13 fl. oz. hot single cream	

Slice onions thinly. Heat the 2 oz. butter but do not brown. Cook onions in butter over medium heat 5 to 7 minutes, or until soft. The onions must remain pale. Butter a shallow baking dish. Arrange alternate layers of hard-boiled eggs and onions. Sprinkle with salt and a little cayenne pepper.

Melt the 2 tablespoons butter and stir in flour. Blend in hot cream and cook over medium heat until sauce is thickened, stirring constantly. Add mustard and cheese, and cook 2 to 3 minutes longer. Beat together egg yolk and milk. Remove sauce from heat and stir in egg mixture. Pour sauce over eggs and onions and grill quickly until top is brown and bubbly. Or bake in hot (425° F., gas 7) oven. Grilling is better, since it will not dry out the dish. For luncheon, serve with Garbanzos Fritos (page 242) and a tomato salad.

French Cheese Soufflé [Soufflé au fromage]

Cheese soufflés are considered difficult to make, for no good reason, since all the cook needs to do is follow directions accurately. There are various recipes for soufflés, but the following one is my favourite – it makes a soufflé that is creamy inside, in the French manner. The lightest soufflés are made with Swiss or Parmesan cheese, which are light cheeses. Cheddar also makes a tasty soufflé, but a heavier one.

2 oz. butter	⅛ teaspoon nutmeg
2 oz. flour	4 eggs, separated
12 fl. oz. hot milk	3 oz. finely grated Swiss or
⅛ teaspoon cayenne pepper	Parmesan cheese

Melt butter. Add flour and cook over low heat until the flour just begins to turn golden, stirring constantly. Add hot milk gradually, and cook about 5 minutes, stirring constantly. Add cayenne pepper and nutmeg. Remove from heat. Beat egg yolks until light. Stir egg yolks carefully into sauce, blending thoroughly. Return to heat, stirring constantly. Heat through but do not allow to boil. Remove from heat and stir in cheese. Beat egg whites until stiff but not dry. Fold into cheese mixture lightly with a slotted spoon or a wire whip. Pour into buttered 3-pint baking dish and bake in hot (425° F., gas 7) oven about 20 minutes. Serve at once.

Austrian Spinach Soufflé [*Spinat Auflauf*]

Central and northern European cooking abounds in souffléed vegetables. Some of these dishes are good, others are not. Spinach soufflé belongs to the first kind. It may be served with melted brown butter as the entrée for a meatless meal. As an accompaniment, I would suggest an artichoke dish, since the flavours of the two vegetables complement each other. The recipe serves 4 but it can easily be doubled.

3 tablespoons (1½ oz.) butter	4 oz. grated Swiss or Parmesan
4 tablespoons flour	cheese
Salt and pepper	6 oz. finely chopped cooked
⅛ teaspoon nutmeg	spinach, well drained
8 fl. oz. single cream or milk	3 eggs, separated

Melt butter and blend in flour, salt, pepper, and nutmeg. Gradually add cream or milk, stirring until well blended. Cook over low heat, stirring constantly, until thick and smooth. Add cheese and spinach and cook until cheese is melted. Cool. Beat the egg yolks until thick. Add to spinach mixture. Beat egg whites until stiff but not dry and fold into spinach. Pour into buttered 2½-pint baking dish and bake in a slow (325° F., gas 3) oven about 45 to 50 minutes.

Italian Potato and Cheese Tart [*Tortino di patate*]

Potato tarts and pies are eaten all over Europe, since potatoes so often have to serve as a main dish rather than as an accompaniment for meats. In fact the meat-and-potato habit is predominantly an Anglo-Saxon and Germanic one. I personally do not care for potato tarts made with pastry, because they seem just too starchy. The following Italian recipe yields a substantial, though savoury, dish.

3 medium-sized potatoes, boiled	Scant 14 fl. oz. olive oil
and mashed	6 oz. canned tomatoes, drained
4 oz. flour	½ lb. Mozzarella cheese, diced
Salt	1 oz. grated Parmesan cheese
Pepper	1 tablespoon rosemary

Work together thoroughly mashed potatoes, flour, and salt and pepper to taste. In large shallow oiled baking dish arrange potato mixture in a layer that is about ½ inch thick. Sprinkle with half the olive oil. Top with tomatoes, Mozzarella, Parmesan cheese, and rosemary. Sprinkle with remaining olive oil. Bake in hot (400° F., gas 6) oven 20 to 25 minutes, or until the cheese is light brown. Serve hot, as an entrée or with cold meats.

Italian Mozzarella Skewers [Crostini alla Mozzarella]

Remove the crust from a loaf of French bread. Cut loaf into slices about ⅓ inch thick. Cut Mozzarella in the same size and thickness as bread. Place alternate slices of bread and cheese on a skewer until there are 3 layers of cheese, beginning and ending with bread. Preheat baking dish and place skewers on it. Bake in a very hot (450–75° F., gas 8–9) oven and bake just long enough for the cheese to melt and the bread to brown.

Melt ½ lb. butter. Chop 8 anchovy fillets and simmer in butter for 5 minutes. Pour some of this anchovy butter over each skewer. Serve as hot as you can.

German Potato Soufflé [Kartoffel Auflauf]

¾ lb. hot mashed potatoes
4 fl. oz. hot single cream
2 oz. grated Swiss cheese
2 tablespoons (1 oz.) butter
1 tablespoon finely chopped parsley
4 eggs, separated

Into hot mashed potatoes beat hot cream, cheese, butter, and parsley. Beat egg yolks until thick and lemon-coloured. Beat egg whites until stiff but not dry. Fold egg yolks into potato mixture, then fold in egg whites. Pile lightly in buttered baking dish. Bake in hot (425° F., gas 7) oven 15 to 20 minutes, or until puffed and lightly brown.

Note: This is often served with Specksauce (page 253), a bacon-onion sauce.

Hungarian Potato and Egg Casserole

6 medium-sized potatoes, boiled	Salt
6 hard-boiled eggs	Pepper
6 rashers bacon, chopped	2 tablespoons chopped parsley
1 tablespoon (½ oz.) butter	4-5 fl. oz. sour cream

Slice potatoes and hard-boiled eggs. Cook bacon in hot butter until crisp. Drain, reserve fat. Place alternate layers of potatoes, eggs, and bacon in greased baking dish. Season with salt and pepper and sprinkle with parsley. Stir reserve fat into sour cream and pour over all. Cover, and bake in moderate (350° F., gas 4) oven about 15 to 20 minutes, or until golden.

Ragoût of Mushrooms and Eggs

2 tablespoons olive oil	4 fl. oz. dry white wine
1 tablespoon minced onion	Salt
1 tablespoon chopped parsley	Pepper
1 lb. mushrooms, sliced	6 hard-boiled eggs, coarsely
1 tablespoon flour	chopped

Heat olive oil over medium heat and cook onion and parsley in it for 2 minutes. Add mushrooms; cover and cook over low heat 10 minutes. Stir in flour and add wine. Cover and simmer for 5 minutes. Season with salt and pepper. Add eggs and simmer, covered, for 5 more minutes, stirring occasionally. Serve as an entrée with hot garlic bread, or with grilled ham or sausages or game.

German Farmers' Breakfast [Bauernfrühstück]

A dish that turns up in practically every Central European country, and one men seem to like very much. It is a good dish for luncheon or supper.

6 rashers bacon, cut in small strips	1 small green pepper, diced
	Salt
2 tablespoons finely chopped onion	Pepper
	2 oz. any grated cheese
3 large boiled potatoes, peeled and cubed	6 eggs

Fry bacon over low heat until slightly browned and crisp. Drain off all but 2 tablespoons of fat. Add green pepper, onion, potatoes, salt, and pepper. Cook over medium heat about 5 minutes, or until potatoes are golden, stirring frequently. Sprinkle cheese over potatoes and stir. Break eggs into pan over potatoes and cook over low heat until eggs are set, stirring constantly. *Do not beat eggs beforehand.*

Swiss Cheese Croquettes [*Délices d'Emmenthal*]

Mouth-melting and divine. The name comes from the Emmenthal, an idyllic valley in the Bernese Oberland, with the prettiest trappings of chalets, fields of wild flowers, happy cows and the *ranz des vaches*, the song of the cowbells. I can't think of a more elegant luncheon dish, with the added advantage that the greater part of the preparation must be done well in advance.

4 tablespoons (2 oz.) butter
5 tablespoons flour
12 fl. oz. hot single cream
1 tablespoon onion juice or
  1 teaspoon onion salt
½ lb. grated Swiss cheese
4 egg yolks, well beaten
White pepper
⅛ teaspoon nutmeg

1 tablespoon finely chopped
  parsley
Flour
1 egg, beaten with 1 tablespoon
  milk
Bread crumbs
Fat for frying
Fried Parsley (page 242)

Melt butter over low heat and stir in flour. Add hot cream and cook over low heat for 10 minutes, stirring constantly. Blend in onion juice or salt and Swiss cheese. Cook until cheese is melted, stirring constantly. Remove from heat and stir in egg yolks, blending thoroughly. Season with pepper and nutmeg, and add parsley. Butter a flat plate or shallow baking dish and spread mixture in it. Chill in refrigerator for at least 3 hours.

Cut mixture into 16 equal portions and shape each portion into a croquette. Use your hands, and keep them lightly floured. Roll the croquettes in flour, shaking off excess, in the egg and milk mixture, and in bread crumbs. Shake off excess crumbs. Chill in refrigerator for 1 more hour. Fry in deep hot (375° F.) fat for 1 to 2 minutes, or until golden. Drain on absorbent paper. Serve very hot in a napkin, with a garnish of Fried Parsley and a tomato sauce.

True Swiss Fondue

The dish poets have sung of, and a natural for chafing-dish cookery. The quantities are for 4.

1 lb. grated Swiss cheese	1 large or 2 small cloves garlic
3 tablespoons flour	Salt and pepper
¾ pint dry white wine (such as Neufchâtel, Rhine, Riesling, or Chablis)	¼ teaspoon nutmeg (optional)
	6 tablespoons Kirschwasser

Dredge cheese with flour. Rub the chafing dish or an earthenware cooking pot or a heatproof china casserole with garlic. Pour in wine and heat over low heat until just below boiling point – when the air bubbles rise to the surface. Add cheese by spoonfuls, stirring with a fork until each spoonful is completely absorbed. Keep stirring until mixture starts to bubble lightly. It must not boil, or the cheese will become stringy. Season with salt, pepper, and nutmeg. Stir in Kirschwasser thoroughly. Remove bubbling fondue from heat and place on preheated table heating equipment. Keep warm to prevent cheese from solidifying, but do not boil.

Eat from pot by dunking pieces of French bread into fondue, stirring it to coat the bread thoroughly and to keep the right consistency. Serve plenty of the same white wine or Kirschwasser with the fondue.

Thin Yellow Boys

A charming name (origin unknown) for the best of egg sandwiches. I serve them for a simple luncheon or late supper, with a salad. This makes 3 sandwiches, but the quantities can easily be doubled or tripled.

6 hard-boiled eggs, finely chopped
2 tablespoons butter (1 oz.), melted
1 tablespoon Dijon or French mustard
1 tablespoon Worcester sauce
1 tablespoon tarragon, fresh or dry
1 tablespoon wine vinegar
1 tablespoon minced fresh chervil
1 tablespoon minced parsley
1 tablespoon minced shallot or finely minced onion
Salt
Freshly ground black pepper
6 slices hot buttered toast

Combine all ingredients except toast, and heat through thoroughly, mixing well. Spread between toast slices and serve very hot.

Wheat, Rice, and Other Cereals

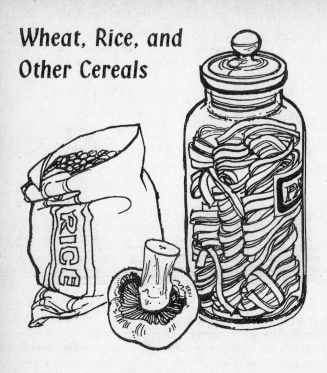

It is to the fruits of the field that we owe the initial transition from animal to human life, and to civilization as we know it. Nomad man, the hunter, in his eternal quest for food could not settle down long enough to create lasting values. The wandering tribes of the African jungle, the desert dwellers, the nomad Arabs, and the natives of the Antipodes prove this to us even in our day and age. Were they to be swept away from the face of the earth, few if any traces of their passage would remain.

Among the fruits of the field, it is the grains that chiefly sustain life. They need not be consumed immediately, they can be stored against need, and in themselves they bear the seed of their renewal. Small wonder then that the religions of the world hold the grains in mystical reverence. Wheat and barley are perhaps the oldest grains known to civilized man of the Western world, and their place of origin is said to have been the fertile plains of the Euphrates from which they spread east and west.

Bread is the staff of life, the Bible tells us, and the Christian ceremonial centres around the bread and wine as divine symbols. Before the Christian era, in ancient Egypt, Greece, and Rome, and even in older civilizations, rites were celebrated to honour the grains.

Demeter, goddess of the fields and fertility (the Romans knew her as Ceres, hence the word 'cereal'), was at the heart of the Eleusinian mysteries, the secret cult that has been called the fountainhead of Greek culture. She is shown in ancient friezes holding ears of wheat, and to the hero Triptolemus the goddesses gave the first grain, bidding him diffuse its blessings throughout the world. Chinese mythology tells of Shen-nung (the divine Husbandman), who taught the Chinese the use of the plough and hoe so that they might cultivate millet and rice, the chief grains of China. In America, the religious ceremonies of the Indians are intrinsically tied up with the mythology of corn, or maize.

From these cursory notes we can see that the cult of the grain existed wherever civilization dawned. To pray for one's daily bread is indeed innate in man all over the earth.

Until very recent times the peoples of Europe subsisted chiefly on grains, as they still do in many parts of the Continent. Potatoes, the starch food of northern Europe, did not cross the sea from their original home in the New World until the end of the sixteenth century. Then they were planted on Sir Walter Raleigh's estate in Cork; they were used as food in Ireland for many years before they became known in England. The majestic roasts of old England were only for the chosen few, and all over the Continent meat was synonymous with riches. Even to this day, in many European countries, a man's position is gauged by the number of times a week he eats meat. Grains were the food of the people, since man can grow them with his labour only, whereas animals must be fed.

Naturally, different ways of using grains developed in the various European countries. Bread, though universal, is grain in a more luxurious form, since it must be baked, consuming much fuel – and fuel was and is precious in Europe. The gruels and porridges of Britain and Scandinavia, the *Mus* or *Musles* of Germany and Switzerland, the barley, buckwheat, and millet dishes of eastern Europe, the dumplings and pancakes of Hungary and Czechoslovakia, the rice of Spain and the Balkans, and the pasta of Italy and the Mediterranean are all the results of man's endeavour to make the grains upon which he must live as filling and as palatable as possible.

Though the Scandinavians still eat gruels in moderate quantities, their use in Britain is obsolete except in oatmeal porridge. The farinaceous mushes of Germany and Switzerland, eaten with milk and perhaps some butter, are alien to today's tastes even in those countries. Dumplings and pancakes are no longer the daily fare in Central Europe now that the machine age has come to those countries. Generally speaking, only the pasta and rice dishes of southern Europe have survived to flourish in modern times, spreading to all of Europe from their native lands and into America.

About Pasta

Amorini (little cupids), *canneroni* (big reeds – which come, like many kinds of macaroni, both big and small, smooth and grooved), *cappelli di prete* (priests' hats), *cappelli pagliaccio* (clowns' hats), *conchigliette* (little shells), *creste di gallo* (coxcombs), *elettrici rigati* (grooved electric ones), *farfalloni* (big butterflies), *fidelini* (little faithful ones), *fusilli* (spindles), *lancette* (little spears), *lasagne* (probably from the Latin *lasanum*, a pot, described in the dictionaries as 'the container for the contained'), *linguine* (little tongues), *lingue di passero* (sparrows' tongues), *lumache, lumachine* and *lumacone* (snails, little snails and big snails), *Margherite* (after a now dead Italian queen), *mostaccioli* (little mugs), *occhi di lupo* (wolf's eyes), *ondulati* (wavy ones), *ricciolini* (little curls), *stelline* (little stars), *stivaletti* (little boots), *vermicelli* (little worms), *ziti* (bridegrooms), as well as *capelletti d'angelo* (angel's hair), are but a few of the 100-odd names given to the various offspring of the pasta family, some enormous, to be stuffed; others minute, to be put into soup.

The very folkloristic sound of these names shows the deep union between the Italian and his pasta. Though there is a misty legend that Marco Polo brought macaroni back from China, where it had been known for thousands of years (this is no legend), macaroni was well known in Italy before Marco Polo's day. In fact it was well enough known there by the year 1200 to be mentioned in a historical document, the *Life of the Blessed Hermit William*. There it says: 'He invited William to dinner, and served macaroni.' Indeed, macaroni may have been known far earlier than this; among the exhibits in the Pompeii museum there is equipment that looks as if it had been used to make, cook, and serve pasta.

The origin of the word 'macaroni' is obscure. It may come from the Greek word *makarios*, which means blessed, but only in reference to the dead, and *makaria*, food eaten in honour of the dead. Perhaps macaroni was the food eaten at funeral banquets. But whatever the origin of macaroni, it flowered beyond belief in Italy throughout the centuries. The people ate it, the writers wrote about it. Boccaccio, in the *Decameron*, describes an idyllic country where no one works and all things are free, with a mountain of grated Parmesan in the middle of it. On top of this mountain there are people who do nothing else but make macaroni, which they cook in capon broth, and then throw it down to all who want it. The eighteenth-century playwright Goldoni tells in his memoirs how he tossed down three platefuls of macaroni and described it as a marvellous moment. Or, as the Neapolitan proverb has it, 'He fell into it, like a macaroni into the cheese', not a surprising saying, considering that during the seventeenth century Naples established herself as the macaroni capital of Italy, and 'Neapolitan' became synonymous with 'macaroni eater'.

Old paintings and other pictures, the kind that tourists brought back from the Grand Tour, show the Neapolitans stuffing spaghetti into their mouths with their hands – both hands – in a steady stream cascading from way above their heads. This was a trick the Neapolitans performed to amuse the tourists, who, according to old travel reports, looked on goggle-eyed. But the fact remained that the best macaroni products came from around

Naples, and many people in Italy still believe this, and will not buy any but Neapolitan macaroni. An aunt of mine, who lives in Milan, is among them; she makes a macaroni-buying trip to Naples several times every year, and one enormous closet in her apartment is choked with cases of the stuff in all sorts of shapes. And the large sheets of dough, drying out in the open before being cut into shapes, can still be seen in some of the more remote southern Italian villages, though no longer in the big cities, where spaghetti and its cousins are made in factories just as anywhere else.

The Italian ways of serving macaroni with about any kind of food known to man are countless, and as popular as they have always been, except for a time in the thirties, when the Italians produced 'Futurismo', a school of philosophy aiming to get Italy away from the dead hand of the past and make it into a super-modern country. Futurismo advocated many things, including making Venice into a factory town and kicking out all tourists, since they insisted on looking upon Italy as the country of museums, *dolce far niente*, *o sole mio*, and other similar antiquated and undignified notions. Little did the Futurists know what the future would bring, and perhaps if they could see the rapid industrialization of Italy today they would sigh for the dear old days when the weekly markets in the provincial towns yielded exquisite handicrafts rather than U.S. Army surplus as they do today.

Marinetti was the chief prophet and poet of the Futurists, and he was a very intelligent man who did many things because 'he knew it teases'. The reform of the Italian diet was among them, and he declared war upon spaghetti. 'Futurist cooking', he said, 'will be liberated from the ancient obsession of weight and volume, and one of its principal aims will be the abolition of pastasciutta [that is, all spaghetti and macaroni dishes]. Pastasciutta, however grateful to the palate, is an obsolete food; it is heavy, brutalizing and gross; its nutritive qualities are deceptive; it induces scepticism, sloth and pessimism.'

These were fighting words, and the nation got into an uproar. Families were divided and villages rent whenever pastasciutta was served, which was daily. The press took the matter up with glee. Even the mayor of Naples, the Duke of Bovino, got into the act with the remark, 'The angels in paradise eat nothing but vermicelli al pomodoro,' to which Marinetti replied that this confirmed his suspicions about the monotony of paradise and the kind of life led by the angels.

Marinetti and his friends also evolved a complete futurist cuisine in which they combined ingredients for no other reason than their shock value, such as cooked salami drenched in hot black coffee flavoured with eau de cologne. All senses were to participate during the eating of a meal; suffice it here to say that perfume was to be sprayed over the diners (warmed, so as not to chill the bald-headed), who were also to stroke materials harmonizing with the meal – velvet or silk or steel – with one hand while the other held the fork.

Marinetti was close to Mussolini, and, with him, he also evolved a campaign to lead the Italians away from such acquired foreign habits as German music and French food, and, of course, American cocktails. All foreign words were to be Italianized – the one I remember is the sandwich, to be known as the *traidue* (between two). Italy has to import most of her wheat for her spaghetti, and Marinetti's influence prompted Mussolini to embark on an all-out campaign to have the Italian-grown rice take the place of spaghetti. Vast sums were spent on popularizing the idea, but it never took. The Italians remained faithful to their pastasciutta, and one of the worst hardships of the Second World War was the horrid, black, and disintegrating pasta of the war and post-war years. White-flour bread and pasta fetched fortunes in the black market of the post-war years, and regrettable as this may be from one point of view, it is also cheering and comforting to think that centuries of civilized eating could not be wiped out by yet another war on Italian soil.

How to Make Good Pastasciutta

Pastasciutta is the general name for all spaghetti, noodle, and macaroni dishes when they are not soups. In Italy there exists the word *minestra*, or soup, whose interpretation has confused many foreigners. There is *minestra asciutta*, or dry soup, and *minestra in brodo*, or broth soup; both are dishes served before the meat or other main course. *Minestre* can be pasta, or rice, or thin soups, or stewlike dishes, but they are never main dishes. If you eat only *minestra*, you are poor and can't afford to do any better. Italian restaurateurs are still confused by foreigners who consider a dish of spaghetti, or rice, and a salad a meal, and frown upon this practice as ungenteel.

To cook pasta properly, it is absolutely essential to have a very big pot with rapidly boiling salt water. Unless the pasta cooks in sufficient water it cannot expand properly and shed its excess starch. Spaghetti, the most popular kind of pasta, also presents the problem of strands sticking together. The addition of a little olive oil to the boiling water helps keep them apart, but this is not necessary (and is seldom done in Italy) when the pasta is stirred properly, as in the step-by-step method that follows below.

Another equally important step is to have the pasta reach the table hot, and piping hot at that – the hotter the better. The pasta must be cooked in violently boiling water, drained quickly, poured immediately on a hot serving dish, served with a sauce that is *hot*, and preferable on really hot dinner plates – as all hot food should be served. Pasta must never be lukewarm or overcooked. It should be cooked *al dente*: to the toothsome stage when it is tender yet still resilient to the bite. If these rules are observed, making good pastasciutta should present no problem.

Obviously the best pasta recipes come from Italy, and equally obviously there are so many superior ones that it would take a whole book to list them. The recipes in this chapter cannot be anything but a guide and an inspiration to look up more in the many excellent Italian cookbooks.

How to Cook Spaghetti and Other Pasta

(1) To cook 1 lb., it is essential to have a very large pan that will hold 10 pints of water; ½ lb. pasta should be cooked in about 5 pints of water. Add 2 tablespoons salt to 10 pints water, and 1 tablespoon salt to 5 pints water.

(2) Bring water to a full, rolling boil. Gradually add spaghetti

or other pasta, stirring with a long-handled kitchen fork. The water should keep on boiling hard.

(3) As the pasta begins to soften, fold it over and over in the water so that it won't stick together. Keep on stirring it frequently during the whole cooking process. Occasionally lift out a strand and taste for doneness. Different pastas have different cooking times. The directions on the package provide some indication as to the length of the cooking time, though in general they make for a pasta that is rather overcooked. Thus tasting is essential to get the pasta right, for one's own taste.

Pasta that is to be cooked further in a casserole should not be more than three quarters done, or the end results will be mushy.

(4) When the pasta is done, drain it immediately into a large strainer or colander. Return to pot and add seasonings. Stir to coat all strands. Serve immediately on heated platter and heated plates.

(5) Never believe that pasta can be cooked in advance (unless for a casserole that will be cooked further). It can't. Never cook pasta until you are ready to eat it. In good restaurants, insist that it be freshly cooked for you, as it is in Italy.

Quantities to Cook

Roughly speaking, macaroni products approximately double in volume when cooked. Small shapes, like sea shells, however, increase less than spaghetti, macaroni, and noodles. 8 oz. will feed 3 or 4 people; 1 lb. 5–8 depending on their appetites.

Stracotto Sauce for All Pastas

Stracotto means overcooked in Italian, and overcooking is the trick behind this sauce, which is one of the best in Italian cooking. It is robust, but not coarse at all, and really an essence of meat, flavoured with mushrooms and Marsala. That meat – beef, in this case – must be of a good quality and absolutely free of fat, tendons, and other such matter. The mushrooms should be the dried kind, since they have much more flavour than the ordinary variety. And, though red or white wine can be used instead of

Marsala, dry Marsala or Madeira will give infinitely superior results.

1 lb. top quality beef (not ordinary stewing beef)	4 fl. oz. dry Marsala or Madeira
4 oz. butter	4 fl. oz. bouillon
1 medium-sized onion, minced	1 oz. dried mushrooms
1 medium-sized carrot, minced	Salt
1 stalk celery, minced	Pepper
1 oz. minced parsley	1 teaspoon grated lemon rind

Cut meat into tiny dice or run through the coarse blade of a mincer; the meat must not be minced fine. In heavy saucepan, heat butter and cook meat, onion, carrot, celery, and parsley in it over medium heat for about 5 minutes, stirring frequently. Add wine, bouillon, and mushrooms, which have been soaked to soften and chopped. Season with salt and pepper and add lemon rind. Cover tightly, and simmer over the lowest possible heat until the meat is *stracotto* – that is, almost dissolved – stirring occasionally. This may take as much as 3 or 4 hours, depending on the cut of meat used. But the sauce must be cooked this way for the flavours to blend. Serve over any pasta, or use for Lasagne (page 23) or similar dishes.

Note: This amount of sauce dresses 1 lb. pasta. Sometimes a peeled chopped tomato is added to the ingredients. This may thin the sauce, which should be thick. Therefore, if the sauce appears to be too thin, cook uncovered until the proper degree of thickness is achieved.

Mushroom Spaghetti Sauce [*Spaghetti al funghi*]

4 medium-sized onions, thinly sliced	Salt
	Pepper
3 oz. butter	¼ teaspoon nutmeg
2 lb. fresh mushrooms, sliced	8 fl. oz. double cream

In a heavy skillet melt 3 tablespoons of the butter. Sauté onions in it over medium heat 5 to 7 minutes, or until golden brown, stirring frequently. Cover and cook onions over very low heat 30 minutes, or until very soft. Stir occasionally. Melt remaining butter in another skillet and sauté the mushrooms until tender. Season with salt, pepper, and nutmeg; add to onions. Keep sauce hot while spaghetti is cooking according to package directions. Five minutes before serving, add cream to sauce and heat thoroughly. Do not boil or the sauce will curdle. Mix cooked spaghetti and sauce thoroughly and serve immediately with grated Parmesan cheese.

Note: This amount of sauce is sufficient for 1 lb. pasta.

Rustic Pasta [Pasta rustica]

Like so many Roman dishes, it starts with a battuto – that is, the mincing together of some of the ingredients. This is done on a chopping board with a mezzaluna, a knife shaped like a crescent moon, which is standard equipment in every Italian kitchen. The chop, chop, chop of the battuto making is the typical sound you hear before mealtime when you are in the country or in Rome's popular districts, where the kitchens are near the street.

Another way of making battuto would be to mince each ingredient separately and then combine them for cooking. The flavour that results, though, is not quite the same; the joint mincing seems to blend the flavours of the ingredients in an inimitable way, which gives the finished dish a subtle though quite unmistakable character. I shall therefore give the Italian way of making pasta rustica.

2–3 oz. parsley	8 fl. oz. bouillon
2 cloves garlic	About 1 lb. cabbage, shredded
1 large onion	2 medium-sized courgettes,
½ lb. bacon	chopped
1 large leek	Salt
2 radishes	Pepper
2 medium-sized carrots	1–1¼ lb. cooked cannellini
3 tablespoons fresh basil	(white kidney beans)
2 fl. oz. olive oil	1 lb. rigatoni
3 large tomatoes, peeled, seeded,	2 oz. butter
and coarsely chopped	2 oz. grated Parmesan cheese

On chopping board, mince together parsley, garlic, onion, bacon, leek, radishes, carrots, and basil. Heat oil in large pan and cook mixture in it about 7 minutes, or until soft and just about to brown. Stir frequently. Add tomatoes, bouillon, cabbage, courgettes, and salt and pepper. Cover, and cook over low heat 10 to

15 minutes, or until vegetables are tender, stirring frequently. Add cannellini and cook 5 minutes longer.

While vegetables are cooking, cook rigatoni in plenty of rapidly boiling salt water. Drain and toss with butter and cheese. Combine vegetables and pasta and mix thoroughly. Serve with additional grated Parmesan cheese. Serves 6 to 8.

Pasta with Parsley, Garlic, and Oil
[Pasta all'aglio, olio, e prezzemolo]

I don't think any other pasta dish illustrates better than this one how the poorest of the poor in Italy can make an excellent, well-flavoured dish out of the simplest ingredients – and the cheapest. This is the pasta for the people who cannot afford meat sauces, butter, or even Parmesan with their daily pasta, and who have to rely on the staples of their diet – olive oil, garlic, and a herb. And strangely enough, this pasta appeals to people with very sophisticated palates.

The amounts of the ingredients are dependent on one's own taste and means, as the case may be. But this is the method. As your pasta is about to finish cooking, warm 8 fl. oz. (or more, or less) olive oil in a small saucepan and stir into it as much finely chopped garlic and chopped parsley as you fancy. I like a great deal of parsley and a medium amount of garlic, but opinions on a medium amount of garlic may differ. The oil should be just warm, not hot, and the garlic and parsley steep in it for 1 to 2 minutes. They should not fry. Toss the whole mixture with the pasta. Cheese can be served with this, and I think it a great improvement, but in Naples, where this pasta is eaten by the poor, cheese is too expensive.

Pasta and Chick-pea Soup [Minestra di pasta e ceci]

This is a Roman speciality, somewhere between a soup and a stew. It is heavy and utterly delicious. The recipe makes 5 pints, about enough to feed 8 to 10 hungry people. I make pasta e ceci for picnics, taking it along in an insulated bag, since it does not have to be eaten absolutely hot. With some ripe tomatoes to be eaten out of hand, wine, bread and cheese, and a slab of bitter chocolate for dessert, the *pasta e ceci* makes most successful picnic food.

6 fl. oz. olive oil	1 tablespoon dry rosemary
3 large cloves garlic, minced	A good 1½ pints water
8 anchovy fillets, minced	1 lb. ditalini or elbow macaroni
2–3 oz. chopped parsley	2 tablespoons salt
2 1-lb. cans chick-peas	8–10 pints rapidly boiling water
4 large tomatoes, peeled, seeded, and chopped	Grated Parmesan or Romano cheese

In large pan, heat oil and cook garlic, anchovies, and parsley in it over low heat for 5 minutes. Add undrained chick-peas, tomatoes, rosemary, and 1½ pints water. Cover and cook over low heat 30 minutes, stirring frequently. Cook ditalini or elbow macaroni in boiling water to which 2 tablespoons salt have been added. Cook uncovered, stirring occasionally, about 8 minutes, or until not quite, but almost, tender. Drain.

Add ditalini or elbow macaroni to soup. Cook another 5 minutes, or until ditalini is tender. Stir occasionally, and serve with plenty of grated cheese.

Note: If you use dried chick-peas, soak overnight and then cook in salt water until soft. Add a little more water when you add them to the soup.

Spaghetti with Fresh Peas [Spaghetti con piselli]

Another speciality, typical of the way the Italians combine vegetables with pasta. Aubergines, courgettes, fennel (finocchio), broccoli – practically every vegetable gets combined with some pasta or other in the Italian rustic cuisine, and very good it is too.

¼ lb. Italian prosciutto or bacon	1 large tomato, peeled, seeded, and chopped
1 medium-sized onion	2 tablespoons fresh basil
1 clove garlic	Salt
1 3-inch piece celery	Pepper
2–3 oz. parsley	1 lb. spaghetti or other pasta
2 fl. oz. olive oil	1 to 2 tablespoons (½–1 oz.) butter
3 tablespoons (1½ oz.) butter	Grated Parmesan cheese
1½ lb. fresh peas, shelled	
3 fl. oz. bouillon	

On chopping board, chop together ham, onion, garlic, celery, and parsley. Heat together olive oil and butter. Cook chopped vegetables in it over low heat for about 5 minutes. Add peas and bouillon. Cover, and simmer until peas are tender, stirring occasionally. Toward the end of the cooking period, add tomato and basil. Season with salt and pepper. If there is too much liquid, cook uncovered to allow for evaporation. The peas should be dry, not soupy.

While peas are cooking, cook pasta in plenty of rapidly boiling salt water. Drain and toss with vegetables. For a nice touch, add 1 to 2 tablespoons butter. Serve with grated Parmesan cheese.

Home-made Noodles Alfredo [Fettuccine alla Alfredo]

The original Alfredo was an excellent restaurateur who ran a famous restaurant in the old Roman street *alla Scrofa* – that is, the Street of the Sow (shown on an antique frieze that used to be there). He was also a born ham, and his customers loved it. He used to celebrate this noodle dish – there is no other word for it – with a golden spoon and fork, tossing the noodles with a flourish and claiming that the implements were given to him by Douglas Fairbanks, Sr, and Mary Pickford. A spotlight used to play on him when this happened.

However, the noodle dish is excellent, even when made with bought noodles. The trick is to use equal parts of noodles, butter, and freshly ground Parmesan cheese and to have everything extremely hot. Also, *the butter must not be melted*. When made with first-class ingredients, this is one of the great noodle dishes of all times.

1 lb. broad noodles (preferably home-made)
1 lb. unsalted butter (it must be unsalted), cut in slices
1 lb. Parmesan cheese (it must be freshly grated)

Cook noodles *al dente*. Drain and put into a big, very hot bowl. Add the butter slices and cheese. Toss very thoroughly so that the noodles are evenly coated. Serve immediately on very hot plates.

Green Lasagne alla Bolognese
[Lasagne verdi alla bolognese]

Lasagne are extra wide and rather heavy noodles, which some-times have crimped edges. Like all noodle products, they are good, but even better when home-made. The dough is a noodle dough, made green with puréed spinach – just like the commercially produced green noodles.

The Bolognese part comes in with the sauces used in this lasagne dish. There are a great many ways of making lasagne creations: with meat sauces, meat balls, shrimps, all with or without several cheeses such as Mozzarella, ricotta, and Parmesan. I think the Bolognese way best, because it is less lethal than those that stem from the heavy southern Italian cuisine, which is full of herbs, spices, and tomatoes. Lovers of these kinds of lasagne will find excellent recipes in all good Italian cookbooks. Not that the Bolognese variety is not rich – after all, it is one of the classical dishes of Bologna la Grassa, Bologna the Rich, Fat One.

Bologna is the eating capital of Italy. This is an incredible city of block-long private houses with fortress walls, towers, arcades, great churches, and squares of a truly theatrical splendour. It is also the home of the oldest European and most famous Italian university (which has earned her the title of 'La Dotta', the Learned One). Its cuisine of noodle products (and others, but this is not the chapter for them) is pure poetry.

As a friend of mine put it when we were watching a plump lady making tortellini, tiny stuffed noodle rings, with a skill and speed that must be inborn: 'La cucina bolognese fa sorrideri gli angeli in paradiso [Bolognese cooking makes the angels in para-dise smile].'

Bolognese meat sauces are made with lean beef, veal and pork, with chicken livers, and with marrow, tenderly pointed up with herbs, seasonings, very little tomato, and with wine and truffles. The Béchamel that goes into this lasagne dish is well seasoned with nutmeg, another favourite of the city's cooking. It takes time to make lasagne verdi alla Bolognese, but the effort is well worth it, especially since the dish can be prepared for a large number of people, and beforehand as well. Lasagne can be stored in the refrigerator, or frozen. It can be made with the bought variety, but since home-made green lasagne are rightfully considered to be very glamorous, I give the recipe. Essentially, it is noodle dough made green, and if you have a pet home-made-noodles recipe, I advise you to follow it, adding the puréed spinach to the dough while decreasing the quantity of the liquid used, be it beaten egg or water.

The spinach must be cooked and retain its fresh green colour. It must be puréed very fine – either by pressing through a sieve or in a blender. And, furthermore, the spinach must be thoroughly drained before being mixed into the dough. If it is still wet, heat it for a moment over high heat to evaporate some of the moisture, stirring constantly. ½ lb. fresh spinach corresponds roughly to one 10 oz. package of frozen chopped spinach, counting in the latter's ice content. For lasagne purposes, the quantities correspond sufficiently. This dough is also good for noodles, ravioli, and the like.

1 lb. sifted flour	½ lb. extremely finely puréed
2 teaspoons salt	spinach
3 eggs, well beaten	

Sift flour and salt into a large bowl. Make a well in the centre and put eggs and spinach in it. Mix gradually with one hand or stir with a fork until the paste is well blended. Since flours vary in their absorption of liquid, in order to obtain a smooth paste you may have to add a little water if the paste is too stiff (1 tablespoon at a time) or a little more flour if it is too wet. Go easy on the flour, adding 1 tablespoon at a time, or the lasagne will be heavy. Knead the dough thoroughly for at least 12 minutes, pushing it away from you on the board with the palms of both hands. Also take the ball of dough in both hands and pummel it hard, banging it on the board until it is thoroughly smooth and elastic. (This banging noise is very characteristic of Italian kitchens.) The dough must be dry and not cling to your hands. If it does, flour your hands lightly and work the flour into the dough. Let the dough rest for 15 to 30 minutes after it has reached the right elasticity. Divide it into 4 pieces. Flour the board and the rolling pin lightly (you will need more flour before you are through, and the less you use for each flouring the better for your lasagne) and roll the dough to about $\frac{1}{16}$ inch thick. As you do so, stretch it around the rolling pin, pulling the dough toward the handles to get it thinner. Lightly flour the flattened paste after each rolling to keep it from sticking. By the time the dough has been rolled and stretched about a dozen times it should be the texture of a piece of cloth which can be folded and manipulated without breaking. Put the pasta sheets that are ready on a clean kitchen towel on the table or hang them over the back of a chair while you are working on the other ones.

Cut the prepared dough into strips 2 by 4 to 6 or 8 inches, depending on the size of the dish in which the lasagne is to be baked. Let them dry on towels for about 1 hour. Boil the strips a few at a time in plenty of rapidly boiling salt water for 3 to 5 minutes, or until almost but not quite tender. Remove them from pan and drop in cold salt water. Drain them again and dry them by spreading on kitchen towels.

Butter a baking dish. Coat the bottom with a small amount of Ragù alla Bolognese (page 250), a small amount of cream sauce, and a sprinkling of grated Parmesan cheese. Place a layer of lasagne on this base, with the ends turning up at the sides of the dish. Repeat this procedure, ending with meat sauce, cream sauce, and a generous layer of Parmesan cheese. Bake in a moderate (350° F., gas 4) oven 20 to 25 minutes, or until the lasagne is golden brown and very hot, and the cheese melted. Cut into wedges.

Note: This recipe makes about 1½ lb. of lasagne. Since you may want to make extra noodle dough while you are at it, here are the quantities of sauces and cheese needed for each ¾ to 1 lb. of lasagne.

1 pint Italian meat sauce from Bologna or any other meat sauce	1½ pints Béchamel Sauce (page 127) or cream sauce 3 oz. grated Parmesan cheese

¾–1 lb. lasagne and the above quantities of sauces and cheese will fill one 8-inch-square baking pan.

Cannelloni Filling

Cannelloni means big rolls in Italian, and any rolls made from dough can be filled and baked. There is the store-bought variety of cannelloni: big (that is, about 4 inches long and rather thick). There are also cannelloni made from egg-noodle dough (more elegant), and (most elegant) cannelloni made from baked French pancakes, cut, like the egg-noodle dough, into 4-inch squares. All of these can be filled with any savoury or creamy mixture, covered with sauce, and baked. Restaurants that specialize in cannelloni usually compose their cannelloni sauce from three, four, or more sauces, which are combined and seasoned again. This is obviously not feasible for the home cook. The following recipe is, however, feasible and good. It can be dressed up further according to the whim of the cook with some sautéed sliced mushrooms, a few chopped truffles, a touch of brandy, and/or any seasonings you fancy. The filling stuffs over 24 cannelloni, depending on size, and serves 8 to 12.

3 chicken breasts, boned	2 oz. flour
6 oz. butter	Good 1½ pints hot milk
6 large chicken livers	8 fl. oz. double cream
8 slices Italian prosciutto or cooked ham	Salt Pepper
½ lb. grated Swiss or Parmesan cheese	¼ teaspoon nutmeg

In a heavy skillet, sauté chicken breasts in 2 oz. of the butter over medium heat for about 10 to 15 minutes, or until golden brown. Push to one side of the skillet and sauté chicken livers for 3 to 4 minutes. Mince chicken breasts, livers, and prosciutto together, using the finest blade of the mincer. Blend in 4 oz. of the cheese.

Over low heat or in the top of a double boiler, melt remaining butter and stir in the flour. Cook 2 to 3 minutes. Blend in hot milk, stirring constantly. Cook 10 minutes, stirring frequently, or until thick and smooth. Add cream, salt and pepper to taste, and nutmeg. Add about 1 cup of the sauce to the chicken mixture and blend thoroughly. Stuff cannelloni with this mixture. If noodle dough squares are used, they must first be boiled in rapidly boiling salt water until tender, drained, and dried on a kitchen towel.

The noodle or pancake squares are stuffed by placing about 2 tablespoons of filling on each square and rolling it tightly. Arrange cannelloni in buttered shallow baking dishes one layer deep – no more. Sprinkle with remaining cheese and a little of the remaining sauce. Dot cannelloni with additional butter and bake in moderate (350° F., gas 4) oven until the tops are golden brown. Serve very hot, with a tossed or a green cooked vegetable salad on the side.

Greek Macaroni Timbale [Pastitsio]

This party timbale must have come from Italy, since it is identical with the Italian version. Like Italian Rice Timbale, it can be made in the morning, refrigerated, and baked at serving time. The Greeks are very fond of their pastitsio, and it is really an excellent, different way of serving macaroni.

10 oz. elbow macaroni	Filling from Italian Rice Timbale
1 pint thick Béchamel Sauce	(page 135)
4 egg yolks	Truffled Madeira Sauce (page
1½ oz. grated Parmesan cheese	257)

BÉCHAMEL SAUCE

6 tablespoons (3 oz.) butter	8 fl. oz. single cream ⎞ heated
6 tablespoons flour	8 fl. oz. milk ⎠ together
2 teaspoons salt	½ teaspoon white pepper

Melt butter. Stir in flour and cook over low heat until it begins to turn golden. Gradually add hot cream and milk, stirring constantly to avoid lumps. Cook over low heat 10 minutes, stirring frequently. Season with salt and pepper.

Cook macaroni in plenty of rapidly boiling salted water until tender. Drain. Add egg yolks and grated Parmesan to Béchamel sauce, blending thoroughly. Combine macaroni and Béchamel and stir until evenly blended. Generously butter a 5-pint casserole and sprinkle with fine dry bread crumbs. Spoon two thirds of the macaroni mixture into it. Press macaroni against bottom and sides, leaving a well in the middle. Fill well with filling from Italian Rice Timbale. Spoon the remaining macaroni over the top of the entire casserole, taking care that the meat is well covered. Bake in moderate (350° F., gas 4) oven about 1 hour, or until macaroni is set. Unmould on a heated platter. Cut into wedges and serve with Madeira Sauce. Yields 8 to 10 servings.

Rice Pilaff

How nice
    Is Rice !
How gentle, and how very free from vice
Are those whose fodder is mainly Rice !
    Rice ! Rice !
Really it doesn't want thinking of twice.
The gambler would quickly abandon his dice,
The criminal classes be quiet as mice,
If carefully fed upon nothing but Rice.
    Yes; Rice ! Rice !
    Beautiful Rice.
All the wrong in the world would be right in a trice
If everyone fed upon nothing but Rice.

This poem comes from a charming book by André Simon, called *Food*, in the Pleasures of Life Series (Burke Publishing Company Ltd, London, 1949). I am very fond of it, particularly because the anonymous author disregarded the fact that all rice-eating people are anything but quiet mice. The Greeks, the Turks, the Arabs, the Chinese and Japanese, rice eaters all, may be free from vice depending on how one looks upon vice, but gentle they are not. Yet the Greeks, Turks, and the people of the Balkans are among the most hospitable and noble, if ruthless, in their approach to many aspects of life. Perhaps this is because rice is their staple cereal. What is sure is that their way of cooking it deserves the crown of all rice cookery.

Rice pilaff is extremely easy to make. All that is needed is a heavy pot with a really tight-fitting lid and a low heat. Pilaff, unlike risotto, should be very dry, each grain separate and distinct. Short-grain rice is not well suited to pilaff, because it cooks rather softly. But long-grain Carolina rice is fine. For a nicer pilaff, however, wash it under cold water to remove some of the outer starch, and dry the rice in a towel.

Once the basic way of making pilaff has been mastered – and I repeat that it is about the world's easiest dish – you can invent hundreds of pilaff combinations of your own. Cooked leftover meat, cut into pieces, or fresh meat, minced or in pieces, bacon, poultry, fish, shellfish, and any vegetables may go into a pilaff. You can season your pilaffs soberly or exotically; you can use canned stuffs to make one up at the last minute. Whatever you do, the pilaff will taste good. A long time ago a visitor to Turkey expressed his opinion on pilaff this way: 'They put before you fortie dishes called by fortie names, as Pelo, chelo, etc., albeit indeed it differ but thus all are of ryce, mutton and hens boyl'd together. Some have butter, some have none, some have termerick [turmeric] and saffron, some have none; some have onions and garlic, some have none; some have almonds and raisins, some have none, and so on ad infinitum.'

Plain Pilaff

2 oz. butter or other fat	1 lb. rice
Good ¾ pint chicken or other bouillon, hot	Salt and pepper

In heavy saucepan, melt butter. Fry the rice in it over medium heat 3 to 5 minutes, until golden and transparent. Stir constantly. Pour in chicken bouillon – the rice will sizzle in an alarming manner. Cover tightly (the Middle Easterners cover the pan with a cloth before putting on the lid) and cook over lowest possible heat about 20 to 25 minutes, or until the rice is just tender and all the liquid absorbed. Season with salt and pepper to taste. Keep the rice hot 5 to 10 minutes before serving. This is not absolutely necessary, but it improves the pilaff. It can be done by standing the rice on the warm stove, or wrapping a cloth around the pan, or keeping it in a warm oven.

Savoury Pilaff

A wonderful party dish. The amounts can easily be doubled
or tripled, with perfect success, provided the pan used is large
enough.

2 oz. butter	Good 1½ pints boiling bouillon
3 medium-sized onions, finely chopped	2 large tomatoes, skinned, seeded, and chopped
½ lb. raw liver or cold roast lamb, cut into small strips	2 tablespoons chopped parsley
1–2 oz. pine nuts or almonds	1 teaspoon powdered sage
1–2 oz. currants or seedless raisins, plumped in water	½ teaspoon ground coriander (or more)
1 lb. rice	¼ teaspoon ground cinnamon

Heat butter in large, heavy pan. Sauté onions in it over low
heat for 5 minutes, or until golden. They must not brown. Add
liver or lamb, and sauté 3 minutes. Add nuts and currants or
raisins and sauté 3 minutes longer. Stir constantly during the
whole sautéing process. Add rice and, over medium heat, cook
5 minutes, stirring all the time. Pour in boiling bouillon, and add
tomatoes, parsley, sage, coriander, and cinnamon. Mix thoroughly.
Cover and cook over lowest possible heat 20 minutes, or until
rice is tender. If possible, stand in a warm place 10 minutes before
serving.

Chicken Pilaff from the Balkans

2 oz. butter	1 lb. rice
2 tablespoons finely minced onion	Good 1½ pints chicken bouillon, hot
¾ lb. raw or cooked chicken, cut into thin strips	2 medium-sized tomatoes, skinned, seeded, and chopped
Salt and pepper	1½ oz. walnuts, coarsely chopped
¼ teaspoon thyme	

Melt butter in heavy saucepan. Cook onion in it over low heat
about 3 minutes, or until golden. Add chicken and cook 3 minutes
longer. Season with salt and pepper to taste, and thyme. Add rice,

and over medium heat cook 5 minutes, stirring constantly. Pour in boiling chicken bouillon, and add tomatoes and walnuts. Cover tightly and cook over lowest possible heat, about 20 minutes, or until all the liquid has been absorbed. Serve with a side dish of yoghurt.

LAMB OR MEAT PILAFF

Instead of the chicken use lamb or other meat cut into strips and proceed as above. Cooked meat may also be used, but the results will not be as savoury.

Risotto

'Rice is born in water, and must die in wine,' the Italian proverb says. The water-born rice of Italy grows in the north, in the plain of the Po, where the paddies are surrounded by the mulberry trees which, with their leaves, feed the silkworms that the farmers' women raise for the silk factories of Milan and Como. The rice harvest is a big annual event, to which men and women from all over northern Italy converge for the abandoned fun of the life and the good wages. For once, the girls are not under the strict supervision of their native villages, or of the signora if they are housemaids in town. They live in dormitories, and as long as they pick their quota, the girls are free to do as they please. When the rice harvest time comes, there is weeping on the part of the signore and even the promise of more wages for the maids in Milan and the other big northern cities, but the girls would rather 'go to the rice fields' where they can display their legs, so the signore say, as they stand in the flooded paddies.

Be that as it may, rice is to northern Italy, Lombardy, the Piedmont and Venice what pasta is to southern Italy. Rice is cooked differently in Italy from the other rice-eating regions: Spain, Greece, Turkey, Persia, the Middle East, and the Orient. Strange to say, the French have never mastered the art of cooking rice.

Risotto – the Milanese variety is most famous – is cooked slowly, the liquid added in small amounts, the smaller the better; and the liquid must be absorbed after each addition. The result is a creamy rice, yet each grain is still separate.

In Italy risotto is served as the dish preceding the main dish of the meal, and never as an accompaniment to the meat, fish, or chicken course, with one exception : Ossi Buchi (veal shanks) is invariably served with Risotto alla Milanese.

The short-grain, starch-coated Italian rice is best, but Carolina long-grain rice will do as well. The rice must not be washed first.

Obviously there are variations in the method of making risotto. I give the one followed in Italian households, which I think the best. Rice is usually cooked in chicken broth, and the better the broth, the better the rice. For lenten dishes, a fish broth or water is used.

Risotto alla Milanese

What makes *risotto alla Milanese* different from other risotti is saffron. It may be served plain or with sautéed chicken livers, mushrooms, truffles, and any savoury sauce. The sauce, though, must be kept on the delicate side – no heavy meat-tomato mixtures – or the delicate risotto will be drowned in the alien flavour. For 4 to 6 people.

2 oz. butter	2 pints chicken bouillon, boiling
2 oz. chopped beef marrow (if marrow is unavailable, use 2 tablespoons butter instead)	½ to ¾ teaspoon saffron, steeped in a little chicken broth
1 small onion, minced	3 tablespoons (1½ oz.) butter
1 lb. unwashed rice	2 oz. grated Parmesan cheese
4 fl. oz. Marsala	

In heavy saucepan, melt butter and beef marrow. Over medium heat, cook onion in it until golden but not brown. Add the unwashed rice, stirring constantly until it becomes transparent in about 3 to 4 minutes. The rice must not brown. Stir in Marsala. When the wine has evaporated, add ½ cup of the bouillon, which is kept boiling hot in a separate saucepan. Cook over medium heat, uncovered, until the bouillon is absorbed. Stir constantly. Add the rest of the bouillon gradually, as the rice absorbs it, stirring constantly. The less bouillon is added at a time, the better the rice. The cooking time should be around 20 minutes from the time the stock is first added, and the stirring constant.

After about 15 minutes' cooking time, or before the rice is tender, add the saffron. When the rice is cooked, stir in the 2 tablespoons butter and the grated Parmesan cheese. Serve immediately and very hot, with additional Parmesan.

Note: Instead of using 4 fl. oz. Marsala and 2 pints chicken broth, a light risotto is made with 8 fl. oz. dry white wine and about 1¾ pints chicken broth. Please also note that the amount of liquid must be gauged as the rice is cooking, since various kinds of rice absorb different amounts of liquid. The results should be a rice that is creamy but not sloppy.

Risotto in Bianco

This white risotto is the basis of many rice dishes that contain shellfish, vegetables, mushrooms (the imported dried ones are best), or whatever is handy to dress the rice. It is also eaten by itself when the Italians feel delicate.

To make it, omit the Marsala in the preceding recipe and use the dry white wine instead, and leave out the saffron.

Venetian Risotto [Risi e bisi]

One of the famous dishes of Venice, and one of the best of the scores of northern Italian risotti. For 4 to 6 people.

2 oz. butter	12 oz. unwashed rice
1 medium-sized onion, finely minced	1½ pints hot chicken bouillon
	Salt
2 slices prosciutto or ham, chopped	Pepper
	2 oz. grated Parmesan cheese
1¼ lb. shelled or frozen peas	

In heavy saucepan, heat butter. Cook onion and prosciutto in it over medium heat for about 5 minutes, or until golden, stirring frequently. Add peas and cook 5 minutes longer. Stir in rice and cook until transparent – about 4 to 5 minutes, stirring constantly. Add hot chicken bouillon and salt and pepper to taste. Cover saucepan and cook over low heat for 15 to 20 minutes, stirring frequently. The rice should absorb all the liquid and be tender but not mushy. Stir in Parmesan cheese and serve very hot, with additional Parmesan.

Roman Stuffed Tomatoes [*Pomodori alla Romana*]

On the food display tables of Roman restaurants, when the big tomatoes are in season, one sees large pans of them stuffed with rice. The dish is an unusually good one, and rather unknown outside Rome. It can be eaten either hot or cold.

It is difficult to give very accurate amounts for the uncooked rice that is used to stuff the tomatoes, since the size of the latter varies so. Roughly speaking, about 2 tablespoons are needed if the tomatoes are large. If any rice stuffing is left over, bake it alongside the tomatoes in the pan.

8 medium to large tomatoes	Good ¾ pint hot chicken broth
4 fl. oz. olive oil	Salt
1 oz. chopped parsley	Pepper
2 cloves garlic, minced	⅛ teaspoon cinnamon (optional)
8 oz. rice	

Cut a slice from the top of each tomato and scoop out centre with a spoon without breaking the walls. Strain and save the juice. Place tomatoes in shallow baking dish. Sprinkle each tomato with a little olive oil – about 2 to 3 tablespoons.

Heat remaining oil in heavy saucepan. Cook parsley and garlic in it over medium heat 3 minutes. Add rice and cook 3 minutes longer, stirring constantly. Add hot chicken broth. Cover, and cook 10 minutes, or until rice is three quarters done. The cooking time varies with the kind of rice used. Remove from heat; season with salt and pepper and cinnamon. Fill tomatoes with rice mixture. Pour tomato juice over tomatoes to the depth of ½ to ¾ inch up the side of the tomatoes. Bake in moderate (350° F., gas 4) oven 30 to 40 minutes, or until rice is tender and liquid absorbed. If during baking time the tomatoes show signs of drying out, add a little hot water. Baste occasionally.

Italian Rice Timbale [*Timballo di riso*]

A handsome and ornamental creation of Milanese cooking, well suited to buffet suppers.

1¼ lb. uncooked long-grain white rice
2 oz. butter

2 oz. grated Parmesan cheese
4 egg yolks
Dry bread crumbs

Cook rice in salt water until tender. Drain. Mix in the butter, Parmesan cheese, and egg yolks. Butter a 2½-pint casserole and sprinkle with fine dry bread crumbs. (The casserole must be thoroughly coated.)

Spoon two-thirds of the rice mixture into the casserole. Press rice against bottom and sides, leaving a well in the middle. Put filling in the well. Spoon the remaining rice over the top of the entire casserole, taking care that the meat is well covered. Bake in moderate (350° F., gas 4) oven about 1 hour, or until rice is set. Unmould on a heated platter. Cut into wedges and serve with tomato sauce. Makes 8 to 10 servings.

FILLING

2 tablespoons (1 oz.) butter
1 small onion, minced
1 lb. veal and pork mixed, minced twice
½ lb. raw chicken livers, chopped
½ small pimento, finely chopped

1 clove garlic, finely minced
8 oz. cooked peas
4 tablespoons tomato paste flavoured with basil leaf
1 teaspoon salt
1 teaspoon sugar
½ teaspoon oregano
¼ teaspoon black pepper

Melt the butter in a skillet. Add onion and garlic. Cook over low heat until onion is golden and transparent. Add minced meat and chicken livers. Cook, stirring occasionally, for about 15 minutes, or until meats are tender. Add pimento, cooked peas, tomato paste, salt, sugar, oregano, and pepper. Cook over low heat for about 20 minutes, stirring frequently.

Spanish Rice

Spain is a rice-eating country, and the dishes made with rice are many, varying from very elaborate ones containing meat, chicken, and fish to very simple ones, eaten by the peasants, which consist of rice with perhaps a vegetable or two and a little piece of fat bacon, which is called *tocino*, or a big piece of fish. In other words, whatever is handy is put into the daily rice to make a change.

The dish we call paëlla, a casserole of rice, chicken, shellfish, and vegetables flavoured with saffron, is the rice dish of Valencia, called in Spain *arroz a la Valenciana*, or simply rice a la Valencia. The name 'paëlla' comes from the dish in which the rice is cooked and served: a flat round or oval pan with two handles, made of metal or earthenware. So paëlla really means pot, and there are many 'paëlla a la so-and-so', depending on the locality of the dish. Unquestionably Paëlla a la Valenciana is the best, and wonderful for a party, since it is scarcely worth while, if at all possible, to make it in small quantities.

Paëlla a la Valenciana

This is a more-or-less dish, for paëlla aficionados to adjust to their own fancy. The only mandatory ingredients are the chicken, the shellfish, the rice, tomato, pimento, and peas or beans. Paëlla is an extremely pretty dish, glowing in the greens, yellows, and reds that are the colours of Spain.

1 lobster
4 fl. oz. olive oil
2 cloves garlic, minced
1 frying chicken (2 to 3 lb.), cut in pieces
1 chorizo or Spanish sausage, sliced (hot Italian sausage will do)
3 green peppers, sliced
3 red pimentos, sliced (fresh or canned)
2 oz. finely diced salt pork
6 medium-sized tomatoes, skinned and cut in wedges

4 medium-sized onions, sliced
1½ lb. rice
2 teaspoons saffron soaked in a little chicken stock
Chicken or fish stock
15 cooked and shelled prawns
15 mussels or clams, well scrubbed
10 oz. green peas or sliced string beans
2 medium artichokes, sliced (remove tough outer leaves and chokes)
Pepper (optional)

Cook lobster until red. Remove meat, but only crack claws and reserve. In large skillet, heat olive oil and garlic. Sauté lobster meat over medium heat for 2 to 3 minutes. Remove and reserve.

Cook chicken until brown on all sides. Return lobster meat to skillet and add chorizo slices, green peppers, pimentos, pork, onions, and tomatoes. Cook about 5 minutes, stirring constantly. Add rice and saffron to cook another 5 minutes. Add stock to cover plus 1 inch. Cover, and cook over medium heat 10 minutes, stirring occasionally. Add prawns, mussels, peas or beans, and artichokes. Season with pepper. Cover and cook 10 more minutes, or until rice is tender, stirring frequently. Check whether more stock is needed. Do add only a little at a time, since the dish should be dry and the liquid all absorbed. Before serving, arrange the paëlla so that some of the prawns will show, and place lobster claws on it. Decorate with additional pimento strips. Serve hot. Makes 8 to 10 servings.

*

Frumenty

This is the name of a traditional harvest dish of medieval England, which was made of new wheat steeped in water and cooked over a slow fire for at least 24 hours, when the kernels of the grain would be very soft and almost melted. The grain was then dried, winnowed and washed, and boiled in milk, spiced and sweetened for eating hot. Sometimes it was also put into pies.

The name comes from the Latin *frumentum* or grain, and shows that the dish goes back to Roman days. It much resembles the Easter wheat pies of Italy, another symbolic food. I have often made frumenty for a one-dish supper, because I like foods with such a pronounced archaic and arcadian nature.

Today's frumenty, which is also called thruminty or ferminty, can be made from cracked wheat. The wheat is boiled in water until soft, and then, after being drained, boiled again in milk. The old recipes call for suet to enrich it, but I add a little butter in its stead. The grated rind of a lemon and its juice are added to about 2 or 3 cups of the cooked wheat, as well as some washed currants and brown sugar. A large apple, peeled and chopped, makes another pleasant addition.

Two Swiss Alps dishes

I give these two recipes for their curiosity value, and for the reader who, like myself, may have lived with the Swiss *Sennen*, the dairymen, up in the High Alps during the summer pasture season. I don't know whether the *Sennen* still eat this food, but they did when I was a child, cooking it over an open fire in the huts. For anybody who wants the atmosphere of those days (which I suspect has vanished since the Second World War) I suggest reading or rereading *Heidi*.

I also think that these two dishes are very much like the food that sustained the European peasantry throughout the ages and that it is eating at its most rudimental.

Cholermus

This is a broken pancake, made by mixing cream or milk, or both, with white flour to form a thick batter. Butter is then melted in a skillet, and the batter poured into it pancake fashion. As the batter fries, it is cut into pieces with a knife or spoon. The pieces are turned to cook golden brown on all sides. The *Cholermus* is eaten with milk. The usual way of serving it is to put the skillet and a bowl of milk on the table; the eaters put a piece of *Cholermus* on a spoon and then dip it into the milk.

Gonterser Bock

This goody comes from the Grisons, best known as the Swiss canton that contains St Moritz. All I can say for it is that it tastes much better than you would think from reading the recipe, especially when eaten at a very high altitude.

Make a stiff batter of flour, milk, and salt. If possible, add a beaten egg to it. (Eggs are scarce on the remote Alpine pastures where the cows are grazed in summer to get the milk that gives the unique flavour to Swiss cheese. When I was a child the Swiss dairymen made their cheese right then and there on the Alp.) Dip a hard-boiled, peeled egg into the batter and fry at once in hot butter. When the egg turns golden, dip it again in the batter and fry again. Repeat the process until the egg is as large as you want it. Cut the whole into pieces, and eat it with milk.

*

Roman Dumplings [*Gnocchi alla Romana*]

Why the Italian word *gnocco* should mean a dumpling when applied to food and a dope when applied to a person, I do not know. What I know is that this recipe makes an excellent substitute for potatoes, rice, or pasta, and a delightful main dish for luncheon or supper.

12 fl. oz. water	4 oz. butter
12 fl. oz. milk	3 eggs
8 oz. semolina	8 oz. grated Parmesan or Swiss
1½ teaspoons salt	cheese (Parmesan preferred)

Bring milk and water to the boil. Gradually stir in the semolina and salt, taking care to avoid lumping. Cook over medium heat until thick. Remove from heat. Beat in half the butter, 2 oz. cheese, and the eggs, and mix well. Spread about ¼ inch thick on a shallow platter or on a baking sheet. Cool. With the rim of a glass or a biscuit cutter cut into circles or any desired shapes. Arrange in buttered baking dish in overlapping layers. Sprinkle each layer with the remaining 6 oz. cheese and 2 oz. butter. Bake in moderate (350° F., gas 4) oven for about 30 minutes, or until golden and crisp.

Note: The dish can be prepared well in advance, stored in refrigerator, and baked when needed.

Spaetzle

There is a 'dumpling belt' in Central Europe, stretching from Alsace to Poland, and taking in southern Germany, northern Switzerland, and the whole of Austria and Czechoslovakia. Here the dumpling reigns supreme, made from bread or bread crumbs, flour, potatoes, semolina, or other grains; stuffed with liver in its classic form, with other meats, cheese, or fruits; boiled, steamed, or fried, or boiled and then fried.

Perhaps the most admirable thing about dumplings is that they are a triumph of ingenuity, making the most of very little. Today, I think that the endlessly varied dumplings are too solid for our lighter tastes in eating, with the exception of Spaetzle, or little sparrows. These tiny dumplings are served with goulash in Austria and Hungary, with a meat sauce in other parts, or even by themselves with butter and cheese. I think them worth making and eating. The dough should be a soft noodle dough – one, however, that will not flow or drop off a spoon. Since flours of various kinds absorb liquid differently, and the size of eggs varies, you may have to do a little adjusting to get the right consistency for the dough.

About ½ lb. flour	1 teaspoon salt
1 medium-sized egg, beaten	Melted butter
About ¼ pint water	

Beat all ingredients together. Let the batter rest for 30 minutes. Have ready a large pan full of rapidly boiling salted water. Put part of the dough on a chopping board, a flat plate, or a large wooden spoon. With a knife, snip off small parts of the dough and flip them directly into the boiling water. Or hold a large-hole colander over the boiling water and force the dough through it. The Spaetzle will rise to the surface when they are cooked. Drain them in a colander. Put them quickly into a heated deep serving dish. Pour 2–4 oz. melted butter over Spaetzle and serve with grated Parmesan, if desired.

Note: In Hungary, and in Austria too, sour cream to taste is often mixed in with, or instead of, the butter. The Spaetzle can also be dressed with poppy seeds, sesame seeds, and any other flavourings used for buttered noodles. Leftover Spaetzle are fried in butter.

Barley Casserole

Barley is much eaten in Eastern European countries such as Poland, and it deserves to come to the English table in lieu of potatoes and other starches. We have mostly relegated it to soup, yet it is excellent with meats, such as lamb, and with poultry. Once the basic preparation is mastered, and very easy it is too, any number of variations can be worked with sautéed chicken livers, herb seasonings, cottage cheese or sour cream, which are mixed with the cooked barley. Fine or medium pearl barleys are best, since the kernels swell.

2 oz. butter or bacon fat	1 medium-sized onion, chopped
½ lb. mushrooms, sliced (optional)	½ lb. pearl barley
	Good ¾ pint boiling bouillon

Heat butter in heavy saucepan. Sauté onion in it over low heat for 5 minutes, or until golden. Do not brown. Add mushrooms and cook 5 minutes longer. Add barley and cook over medium heat 5 minutes or until it just begins to brown. Pour boiling bouillon over barley. Cover tightly, and cook over lowest possible heat about 25 minutes, or until barley is tender, each grain separate and the liquid all absorbed. If casserole is too liquid, cook uncovered to allow for evaporation. Conversely, add more bouillon, a little at a time, if the casserole is too dry.

Note: Chopped toasted almonds (about 3 oz.) can be mixed into the cooked barley. Or use more mushrooms. Or sauté ½ lb. chicken livers and add to casserole.

Russian Buckwheat [Kasha]

The Russians eat this grain as one of their staples, the way the Italians eat pasta and the Chinese rice. Buckwheat is extremely healthy, and it can be bought in delicatessens. Kasha is served in Russia as a side dish with meats, soups, fish and by itself, and dishes are made with it by adding sautéed mushrooms, minced meat, and/or sour cream.

Kasha can be made by following the directions for Pilaff (page 129) but the method that follows, which uses an egg, gives better results. It can also be boiled or steamed, like rice.

1 lb. buckwheat, whole or split	Boiling water or bouillon (about
1 egg	1½ pints)
2 tablespoons (1 oz.) butter or any fat	Salt

Place buckwheat in ungreased skillet. Add unbeaten egg and mix well. Cook over low heat, stirring constantly, until each grain is coated with egg and separate. Transfer mixture to buttered baking dish. Add butter, salt to taste, and boiling water to cover. Cover baking dish and bake in moderate (350° F., gas 4) oven for 1 hour. Every 10 minutes, check to see if more boiling water is needed to prevent kasha from scorching. When done, the kasha grains should be tender and perfectly dry.

Kasha and Mushrooms

A favourite Russian dish.

To cooked Kasha, add ½ lb. sliced mushrooms which have been sautéed in butter with 1 tablespoon minced onion and salt and pepper to taste. Serve hot, with sour cream on the side.

Finnish Barley Pudding [Uunipuuro]

In the Finnish countryside barley, rice, rolled oats, buckwheat, and rye porridges and gruels are eaten hot, with butter and cold milk. The following barley pudding, which can also be made with buckwheat, is a nice substantial side dish that I serve instead of potatoes with meats, though the Finns eat it *per se*, with hot milk. It must be baked very slowly.

½ lb. whole barley (the large kind)	Good 2 pints boiling milk
Good 1½ pints water	2 oz. butter

Soak barley overnight or for several hours in water. Cook in the same water. As the barley begins to absorb the water, add the boiling milk gradually, stirring constantly. Cook the barley over the lowest possible heat, or in the top of a double boiler, for about 30 minutes, stirring frequently. Transfer to buttered 1½-pint baking dish. Stir in butter and bake in slow (250–75° F., gas ½–1) oven until the pudding is golden brown. Depending on the oven, this may take 2 to 3 hours.

Italian Polenta or Rumanian Mamaliga

In the Balkans, especially Rumania, mamaliga is the staple national food, and so it is in northern Italy, though not quite to the same extent. The peasants in these countries make it in the same way: a large, deep pan, filled with water and hanging over the open hearth, is brought to the boil. Corn meal is dumped into the boiling water and cooked for at least 1 hour, while being constantly stirred with a long wooden stick that is reserved for this use. When a crust (which is delicious) has formed inside the pan the corn meal is turned out on a plate or a wooden board – it will be the shape of the pan. It is cut into slices with a piece of string and eaten in lieu of bread, or with a meat sauce, with cheese, with sweet or sour cream, or just with plain milk. Cold polenta or mamaliga is fried, stuffed, or baked with cheese. In Bergamo and Venice polenta is the classic accompaniment to *baccalà* (dried cod) and to the roasted little songbirds the Italians are partial to.

An easy way of making a polenta or mamaliga pie is to cut it into slices and alternate them in a buttered baking dish with Mornay Sauce (page 255). Sautéed mushrooms and truffles of course add immensely to the dish, which is baked in a moderately hot (400° F., gas 6) oven until the top is brown and crusty.

Chicken and Other Birds

The number of ways of cooking chicken is indeed legion, perhaps because this most domesticated of all birds has the great advantage of producing edible flesh with far less trouble than any other animal. Chickens will fend for themselves if not fed, and though their meat may be tough, it certainly is edible. In this context I remember the chickens in the country around Seville. They were fierce and determined birds with more than one strain of fighting cock derived from straying into the preserves of that time-honoured local sport. Since the barren soil of their yard was most unrewarding, these enterprising fowl lived in the orange groves and supported themselves on orange windfalls. These Spanish chickens were not afraid of man or dog and had to be chased away with a stick. When they came to the table, everybody felt a sense of personal triumph, seeing the enemy down at last. They tasted uniquely and wonderfully of orange, and the toughness of their athletic bodies mattered no longer, since they had been stewed gently and for long in fragrant, spur-of-the-moment casseroles made with tenderizing white or red wine, tomatoes and whatever vegetables were at hand, with a pinch of coriander, cinnamon, or saffron thrown in, depending on the whim of the cook.

On the other hand, the plump pullets of Bresse, the tender English roasting chickens, the Swiss and German chickens, the flighty Austrian *Backhändls* were all carefully raised for men. However excellent our mass-produced poultry, it cannot compare with the taste of a fine, free-range and freshly killed bird.

As I said, the number of chicken dishes transcends belief. André Simon, in his *Concise Encyclopaedia of Gastronomy*, devotes thirty pages to the bird, and he limits himself mostly to the classic French and English recipes. Therefore, it would be hopeless to try to list here the chicken dishes that are characteristic of each European country. The recipes that follow have been culled from my own and my friends' favourites, and I beg my readers' indulgence if they miss some dish they may have admired on their travels. I should also like to remind them that many chicken dishes are specialities that a chef creates for his own clients and may not be typical of a country.

What surprises me is the similarity of all chicken dishes and their basically utilitarian nature. Young, tender chickens are roasted and though the seasonings or stuffings may vary roast chicken is still roast chicken, whether it is flavoured with tarragon in the French manner, parsley in the English, marjoram or olives in the Spanish, or mushrooms in the Slavic manner. Also, over all the Continent, a bird is cooked slowly in tenderizing agents such as wine, tomatoes, or sour cream, with the addition of whatever vegetables are within reach. Stewed chicken and vegetables prevail because tough barnyard chickens are the norm, especially in southern and eastern Europe, where the purchase of a chicken is a serious matter, accomplished with much critical scrutiny and pinching of flesh.

Cooking Methods

Roasting. I do not intend to get in on the great controversy as to whether chickens should be roasted at a high heat, with constant

basting, or at a medium heat. Personally, I roast birds up to 3 lb.
in a 400–25° F., gas 6–7, oven, and larger chickens in a 350° F.,
gas 4, oven, with excellent results. Again, and this is my own
opinion, I think that a small bird dries out if cooked at the lower
temperature. Agreed that poultry, like other meats, is only roasted
if cooked on a spit in circulating dry air, and incomparably better
than if done in any other way – I leave it to the cook to roast
her chickens the way that has given her best results. But I do
think that in oven roasting the birds should first be salted and
peppered both inside and outside and rubbed with butter that is
soft, or with a mixture of butter and olive oil. Bigger birds ought
to have a piece of larding pork or bacon tied on to their breasts
to prevent the breast from browning too quickly and from drying
out while the slower-cooking legs are being roasted. The chicken
should be laid on a rack, so that it will be roasted all around,
rather than roasted on top and steamed in its own juices underneath, which will happen if it is allowed to lie in the pan bastings.

I am a great believer in constant basting, and here I agree
with the French chefs that only fat – especially butter – should
be used for basting a roasting chicken. Some authorities claim
that butter mixed with chicken broth or hot water makes for a
more succulent gravy, and I dare say they are right if you are
interested in gravy. But as for the chicken, I say : baste it with
melted butter which is kept hot on the stove. Pan bastings are
apt to deposit the little burned bits on the chicken, which are
delicious in the gravy but not on the chicken's complexion.

And don't forget to turn the chicken during the roasting process, so that the underside will be done as perfectly as the breast
side.

Casseroled chicken. Chicken casseroles can be made up on the
spur of the moment with whatever vegetables and herbs and
seasonings are available. The beginning is always the same : the
fowl, either whole or cut in pieces, is sautéed in fat until golden
on all sides. The fat can be butter, bacon, lard, salt pork, or olive
oil, depending on the flavour the finished dish is to have and the
ingredients that will be cooked with the chicken. Heavy vegetables,
such as turnips, carrots, potatoes, etc., benefit from the fat of the
pig. Delicate vegetables, such as peas, young string beans, arti-

choke hearts, are better off with a butter beginning. Perfectionists differentiate between the vegetables used to season the casserole (onions, carrots, celery, for instance) and the vegetables that are to be eaten. They say the first vegetables should be strained out of the sauce when the fowl is three-quarters cooked, and the eating vegetables added, after having been browned in a little butter.

The liquid for a classic chicken casserole is hot chicken stock, wine, sometimes tomato juice or apple cider, and even the chicken's blood. Or there are mixtures of these liquids. Excessive fat is to be strained from the sauce before serving the chicken. This is not easy, and in my experience it is better to use no more than the barest amount of fat needed to brown the bird, in order to make this defatting process easier.

Often, sweet or sour cream and egg yolks are added to a casserole to thicken and flavour the sauce. The prevailing practice is to add the creams to the finished dish and let it heat through without boiling, to avoid curdling the sauce. But in some French and Slavic casseroles the chicken is cooked, or rather simmered, in the cream. This makes for a tastier though less attractive dish.

Skinning, trimming, etc. Experts disagree as to whether birds other than roasters should be skinned before cooking. I skin and trim away every bit of skin, fat, tendons, and other superfluous matter before cooking any chicken other than a roaster.

Since chicken is inexpensive nowadays and can also be bought in parts, I never use the wings and backs of a cut-up chicken for anything but making stock. Why penalize people with the lesser parts of the bird when it costs but little more to make a casserole of legs and breasts, if not breasts alone?

A cook's native good sense should prevail when it comes to the cooking time of chicken and their sauces. The cooking time in the following recipes is as nearly correct as I can make it. But most chicken dishes can be done with any kind of fowl, and furthermore, any bird's tenderness varies with its age, so that the cook has to test for doneness. Chickens should not be overdone, but they should be well done, and cooked through thoroughly and completely.

The cook has also to rely on her judgement when it comes to the consistency of the sauce. If it is too thin, it can be either boiled down after the chicken is ready and kept hot on a separate plate, or else the dish can cook without a cover. The sauce can also be thickened with *beurre manié*: equal parts of butter and flour (or 2 parts butter to 1 part flour, depending on how rich the sauce is to be) kneaded together into small balls, which are stirred into the sauce until the right consistency is reached.

A sauce that is too thick can be thinned with a little more wine or broth or water – all added very hot, a tablespoon at a time, until the right consistency has been achieved.

As a final word of cheer, I should like to say that casseroles made with fowl, like all casseroles, do not have to be measured with the utmost accuracy, as the ingredients for a cake must be measured. Let expediency and one's own taste triumph in this case.

The number of servings to be derived from a chicken is a moot point. When buying a roasting chicken, allow 1 lb. for each person. But when the chicken is cut up, the cook will have to decide on the number of servings. A 2½- to 3-lb. chicken can serve 4 if every bit is utilized and if some of the eaters are to have little meat. If only legs and breasts are used, it is for the cook to decide whether each guest is to have one or two pieces. All I can describe in the following recipes is how to cook a chicken of a certain size, and leave it to the cook to double the recipe if necessary.

It is taken for granted that the chicken is truly ready to cook – that is, properly cleaned and plucked, washed and dried.

*

English Roast Chicken

In this country we usually stuff chickens with a standard bread and herb stuffing, to which sausage meat is added occasionally. The bird's breast is covered with bacon, which is removed towards the end of the roasting period to let the breast brown. The basting is done generally with bacon fat.

The roast chicken is served with crisp bacon curls, and also sometimes with chipolata sausages. The gravy is plain and the characteristic accompaniment is Bread Sauce. Potatoes roasted in the drippings and green peas, with or without mint, are usually served with English roast chicken.

BREAD SAUCE (for roast chicken, turkey, and other birds)

Bread sauce should be the consistency of a medium-thick oatmeal porridge, creamy, and utterly free of lumps. It should also be well flavoured. The following recipe makes about 4 servings.

3 cloves	Pepper
1 medium-sized onion	⅛ teaspoon nutmeg or ½
1 bay leaf	teaspoon cayenne pepper (both
¾ pint milk	ingredients and quantities are
3 to 4 tablespoons fresh white	optional)
bread crumbs (without crusts)	1 tablespoon (½ oz.) butter
Salt	1 tablespoon cream

Stick cloves into the onion and put it with the bay leaf and milk into a saucepan. Cover, and barely simmer over very low heat 15 to 20 minutes, or until the milk is well flavoured. Remove onion and bay leaf, and stir crumbs into milk. Simmer over low heat about 5 minutes, or until sauce is thickened and creamy, stirring constantly. Remove from heat and season with salt and pepper and nutmeg or cayenne. Blend in butter and cream. Reheat gently and serve at once.

Note: Depending on individual tastes, this sauce can be made thicker or thinner. If a thicker sauce is wanted, add 1 to 2 more tablespoons bread crumbs. If a thinner sauce is called for, decrease the bread crumbs accordingly. The main thing is to have a sauce that is well flavoured with onion and seasonings.

French Chicken Normandy [Poulet à la normande]

This is one of the best chicken dishes I know, and it comes from Normandy, the French province that's famous for apples and Calvados (apple brandy). It is the Calvados and the apples that give the dish its unique, subtle flavour, which cannot be duplicated with any other brandy. Like all brandies, Calvados can be old and smooth, or quite rough, and it is worth while to spend the money to get a good quality.

2 1½- to 2-lb. broilers, cut in pieces	4 oz. butter
1 medium-sized onion, thinly sliced	¼ pint Calvados
	1 tablespoon chopped parsley
2 hearts of celery (white part only), thinly sliced	⅛ teaspoon thyme
	Salt
2 tart apples, peeled, cored, and chopped	Pepper
	3 fl. oz. double cream

Sauté chickens in hot butter until golden but not brown. Pour 4 tablespoons Calvados over chicken pieces and light the brandy. Let it burn out. Remove chicken pieces and keep hot. In the pan juices remaining in the skillet, sauté slowly the onion, celery, and apples until they are soft and nearly cooked. Add parsley and thyme. Stir in remaining Calvados. Transfer chicken back to sauce. Cover, and cook over low heat for 30 to 40 minutes, or until chicken is tender. Season with salt and pepper. Just before serving, remove from heat and stir in cream. Do not boil again. Serve with plain buttered rice or noodles, or with boiled new potatoes.

Poached Chicken Albuféra [Poularde Albuféra]

The queen, nay, the empress, of all poached or boiled chickens. The stuffing is equally good in a roast chicken, but the long, slow simmering seems to blend its flavours into the chicken meat in an ineffable way.

1 4- to 5-lb. chicken	½ white onion
Boiling water and white wine in equal quantities to cover	1 teaspoon white pepper
	2 teaspoons salt

Stuff chicken in the usual manner and truss. Place in deep, heavy pan that fits chicken tightly. Barely cover with boiling water and white wine mixed. Add onion and pepper. Cover tightly and simmer gently for 1 hour. Do not boil. Skim if needed. Add the salt and continue simmering until done. This might take another hour or less, depending on the age of the chicken. Test for done-ness with a fork.

Arrange chicken on deep serving dish. Remove strings or skewers that trussed the chicken. Garnish with whole mushroom caps sautéed in butter and additional truffle slices that were soaked and cooked in Madeira. Serve with a rich white sauce made from chicken stock and cream and accompany with a dish of creamed spinach or poached artichokes.

STUFFING

3 medium-sized truffles	2 tablespoons (1 oz.) butter
Madeira	Grated rind of ½ lemon
5–6 oz. foie gras or pâté de foie gras	4 oz. cooked white or wild rice

Wash truffles thoroughly in cold water, dry, and chop into coarse pieces. Soak in Madeira to cover for 1 hour. Then simmer in same Madeira for 15 minutes. Drain. Sauté foie gras or pâté by the spoonful in hot but not brown butter for 2 minutes. Com-bine truffles, foie gras, and lemon rind. Mix thoroughly with cooked rice.

Note: For a richer dish, poach chicken in chicken bouillon and white wine. Perfectionists do not let the chicken come in contact with any liquid at all, but encase it in a waterproof container which is placed in another, larger, waterproof container. The containers are then plunged in a deep pan full of simmering water and simmered for about 3 to 4 hours. I have done it this way but found that the trouble involved is greater than the difference in the end result.

Chicken Marengo [Poulet Marengo]

This is a classic of French cooking, and a dish that is universally liked. Basically, it is nothing but a cut-up chicken that has been first sautéed and then stewed in a wine-tomato sauce to which mushrooms are added at a later stage of cooking. As with all household recipes, there are slight variations in the cooking methods, yet the result is always the same. The garniture of fried eggs and cooked shrimps or lobster tails is entirely optional, though most worth while when the hostess wishes to create an effect. It is an excellent party dish for buffets, since it will wait for the guests, who are invariably impressed by it. This recipe is for 4 people, but it can easily be doubled.

3 tablespoons olive oil
1 tablespoon (½ oz.) butter
1 2½- to 3-lb. broiler, cut in pieces
1 tablespoon flour
Salt
Pepper
1 clove garlic, crushed
4 fl. oz. dry white wine
2 oz. canned tomatoes or 1 to 2 tablespoons tomato paste dissolved in a little water

3 tomatoes, peeled, seeded, and chopped
½ teaspoon thyme
½ lb. mushrooms, sliced
2 tablespoons chopped parsley
4 slices bread, trimmed of crusts (optional) and fried in butter
4 eggs, fried in hot olive oil (optional)
Shrimps or lobster tails (optional)

Heat oil and butter together in large, heavy skillet. Sauté chicken in it until brown on all sides. Remove chicken pieces to casserole and keep hot. Blend flour into the pan juices left in skillet. Cook for 2 to 3 minutes, stirring constantly. Add salt and pepper to taste, garlic, wine, and canned tomatoes or tomato paste. Bring to the boil, then add fresh tomatoes, thyme, and mushrooms. Cook over medium heat for about 5 minutes. Pour sauce over chicken pieces in casserole or transfer chicken back to sauce. Cover and cook over low heat for 15 minutes, or until chicken is tender. Sprinkle with parsley before serving. Garnish with bread slices topped with fried eggs, and shrimps or lobster. Or pile chicken on hot serving dish, pour sauce over it and arrange bread, eggs, and shrimps or lobster around it.

Note: Chicken Marengo can be made with fresh tomatoes entirely, though in this case the colour of the sauce will not be as red nor the tomato flavour as pronounced. It is impossible to give absolutely accurate quantities for the sauce ingredients, since the juiciness of the tomatoes and the mushrooms varies. If the sauce is too thin, cook uncovered to allow evaporation until the right consistency is reached. If it is too thick, add a little wine or hot bouillon.

French Chicken Capilotade [*Poulet en capilotade*]

This is an excellent way of using up leftover chicken or other birds, and a welcome change from the eternal creamed chicken. It is an old French recipe, and the ingredients of the sauce have to be increased or decreased depending on the amount of chicken to be used up. The following amounts will do for about ¾ lb. of chicken. But again, this is one of the more-or-less recipes.

2 tablespoons (1 oz.) butter	Salt
2 medium-sized onions, minced	Pepper
4 fl. oz. dry white wine	½ bay leaf
1 teaspoon vinegar	⅛ teaspoon thyme or marjoram
2 tablespoons tomato sauce or 2 teaspoons tomato paste	1 tablespoon chopped parsley
8 fl. oz. chicken stock	2 tablespoons flour or bread crumbs

Heat butter until golden but not brown and sauté onion over medium heat for about 5 minutes, or until soft and light brown. Stir in wine and vinegar and simmer gently until the liquid has boiled down to a quarter of the original quantity. Add tomato sauce or paste and chicken stock. Season with salt and pepper, and add bay leaf, thyme, and parsley. Add chopped chicken or other fowl. Cover, and simmer over low heat 10 to 15 minutes. Moisten flour or bread crumbs with a little water and blend into chicken mixture. Cook 5 minutes longer. Serve with mashed potatoes and creamed spinach.

Note: 1 tablespoon of capers may be added for piquancy.

French Minced Chicken à la Ritz
[*Hachis de poulet à la Ritz*]

Serves 3.

4 chicken breasts	1½ tablespoons minced pimento
Chicken stock	¼ pint dry sherry
2 tablespoons (1 oz.) butter	8 fl. oz. double cream
4 oz. sliced mushrooms	12–16 fl. oz. cream sauce
3 tablespoons minced green pepper	1 teaspoon salt

Simmer chicken breasts in chicken stock to cover until tender. Skin and trim free of bones, fat, and tendons. Mince fine (or use about 1 lb. of the white meat of leftover chicken). Heat butter until golden, not brown, in heavy skillet and sauté mushrooms, pepper, and pimento in it for about 5 minutes. Add the chicken, half the sherry, and the double cream. Simmer over low heat for about 10 minutes, or until the sauce has cooked down to half. (It is not necessary to be deadly accurate about this – the purpose of this step is to have the chicken absorb most of the sherry and cream.) Add cream sauce and blend thoroughly. Season with salt. Just before serving, stir in remaining sherry and a little more cream if the sauce looks too thick. Serve with cooked plain or wild rice, or on buttered toast.

Swiss Baked Chicken [*Poulet Quai des Bergues*]

As a student, I lived in a pension in Geneva. The pension was on the Quai des Bergues, the city's spectacular water-front promenade that overlooks the lake and the Mont Blanc massif – the kind of view that is declared to be exaggerated when seen on picture postcards. Madame often served this baked chicken, with the remark that she had learned to make it from her 'own, poor, sainted *maman*, God rest her soul'.

The trick of the dish is to use fresh coarse bread crumbs, or rather shreds of fresh white bread, and plenty of unsalted butter. The best way of making these coarse crumbs is to trim the crusts from the bread and pull the slices apart with the hands.

1 2½- to 3-lb. frying chicken, cut in pieces	½ lb. butter (or more)
Salt	½ loaf fresh white bread, shredded into coarse crumbs
White pepper	

Skin and trim chicken pieces. Sprinkle with salt and pepper. Cream butter until very soft. Spread each chicken piece thinly with creamed butter. Place chicken in buttered baking dish. Scatter bread crumbs evenly over chicken. Dot with more butter. Bake in moderate (350° F., gas 4) oven 30 to 40 minutes, or until chicken is tender and crumbs golden and crisp. Serve from baking dish.

Note: A fairly tart salad — watercress, for instance – goes well with this dish. Or a salad of hot broccoli or string beans dressed with a vinaigrette dressing. No potatoes, rice, or noodles are needed, since the bread takes their place.

Milan Fried Chicken or Turkey Breasts
[*Petti di pollo o di tacchino alla Milanese*]

This is perhaps *the* party dish from Milan, especially when made with turkey breasts. Poultry is a luxury in Italy, and served when guests are to be honoured.

Since the size of chicken breasts is more predictable than that of turkey breasts, the recipe below has been adjusted to them. If turkey breasts are used, they should be cut into the size of a *suprême* – that is, ½ a chicken breast; 1 whole breast makes 2 *suprêmes*. The recipe serves 4, and it is a very easy one, bearing out the old adage that some of the simplest food can be the most elegant.

4 chicken breasts (8 slices)	Very fine dry white bread
Salt	crumbs
Pepper	2 oz. butter
Flour	3 tablespoons olive oil
2 eggs, well beaten	

Remove all bones from chicken breasts. Skin and trim them, and flatten as thin as possible with a rolling pin. The breasts should be as even in size as possible. Season with salt and pepper. Dip in flour and shake off excess. Dip in beaten egg and bread crumbs. Shake dry. (This can be done before cooking time and the breasts stored in the refrigerator.) Heat butter and oil in large skillet. When fat is no longer bubbling but not brown, put in chicken breasts. Cook over heat that is a little hotter than moderate (but not too high) for about 4 to 7 minutes on each side (depending on size), or until golden. Dry on absorbent paper and serve very hot, garnished with parsley and lemon slices. Any of the nicer green vegetables, such as asparagus or tiny peas cooked with ham, would be a good accompaniment.

Italian Hunter's Chicken [*Pollo alla cacciatore*]

There are two versions of this dish – one from northern and the other from southern Italy. The latter is a much more powerful dish, containing tomatoes and hot peppers. I prefer the former, since it is more delicate, and rather fragrant.

4 oz. butter
2 medium-sized onions, minced
1½ oz. chopped parsley
1 2½- to 3-lb. frying chicken,
    cut in pieces
8 fl. oz. water
4 oz. sliced mushrooms

3 tablespoons minced fresh basil
    or 1 tablespoon dried basil
1 teaspoon dried rosemary
1 bay leaf
Salt and pepper
4 fl. oz. dry white wine

In large skillet, sauté onion in hot butter for 5 minutes, or until soft. Add parsley and cook 1 minute. Add chicken pieces and cook until golden brown. Add water, mushrooms, basil, rosemary, bay leaf, and salt and pepper to taste. Cover, and simmer 15 to 20 minutes. Add wine, and cook another 15 to 20 minutes, or until chicken is tender. Serve with buttered noodles.

   Note: For a less aromatic dish, reduce quantities of herbs to taste.

Italian Chicken Livers with Sage 1
[*Fegatini di pollo alla salvia*]

Chicken livers and fresh sage are an excellent combination, and one that is virtually unknown outside Italy. Dried sage can be used at a pinch, but it is worth while to take the trouble to find fresh sage for this dish.

1 lb. chicken livers
Salt and pepper
12 chopped fresh sage leaves or
    1 tablespoon dried sage

2 oz. butter
2 slices bacon, diced
2 fl. oz. dry white wine

Cut chicken livers into halves if they are large. Season with salt and pepper and coat with fresh or dried sage. Heat butter and bacon together in skillet. Sauté livers 5 to 6 minutes. Add white wine and simmer 2 minutes longer. Serve on spaghetti, rice, or Polenta (page 143).

Italian Chicken Livers with Sage 2
[Spiedino di fegatini di pollo con salvia]

This version of the dish is cooked on small skewers. Keep chicken livers whole, season with salt and pepper and coat with chopped fresh or dried sage. Wrap chicken livers in strips of Italian prosciutto or bacon. If Italian prosciutto is used, all fat must be trimmed off. String on small skewers. Cook over a campfire, a grill, a rotisserie, or in the oven.

If the livers are wrapped in bacon, there is no need for basting. But if lean Italian prosciuto covers the livers, the skewers should be basted with melted butter.

Italian Devilled Chicken [Pollo alla diavola]

On a beautiful day, few places in the world can rival the setting of the Tre Scalini restaurant in Rome, right in the middle of the spectacular Piazza Navona, where Bernini's enormous baroque fountains splash in the square's perfect oblong shape. The food is as beautiful as the surroundings, Roman cooking at its best. *Pollo alla diavola* is a classic Roman dish, a recipe that could not be simpler, yet is infinitely more delicious than almost all grilled chicken. The following recipe serves 2.

1 2½-lb. chicken	Olive oil
1 tablespoon crushed red pepper flakes (or less, if a milder dish is wanted)	Salt
	About 2 fl. oz. dry white wine

Split chicken in half and crush flat (bones and all) with a meat mallet or a rolling pin. Brush both sides lavishly with olive oil. Sprinkle with red pepper flakes and salt. Preheat grill and grill chicken not too close to the heat. Cook about 15 minutes on each side, basting with a little more oil. The chicken should be golden – take care not to burn. Transfer chicken to hot dish and keep hot. Place grill pan with chicken juices over direct moderate heat and stir in wine. Bring to the boil and pour sauce over chicken. In Rome, this dish would be served with a tossed green salad.

Note: A very good variation of *pollo alla diavola* can be made by substituting an equal amount of crushed rosemary leaves, dried or fresh, for the red pepper flakes.

Portuguese Chicken in Cream
[*Frango guisado a moda de Maria Gloria*]

Once, when I was travelling between England and Brazil, the ship stopped for a day in Lisbon. The city sparkled, as always, with colour. The cubed houses looked newly washed with pastel colours, the azulejos, the square blue tiles that frame the windows and doors of most Portuguese buildings, shone bluer than ever, and the mosaic-covered street pavements swirled dizzily with black and white and red patterns. I spent the day wandering around that most enchanting city, and finally, in the evening, I sat down for supper in a small, obscure restaurant in an equally small and obscure – and charming – square, to the sound of a little fountain. The owner was a formal, sparse, and black-dressed lady who would not talk, except to tell me her name, but who cooked me one of the most delicious chicken dishes I've ever tasted. Though I pressed her, she did not tell me the ingredients, and the recipe that follows is reconstructed from memory. What struck me about it was the very difference from typical Portuguese cooking, which has a penchant for tomatoes, peppers, onions, and herbs. With it, I drank Portugal's *vinho verde*, a young, white table wine, crisp, slightly sparkling, and chilled.

1 2½-lb. broiler, cut in pieces	1 teaspoon ground coriander
2 oz. butter	8 fl. oz. dry white port
1 to 2 tablespoons flour	Hot water
Salt and pepper	8 fl. oz. double cream
3 garlic cloves, cut in halves	

Sauté chicken pieces in hot (but not browned) butter in heavy skillet over low heat for about 5 minutes. They must be pale gold, rather than brown. Sprinkle with flour and blend flour into pan juices. Season with salt and pepper. Add garlic, coriander, white port, and enough hot water to cover the chicken three quarters of the way. Cover tightly and simmer over low heat for 30 to 40 minutes, or until chicken is tender. Place chicken in deep platter and keep hot. Remove garlic pieces. Boil down stock to about 1 cup. Add cream and simmer for 3 to 4 minutes, but do not boil. Pour sauce over chicken. Very thin buttered noodles might accompany this dish.

Elegant variation: Omit garlic and coriander and use instead 2 or 3 white or black truffles (canned ones will do, *faute de mieux*). Proceed as above.

Scandinavian Chicken

In the Scandinavian countries poultry is generally regarded as a party dish, especially when it is roasted. Roasting fowl are usually stuffed with butter and parsley and browned in butter in a heavy iron pan before being pot-roasted. Sometimes cream is added after browning, sometimes stock. The bird is served with a rich cream gravy, to which horseradish is sometimes added, an excellent touch.

Quite a number of Scandinavian recipes deal with boiled fowl, served with rice and a cream sauce or fricasséed. The Scandinavians are fond of sweet and sour flavour contrasts, and serve compotes with their poultry, such as rhubarb in Denmark or cranberries in Sweden and Norway, as well as potatoes and perhaps a creamed vegetable.

Though Scandinavian chickens are very good, the dishes are not highly original. Where the Nordics excel is in the cooking of geese and duck, which are very popular all the year round, and more characteristic of their countries' cooking than chicken.

Stewed Chicken from the Canary Islands
[*Pepitoria de pollo a la Canaria*]

Contrary to what one may think, there are no canary birds in the Canary Islands. They were known to the ancients under the name they now bear, allegedly derived from the number of dogs

(Latin *canis*) found there. The ravishing Canaries rise steeply out of the blue sea as you approach them by boat. Ashore, in Tenerife where most of the ships dock en route to South America, they look and are indeed the 'Happy Isles' of antiquity. Since this, however, is a cookbook and not a travel panegyric about one of the loveliest of Spain's provinces, I shall limit myself to giving the recipe for an excellent stewed chicken I ate in a restaurant in Tenerife.

1 4-lb. roasting chicken, cut in pieces
Flour
Salt
Pepper
6 fl. oz. olive oil
2 cloves garlic, minced
1 medium-sized onion, chopped
¾ pint dry white wine
Hot chicken stock
1 bay leaf
⅛ teaspoon thyme
1 teaspoon saffron
15 blanched almonds, freshly chopped
2 hard-boiled eggs, chopped
1 oz. coarse bread crumbs
Olive oil for frying crumbs
½ oz. chopped parsley

Coat chicken pieces in flour that has been seasoned with salt and pepper. Shake off excess flour. Heat olive oil in heavy skillet. Sauté garlic and onion in it for about 5 minutes, or until soft. Add chicken pieces and sauté over medium heat until just golden. They should not be brown. Add white wine and enough chicken stock barely to cover chicken. Taste for seasoning and add salt and pepper if needed. Add bay leaf and thyme. Cover and simmer over low heat about 45 minutes or until chicken is almost tender. Dissolve saffron in a little hot water and add to chicken with almonds. Simmer about 15 minutes longer, or until chicken is tender. If the sauce looks too thin, cook uncovered to allow evaporation. Fry bread crumbs in a little olive oil until crisp and brown. Before serving, sprinkle chicken with hard-boiled egg, bread crumbs, and parsley. Accompany with boiled new potatoes and a green hot vegetable salad.

Circassian Chicken

This is a highly original dish from the Caucasus and its Circassian tribes; it is found in Turkish and Russian cooking. The chicken is a plain boiled one, but the sauce is made from walnuts, put

5 times through the meat mincer. This is a most laborious process, and it prevents this excellent dish from coming to the table as often as it should. Therefore I make my Circassian chicken sauce in my blender, and it saves a world of time and effort.

The taste of the hand-made and the blended sauce is the same. The appearance differs, since the mincing separates the walnut oil from the paste, whereas the blended nuts are homogenized. In the original dish, the walnut oil is coloured with paprika and dribbled over the paste-coated chicken. In the blended version, the paste is used as it is.

This Circassian chicken is a great success with gourmets, and it has the advantage that it can be made in advance, and as easily for a crowd (in the blender) as for a few people.

5 pints water	1 teaspoon cayenne pepper
1 medium-sized onion	1 4-lb. boiling chicken
1 carrot	8 oz. walnuts
1 stalk celery	3 slices white bread, crusts
1 oz. parsley sprigs	trimmed off
1 teaspoon salt	1 tablespoon paprika

Combine in a large pan water, onion, carrot, celery, parsley, salt and cayenne pepper. Bring to the boil and add chicken. Cover and simmer over low heat 1 to 1½ hours, or until chicken is tender. Remove 1 cup chicken stock. Cool chicken in remaining stock.

Grind together walnuts and bread in blender at high speed, 1 cupful at a time. Remove from container. Into container put 1 cup stock and 1 cup walnut and bread mixture. Blend on high speed until smooth. Turn off motor each time, and add 1 cup walnut and bread mixture at a time until mixture is a smooth paste, and all walnuts and bread have been used. Stir paprika into paste until thoroughly mixed.

Slice chicken and spread with walnut paste. Arrange on serving dish and garnish with parsley. Chill and serve with a cold vegetable salad.

Russian Chicken Kiev

This is one of the showpieces of Russian cooking. The theory of chicken Kiev is simple, since it is nothing but half a breast of chicken stuffed with butter, and then rolled up and fried. In practice, it takes a little learning to produce it perfectly – that is, so that it looks neat. However, it is well worth while to learn to make a good chicken Kiev, because the dish is delicious and never fails to impress guests enormously.

Boned breasts of chicken, cut in half	Flour
Butter, ice cold and very hard	Beaten eggs
Salt	Fine dry white bread crumbs
White pepper	Deep fat for frying

Remove all bones from chicken breasts. Skin and trim them free of all fat, membrane, and tendons. The breasts must be as supple as a piece of cloth. Place each piece between 2 sheets of wax paper and flatten them to ¼-inch thickness with a meat mallet or a rolling pin. It is essential that the breasts be this thin. Cut breasts into even shapes.

Cut butter into sticks about 2 inches long and ½ inch thick. If the breasts are large, the butter sticks should be larger. Conversely, they should be smaller for small chicken breasts. Place 1 butter stick in the middle of each chicken breast. Season with salt and white pepper. Fold one end over the butter. Roll the breast up, tucking in the other end and the sides, until the breast resembles a cigar. Make sure that the butter is completely enclosed, or it will ooze out during the frying. The breasts will stay rolled up with a little practice, but they can also be secured with toothpicks. Dip in flour, beaten eggs, and bread crumbs, shaking off excess. Chill for at least 1 hour. Fry in deep fat at 325° F. until golden brown, between 5 and 10 minutes, depending on the size and thickness of the chicken breast rolls. Drain on absorbent paper and serve very hot, with a garnish of lemon quarters and watercress. Allow 1 breast for each serving.

Note: Be careful when cutting into chicken Kiev at the table since the butter has a tendency to spurt out.

I realize that this is a heretical remark, but I think the flavour of chicken Kiev rather flat, though very delicate. To my mind, the dish is improved by placing a slice of ham on each chicken breast before proceeding with the butter. The ham should be a little smaller than the chicken.

Polish Poultry Livers Smothered in Madeira
[*Watrobki w maderze*]

This is Polish cooking, yet it could be French. Madeira is excellent for cooking, far better than sherry or Marsala, and it is particularly suited to poultry. The novel touch of this dish is the soaking of the chicken livers in milk. I think it improves them greatly, taking away much of that very liverish taste of chicken livers. The recipe serves 2 or 3, but it can easily be doubled if it is to be a main dish.

½ lb. chicken, turkey, or goose livers	Salt
	Pepper
Milk	1 to 2 tablespoons flour
2 tablespoons (1 oz.) butter	2 fl. oz. chicken stock
1 small onion, minced	2 fl. oz. Madeira

Soak chicken livers in milk to cover for 2 hours. Drain and dry. Cut large livers into halves. Heat butter and sauté onion about 5 minutes, or until soft and golden. Increase heat and sauté livers for 2 to 3 minutes, or until brown on all sides. Season with salt and pepper. Sprinkle flour over livers and blend into pan juices. Add chicken stock and Madeira and bring to the boil quickly. Lower heat and simmer 5 minutes. (The livers should not cook more than 6 to 8 minutes altogether.) Serve with Risotto alla Milanese (page 132).

Rumanian Smothered Chicken with Sour Cream and Lemon

A dish that turns up, with variations, in most eastern European countries, such as Poland, Russia, Hungary, and Bulgaria. This Rumanian version adds a little lemon juice and rind to the dish, which improves the flavour of the sauce greatly.

1 2½- to 3-lb. chicken, cut in
  pieces
2 oz. butter
2 tablespoons flour
12 fl. oz. sour cream
Salt
Pepper
4 oz. sliced mushrooms

1 tablespoon chopped parsley
1 tablespoon fennel or poppy
  seeds
1 tablespoon chopped chives or
  the green part of spring onions
1 tablespoon lemon juice
Grated rind of ½ lemon

Brown chicken on all sides in hot butter. Transfer to casserole. Stir flour into remaining pan juices. Blend in sour cream and simmer 3 to 5 minutes. Season with salt and pepper. Scatter mushrooms over chicken pieces, together with parsley, fennel, and chives. Pour sauce over chicken. Cover and simmer over low heat about 30 minutes, or until chicken is tender, stirring occasionally. Before serving, remove from heat and stir in lemon juice and rind. Crisp fried Mamaliga (page 143) or boiled potatoes and a salad would be good accompaniments, though the Rumanian lady who made this dish for me served a sour cherry compote as a side dish instead of the salad.

Note: I have also made this dish with sweet rather than sour cream, in the French manner. It is also very good, though of course quite different in taste. The Poulet à la Crème, which the dish becomes when sweet cream is used, can be varied by omitting the fennel or poppy seeds, and adding 1 tablespoon grated onion in their place. For an even richer dish, the sauce can be thickened by stirring in 2 egg yolks which have been beaten with lemon juice and rind.

French Duckling with Olives [Caneton aux olives]

If a very fat duck is being used for any of the following stewed or braised duck recipes, the dish will be far better if the duck is roasted for a certain period of time to allow the fat to escape (as in the recipe below) and then braised. In any case, all the excess wads of fat around the openings of the duck are to be removed before cooking. Duckling with olives is a classic recipe. It should be made with green olives, not black ones, and the kind that is stuffed with pimentos makes for a tastier and prettier dish.

1 5- to 6-lb. duckling
1 lb. green olives, stoned
1 tablespoon flour
4 fl. oz. chicken stock
4 fl. oz. dry Madeira

¼ teaspoon pepper
⅛ teaspoon thyme
2 sprigs parsley
1 stalk celery
1 small bay leaf

Stuff duckling with ¾ lb. olives in the usual manner and truss. Prick all over with the tines of a fork. Place on a rack in a shallow roasting pan and roast in hot (425° F., gas 7) oven 10 minutes. Lower oven temperature to moderate (350° F., gas 4) and roast 20 minutes longer. Remove duckling from pan and keep hot. Pour off all fat except 2 tablespoons. Add flour to pan drippings and blend. Cook, stirring constantly, over low heat until the flour is golden brown. Add chicken stock and Madeira and cook, stirring constantly, until the sauce is thickened and smooth. Add pepper, thyme, parsley, celery, and bay leaf to sauce. Return duckling to pan. Cover, and cook in moderate (350° F., gas 4) oven 45 minutes to 1 hour, or until tender. Remove duckling and place on hot platter. Slice remaining olives and add to sauce. Pour sauce over duckling and serve immediately.

French Roast Duck with Orange [Caneton bigarade]

1 5- to 6-lb. duckling
8 fl. oz. orange juice
Salt
Pepper

1 orange, cut in quarters (do not peel, but remove pips)
4 fl. oz. dry white wine

Simmer giblets and duck neck in a scant ¾ pint of water for 35 minutes. Drain and reserve broth to use in sauce. Rub duckling cavity and skin with a little salt and pepper. Stuff with orange quarters. Truss. Prick all over with the tines of a fork. Place on rack in shallow roasting pan and roast in hot (425° F., gas 7) oven 10 minutes. Lower oven temperature to moderate (350° F., gas 4) and roast 20 minutes longer. Pour off all fat. Combine orange juice and wine. Roast duckling in moderate (350° F., gas 4) oven 45 minutes to 1 hour, depending on age of bird, basting frequently with the orange juice and wine. Remove from pan, place on hot platter, and keep hot. Spoon a little of the sauce over the duck and hand remainder separately. Decorate with watercress sprigs and serve with a Rice or Barley Pilaff (page 128) with mushrooms and a plain green salad.

SAUCE

8 fl. oz. duck broth	1 tablespoon flour or cornflour
8 fl. oz. orange juice	1 orange, peeled and coarsely
Juice of ½ lemon	diced
2 tablespoons brandy	

Combine duck broth, orange juice, lemon juice, and brandy. Blend flour with a little water and stir into mixture. Simmer, uncovered, for 10 minutes, stirring occasionally. (This can be done while duckling is roasting.) Add orange pieces.

Note: I am fully aware that the orthodox method of making the sauce would be to use the pan juices. I also realize that, by making the sauce as I do, I lose the delicious little brown drippings in the pan which make for a good sauce with any bird. However, I have found that the pan drippings are too fat for my taste and that it is better to lose them in favour of a greaseless sauce. Since duck has a well-defined flavour, the loss of taste that comes from omitting the drippings is not very great.

Polish Duck Braised in Red Cabbage
[Kaczka Duszona z Czerwonq Kapusta]

Aside from duck, goose and any game bird can be cooked in this manner with great success. The cooking time will vary, naturally, depending on which bird is used. Cooking fowl with cabbage is a common practice in eastern Europe and Scandinavia.

1 5- to 6-lb. duckling	1 medium-sized onion, chopped
Salt	2 tablespoons flour
Pepper	8 fl. oz. red wine
1 medium-sized red cabbage, shredded	1 to 2 teaspoons sugar
	Pepper
Juice of ½ lemon	1 teaspoon caraway seeds
4 oz. diced salt pork	

Rub duckling cavity and skin with a little salt and pepper. Truss. Prick all over with tines of a fork. Place on rack in shallow roasting pan and roast in hot (425° F., gas 7) oven 10 minutes. Lower oven temperature to moderate (350° F., gas 4) and roast 50 minutes longer. Remove duckling from pan and keep hot.

While duckling is roasting, pour boiling water over cabbage and drain immediately. Sprinkle with lemon juice to preserve colour. If salt pork is too salty, soak in cold water 10 minutes, changing water twice. Drain pork and dry. In heavy pan, cook salt pork over medium heat until transparent. Be careful not to burn. Add onion and flour, and cook 5 minutes, stirring constantly. Add cabbage, red wine, sugar, pepper to taste, and caraway seeds. Cover, and simmer over low heat for 30 minutes, or until duckling is roasted. Stir occasionally.

Transfer duckling into pan with cabbage. Cover, and simmer for 45 minutes or 1 hour, or until duckling is tender. Place on hot platter and serve red cabbage in separate dish. Plain boiled potatoes and a hearty vegetable, such as braised celery or turnips, are good accompaniments.

French Truffled Turkey de Luxe
[*Dinde truffée grand luxe*]

1 8- to 10-lb. turkey	Madeira
4 large truffles or 2 small cans truffle peelings and 1 large can whole truffles	Salt
	Pepper
½ lb. diced salt pork	Slices of fat bacon
	Watercress

Buy turkey at least 2 days before serving. Wash and peel truffles. Chop coarsely. Or chop together truffle peelings and whole truffles. If salt pork is too salty, soak in cold water 10 minutes, changing water twice. Drain and dry. Cook salt pork until transparent. Remove pork pieces and add truffles. Sauté 3 minutes over medium heat. Add Madeira to cover and season with a little salt (if necessary) and pepper. Cover, and simmer 20 minutes. Drain and cool. Stuff turkey with truffle pieces, fasten the openings, and truss. Place turkey in refrigerator for 2 days so that the taste of the truffles will penetrate the turkey.

Before roasting, cover turkey breast with slices of fat bacon and tie with thick white thread or kitchen string. Roast turkey in moderate (350° F., gas 4) oven, allowing 25 minutes to the pound. Baste frequently with melted bacon fat and pan drippings. About 20 minutes before turkey is cooked, remove string and bacon slices and allow breast to brown. Serve on a bed of watercress.

Turkey Stuffing from the Eastern Mediterranean

This rice stuffing is also used for chickens and for *dolmas*. It is very good indeed and not too exotic. The following recipe makes about 4 cups stuffing, enough for a 5- to 7-lb. turkey. If a larger bird is to be stuffed, double the quantities.

1 medium-sized onion, chopped	1½ oz. currants
2 tablespoons (1 oz.) butter	Salt
1½ oz. pine nuts or almonds	Pepper
½ lb. uncooked rice	Turkey liver and heart, chopped
¾ pint turkey or chicken broth	Butter
1 tablespoon tomato paste	Dill

Sauté onion in butter 3 to 4 minutes, or until soft and golden. Add pine nuts and sauté 3 minutes. Add rice and sauté over medium heat 5 minutes, stirring constantly. Heat turkey broth to boiling point and pour over rice. (The rice will sizzle alarmingly.) Add tomato paste, currants, and salt and pepper to taste. Cover tightly and simmer over lowest possible heat 20 to 25 minutes, or until rice is tender. The liquid should have been entirely absorbed by the rice, leaving it fluffy and dry.

Sauté turkey liver and heart in a little butter for 5 minutes. Add to rice, together with a little chopped dill. Cool rice and stuff turkey as usual.

Swedish Roast Goose [*Stekt Gas*]

The goose is a bird much beloved by Germans, Scandinavians, Czechs, Poles, Hungarians, and other European people. 'The only trouble with the goose', say the Germans, 'is that it is too much for one, and not enough for two.' There is little that is not eaten in a goose. Rendered goose-fat sandwiches are a delicacy, and so are the cracklings, the gizzards and liver, of course, and the neck, which is stuffed. Poems have been written about the goose, and strong men have waxed mushy over the beauty of the roasted bird before them.

European geese are stuffed with all kinds of bread, onion, apple, herb, chestnut, and sauerkraut stuffings. The Scandinavians stuff theirs with apples and prunes, and I think it is one of the best, since it cuts the greasiness of that fat bird.

1 10- to 12-lb. goose	5 tart apples, quartered, peeled,
½ lemon	and cored
Salt	20 stoned prunes
Pepper	

Rub goose inside and out with lemon, salt, and pepper. Stuff loosely with apples and prunes. Sew up cavities or fasten with poultry skewers. Truss. Prick skin all over with tines of a fork to let fat run out. Place goose on a rack of a shallow roasting pan, breast side up. Roast in a moderate (350° F., gas 4) oven for 2½ to 3 hours, or about 15 to 18 minutes to the pound. (If the goose is young and tender, 15 minutes to the pound ought to be sufficient.) Test for doneness by moving drumstick. If the goose is very fat, pour off fat from the pan several times during roasting, leaving just enough in the pan for basting. Baste occasionally. For about 10 minutes before the goose is done, keep oven door slightly open to crisp skin (this is a Scandinavian trick). Remove goose to hot platter and keep hot. Make gravy any usual, preferred way. Garnish in the traditional way with Cinnamon Apple Slices and whole cooked prunes and serve with browned potatoes and red cabbage.

CINNAMON APPLE SLICES
Boil together for 5 minutes ½ lb. sugar, 8 fl. oz. water, and 2 teaspoons ground cinnamon or 1 2-inch cinnamon stick. Add a few drops of red food colouring to make syrup pink. Core but do not peel 5 medium-sized tart apples. Cut apples into thick slices. Poach a few of the apple slices at a time in the syrup, simmering over low heat. When tender, remove with slotted spoon and drain carefully on a baking sheet.

Game Birds

The general rule for cooking game birds is to roast the young ones, stew the middle-aged, and marinate and stew the elderly birds. For more specific information on how to recognize a bird's age, consult a poultry and game cookbook or the source of the bird. I do not wish to be involved in the ancient controversy on how long a bird should hang. Each to his or her own taste is my motto, as I take my birds rather fresh, without the excessive gamey flavour that comes from longer hanging.

As for cooking birds: let us remember that a hot or cold roast bird and a good bottle of wine, with perhaps a little watercress on the side, are just plain wonderful eating.

Pheasant in Sour Cream

This recipe was recommended to me by a Hungarian lady whom I can only describe as a steel butterfly. She said it helped to attract men when one is no longer young. It does.

1 oz. fine dry bread crumbs	4 oz. butter
2½ oz. finely ground hazelnuts	2 tablespoons brandy
Grated rind of 1 lemon	4 fl. oz. pheasant stock or
Sherry to moisten	chicken bouillon
4 small pheasants	4 fl. oz. dry white wine
Salt	8 fl. oz. hot sour cream
Pepper	Chopped parsley

Combine bread crumbs, hazelnuts, and lemon rind. Moisten with sherry; squeeze dry. Place 2 to 3 tablespoons of this stuffing in the cavity of each pheasant. Sew up cavities. Rub birds with salt and pepper. Sauté each pheasant in hot butter until brown on all sides. Blaze brandy in warmed spoon and pour over birds. Transfer pheasants to casserole and keep hot. Add stock and wine to skillet in which pheasants were browned. Stir thoroughly, scraping off the brown bits from the bottom of the skillet. Pour sauce over birds. Cover tightly and simmer over low heat 30 to 45 minutes, or until tender. Add hot sour cream to pheasants and simmer over low heat 10 minutes. Do not boil. Place birds on hot deep serving platter and pour sauce over them. Garnish with mushroom caps sautéed in butter and little mounds of buttered flageolet beans. Sprinkle parsley over birds, mushrooms, and flageolets.

Note: One small pheasant feeds 1, a larger bird 2 to 3 people.

German Partridges with Orange Sauerkraut
[Rebhühner mit Orangenkraut]

This method of cooking small birds of different kinds is a very popular one in Germany, Poland, and the countries of the old Austro-Hungarian Empire. The oranges in the sauerkraut are not strictly necessary, but I once had kraut done this way at a small and delightful inn in Rothenburg-ob-der-Tauber (a picturesque medieval town) and I thought it a great improvement over ordinary sauerkraut. With the partridges we had a fine vintage burgundy, and it was a meal fit for the gods. The recipe is for small birds – 1 makes a portion.

Partridges (1 per person)	Double cream (about 2 fl. oz. per partridge)
½ lemon	
Juniper berries	Butter
Salt pork slices or fat bacon slices	Sauerkraut
Brandy	Salt
Oranges	Pepper

Singe, clean, and draw partridges. Wash thoroughly and dry. Rub cavity and skin with lemon. Put 2 juniper berries into cavity of each bird. Wrap salt pork or bacon slices around the breasts and tie with white thread or kitchen string. Truss the birds or push legs toward the breast and fasten them with a skewer pushed through both legs and the middle of the bird. Roast in hot (400° F., gas 6) oven 20 minutes, basting frequently. Five minutes before the birds are done increase oven heat to 450° F., gas 8, and remove salt pork or bacon slices. Brown breasts thoroughly. Blaze brandy by lighting it in a warmed ladle. Pour over birds. Remove birds to hot platter and keep hot. Stir cream into pan bastings and simmer over moderate heat 3 to 4 minutes. Pour over birds.

For each quart of sauerkraut, use 1 large orange. Peel and remove all white membranes from orange flesh. Cut into pieces. Sauté in hot butter (2 oz. for each quart of sauerkraut and orange) 3 to 4 minutes. Drain sauerkraut and add to orange. Season with salt and pepper to taste. Cover, and simmer 10 minutes. Drain.

Serve each bird on a mound of rather stiff, rich mashed potatoes. Surround with sauerkraut. Decorate platter with thin orange slices and parsley or watercress sprigs.

*

Lemon Compote for Roast Duck or any Hot or Cold Roast Fowl

6 fleshy, thin-skinned lemons
1 lb. sugar
Good ¾ pint water

6 small sprays tarragon or 2 tablespoons dried tarragon (or less, if desired)

With a sharp knife or potato peeler, pare the yellow part of the rind of 2 of the lemons. There should be no trace of white skin. Cut rind into fine strips and pour boiling water over them. Drain and reserve. Cut peel and all white skin from the lemons. Cut lemons into thin rounds and remove seeds. Places slices in a shallow heatproof serving dish and scatter with tarragon. (If fresh tarragon is used, dip for a moment into boiling water.) Boil sugar and water together 3 to 4 minutes, or until thick. Add lemon strips; pour over lemon slices and chill.

Meat

The cooking of meat is a vast, noble, and controversial subject – at least in its finer points. Much has been written about it by great and small European masters, often in acrimonious tones. Nevertheless, there are a number of common principles. The first of these is that the meat must be suited to the purpose it will be put to, and the second, that the correct method of cooking must be used.

Since any good standard cookbook tells the proper use for every kind of meat, there is no need to repeat this information here. But it is well to bear in mind that in these days of the vanishing butcher, when most meat is cut behind the scenes by invisible and unskilful gnomes, it is extremely important to trim one's own meat. A good butcher will do it, but most butchers are not good and they are too conscious of the fact that fat is cheap and meat is not, and that you are paying for the latter. You can't forever fight your butcher, but you can at least get what meat you have into perfect shape. Now, a few basic rules to be observed in meat cookery:

Roasting. Roasted meats should be cooked so they are full of their own juices, sealed within. Red meats should have rosy – not bloody – juices, white meats, white – and never pinkish – juices. There is but one true roasting process: the spit turning over an open fire, or its nearest modern equivalent, the electric rotisserie. Both allow the fundamental principle of roasting to take place: namely, to let dry air circulate freely around the meat while it cooks. The taste and succulence of genuinely roasted meats cannot be reproduced by any other process.

Oven roasting, even in an open pan, as it should be done, is really a baking process. Fresh, dry air cannot circulate freely in an oven and some steam will accumulate. But as oven roasting is the method we must use in daily cooking, let us observe a few rules for best results. In order to let as much air as possible flow around the meat, it should always be set on a rack. The meat should not sit directly in the roasting pan, or the liquid dripping from it will braise the underside. The roasting pan should not be larger than necessary, or the meat drippings will spread around and burn, giving the roast an acrid taste and reducing the pan juices which are the roast's finest gravy. I also think that no oven roast should exceed 6 or 7 pounds. If it is much larger, the outside tends to be overcooked, whereas the inside is insufficiently done.

Preheating the oven. It will always be a mystery to me why people can't understand that there is a world of difference between putting a dish into an oven that's already hot and allowing it to heat up with the oven. Since this simple fact is so hard to grasp, let me say that, in roasting, it is of the greatest importance that the oven be preheated and really hot, since the heat is to sear the meat and keep the juices inside. The same goes for grilling. The grill should be as hot as can be (some chefs says this takes 10 minutes to achieve), and well greased.

Searing or not searing. Searing means placing the roast into a very hot (450° F., gas 8) oven and leaving it there for 20 to 25 minutes to close its pores and seal in the juices. The oven temperature is then lowered to 300–50° F., gas 2–4, depending on the meat, and the roast is cooked with frequent bastings of melted fat. This is the old-fashioned way of starting a roast and is decried as obsolete by many moderns. They advocate roasting the meat at *one* low temperature, saying that there is less shrinkage, a more evenly cooked product, and that the fat does not spatter. Having given the arguments for the other side, I now go on record as saying that I think the low-temperature method is inferior, except for some bird cookery, and I have the French *haute cuisine* to support me. Low-temperature cooked meat is tasteless, compared to the other. The economy factor is very small and leaves me stone cold when I think of the other waste in some kitchens. As for the spattering fat, there are several excellent, fast oven cleaners. As to whether all oven-roasted meats should be seared, I agree with those experts who say, 'Yes, even veal, lamb, and poultry.' Their juices are not as copious as that of good beef, but that makes them all the more worth preserving.

Basting. The theory of the French *haute cuisine* and the great English roasting masters (and none are greater) is that meat must be basted, basted frequently, and only with clean fat containing no burned particles. Often it will be necessary to keep melted fat in a dish apart for basting, since the pan drippings may be burned. Stock is permissible for use in basting in some instances, but it is not a classic procedure, one of the reasons being that the water in it will open the meat pores that have been so carefully closed. Another reason is that it will evaporate and cause steam, which consumes the little dry air there is in the oven. However, at times, dry wine, mixed with the pan juices, is used for basting to give the meat more flavour.

Braised meats, pot roasts, stews, and casseroles. These are slow-cooking methods to make the meats tender, using more or less liquid. The liquid in stews is water, wine, or bouillon, or a combination of these, whereas casseroles are cooked in a sauce that's already made. Braised meats, which are extremely popular in all of Europe, are cooked in a minimum of liquid – just enough to generate sufficient steam to cook the meat. All of these processes require pots with extremely tight-fitting lids. The steam must not escape. And they must be simmered over low heat. Simmering can be done in a low oven or over a top burner. An asbestos plate placed over the burner helps tone down the heat and allows true simmering. Since more dishes have been spoiled my misunderstanding of what simmering is, and as a result are boiled instead, let me stress this. A liquid simmers when the movement on the surface is agitated in the gentlest manner, with an occasional bubble here or there. There is no rapid bubbling or strong movement. When this does occur, the liquid boils. And boiling ruins the meat that should be simmered (stews, pot roasts), since it toughens them.

Controversy is rampant as to whether the meats for the above dishes should be seared in hot fat. If there is no searing, the juices escape and flavours intermingle in an uninhibited manner, says one school. I adhere to the other, or French, school, which says that all the ingredients, even the vegetables, should be seared or fried in fat before the liquid is added, regardless of whether they go into the dish at the very beginning or are added later, as in the case of the tenderer vegetables. They taste better and keep their shape, and the juice of the dish is just as good. However, to be authentic, some national dishes, such as Irish stew, require the first – no searing – method and that is that.

A great many cooks labour under the misapprehension that stews, casseroles, or braised meats are, so to speak, timeless, and can be kept cooking at will. They can't. They overcook, just like any other food, though not as spectacularly as a steak or soufflé, since their cooking span is longer. But overcook they do, and the reason that often few of these dishes are worth eating is that the cook thinks stewing is stewing, and lets the dish stand without considering that chicken or veal do not take as long to stew as beef or mutton, and that their flesh will disintegrate, whereas the other meats will retain their firmness much longer.

Unfortunately, snobbery, foppishness, and laziness have reared their silly heads in the matter of stews and pot roasts. They must be cooked with the greatest of care to raise them from the odium into which they have sunk.

Larding. Larding is a process which makes dry meat more succulent by the insertion of lardoons – long strips of pork or ham fat about ½ inch wide. This is done with a 4-tined larding needle on which the lardoons are threaded and then inserted across the grain of the meat. It immensely improves the flavour if, before use, the lardoons are rolled in salt and pepper, chopped parsley, and a pinch of spice such as cloves or nutmeg, or even soaked in brandy. However, few home cooks are willing to lard at home. They should ask the butcher to lard their pot roasts, and generally he will. The French, masters of pot roasts, are great ones for larding, and cooks do it as a matter of course.

Since larding really makes a world of difference to the succulence and tenderness of the meat, it is worth while to acquire a needle and the technique. At a pinch, meat can be larded with a thick knitting needle. You insert the needle into the meat and poke a hole for the lardoons. Then you push them in with the needle.

Marinating. A process by which meat is soaked in wine or vinegar, oil or not, and seasonings. It is used a great deal where the meats are tough, as in Spain, and certainly tenderizes them. However, marinating also impregnates the meat and the dish with the flavour of the red or white wine or vinegar in which it was soaked. Some like this flavour, others don't.

Size of vessel, lids, cooking time. Meats cook differently in vessels of different sizes. For the sake of uniformity, the amount of liquid for a dish will be specified, but it may be necessary to increase or decrease this amount, if the surface of the pot is unusually large or small, and to adjust the cooking time accordingly. Cooking utensils are by no means standard, and we must cook in what we have. Fortunately, stews, casseroles, and braised meats are not subject to the deadly accuracy required in baking, where even the smallest deviation in ingredients can cause disaster. The beauty of stews is that they are 'more-or-less' dishes as to both quantity and flavouring, subject to the invention and ingenuity of the cook. Damage is easily repaired. If the dish is too liquid, reduce by evaporation – that is, cooking without a cover – or by thickening with a little *beurre manié* (butter and flour kneaded together), with butter alone, or with an extra egg yolk if the dish calls for eggs. If too thick, add more water, wine, or broth, whatever the case may be. But be sure it is hot, since sudden temperature changes improve meats no more than they improve human tempers.

Lids must be tight. So tight that no steam escapes. Many a dish has been ruined by a loose lid.

Not only the shape and size of the pan but the shape of the

meats also affects their cooking time, as do the age, quality and kind of the cut. This is the reason that recipes invariably state, after an approximate estimate of cooking time, 'until tender'.

How much meat to allow for one serving depends entirely on the kind of dish, the kind of meal, and, naturally, the appetite and capacity of the eater. Speaking very roughly, allow ½ lb. of meat per person; more if the meat is bony, less if it is cut thin, as for scaloppine.

Serving. On the Continent, meats are carved in the kitchen and not at the table. The advantage of this method is that meats can be eaten really hot, since there is no delay in serving. The slices of meat are laid on a big, heated platter and the vegetables and other garnishes put around them in a pleasing and often very artistic manner, even for family meals. Vegetables and potatoes are arranged in neat piles or bundles with an eye to colour and shape, so that the whole platter presents an edible picture. The Scandinavian countries and Germany particularly excel at this method of serving.

Meat Dishes from Spain and Portugal

Spanish food, like Spanish songs and dances, is strongly regional, and meat is no exception. As the Spaniards put it, linking their climate and their cooking: 'In the north they stew, in the centre they roast, and in the south they fry.' As in most southern countries, the best meat comes from the north where there is good pasture, but nowhere in the peninsula is the meat on a par with the fish. By our standards, since hanging is practically unknown, the meat is tough unless the animal has been killed off in its first infancy. Spaniards, however, have no compunction about slaughtering their beasts while they are still suckling babes. *Lechón* (suckling lamb) is delicious, and sucking pig (*cochinillo* or *tostón*) equally wonderful. Both are extremely popular, and travellers from more squeamish countries are sometimes unnerved by the sight of so many tiny lambs and pigs, split down the middle, reposing in the butchers' windows.

Once past babyhood, Spanish lamb becomes rather tough, since the sheep have to be good milkers to make the cheese which is one of the country's staples. And good milch sheep make no tenderer meat than good milch cows.

Pig, even when grown to porker, remains good, which seems rather surprising since the Iberian pig is an animal used to fending for itself, rather than leading the coddled existence of Anglo-Saxon and Teutonic pigs.

Both Spaniards and Portuguese are fond of highly seasoned and often highly smoked sausages and hams. These are usually delicious indeed and, since they vary from region to region, are a source of great and justified local pride. Their very spiciness is a tribute to the Iberian's cleverness in making a virtue of necessity; the people are poor and meat is a luxury. A little cured meat, provided it is assertive (and Iberian cured meats are), goes a long way toward making the beans, rice, chick-peas, cabbages, potatoes, and bread, which are the staple Iberian foods, taste better and more varied. Sausages also provide some much-needed animal fat and protein.

Beef (*vaca*), for excellent reasons, is usually marinated first and then fried or stewed. *Ternera* (veal) is not like the white French or Italian veal but more nearly resembles our beef. All in all, the Spaniards know what they are doing when they cook these meats in an endless variety of stews. These go under many regional names: *cocido*, *calderada*, *olla podrida*, and suchlike. Often the soup and meat are eaten separately.

Of course, in the fine restaurants of Madrid and Lisbon, and in the big cities, it is possible to eat the standard dishes of the international cuisine, done up in an elegant and very tasty manner. But the food of the people is an entirely different matter. It has the pastoral, archaic, aromatic flavour of the Mediterranean – since garlic, herbs, and nuts, pounded with mortar and pestle, are much used – evoking the foods of distant and exotic lands, brought home by the seafaring Spaniards and Portuguese. After all, the Moorish shores are but a crow's flight away.

I think that Spanish food is the reddest and yellowest food there is, owing to the free use of tomatoes and saffron. Both figure in all meals as a matter of course, and turn up on meats and other unexpected places.

There is quite a difference between Spanish and Portuguese food, just as there is a difference between the two countries. Spanish food is fiercer. Portuguese food is milder, relying more on the wonderful fruits and vegetables which abound in Portugal. But basically the food habits of these neighbours are similar. Both share an addiction to eggs, for instance. And, since Spanish and Portuguese food is filling, the traveller is apt to feel rather startled when, at the end of an excellent meal, the waiter asks, 'Como comer los huevos?' – just in case you are still hungry and would like another round of eggs.

In Spain there is still much game; even wild boar is to be found. I have eaten boar, since my host hunted it with pride, but I would not go to the trouble of seeking wild boar, or any other Spanish game, alive or dead. There are too many other original and superlative Spanish dishes which are more easily achieved.

The reason I have omitted Spanish recipes for sucking pig and lamb is that neither is easily come by here, and even when obtainable, they are never as babyish as those of the Iberian Peninsula, where they are often as young as a few days, and weigh as little as 3 or 4 pounds. My choice of Spanish and Portuguese meat dishes has turned to those not requiring infanticide.

Stew from Andalusia [Cocido andaluz]

I've eaten many regional cocidos in Spain and cozidos in Portugal and, to my mind, this is one of the best. It comes from Seville, the pearl (and I use the word deliberately) of Andalusia, the only city, besides Venice, whose streets and squares give you the feeling of being not out of doors but in an elegant interior. It's the Moorish influence in both towns, I dare say, that produces this unexpected and totally delightful effect.

There are simpler cocidos in Spain; there are others, such as Portuguese cozidos, made with turnips, carrots, and cabbage. But this one seems to me the Iberian cocido personified, and a great dish of its kind.

1 lb. lean stewing beef
¼ lb. streaky bacon in one piece
2 big beef bones, preferably
   with marrow
3–5 pints water
½ lb. chick-peas, soaked
   overnight

Salt and pepper
1 lb. string beans, sliced
1 lb. potatoes, sliced
1 lb. chorizo or other spicy
   sausage
½ lb. noodles or spaghetti

Place beef, bacon, and bones in deep pan and cover with water.
Season to taste. Bring slowly to the boil and simmer till three
quarters tender – about 1 to 1½ hours – skimming as needed.
Boil chick-peas and string beans together until half done; if
canned chick-peas are used, parboil string beans alone. Drain
beans, add with chick-peas to meat, together with the potatoes
and sausage. Cook everything until tender. Strain, skim well,
and reserve stock. Cook noodles in it – this makes the soup, which
is served separately.

Slice beef, bacon and sausage and place on heated platter.
Arrange the vegetables in a ring around the meat. Keep hot. Pour
sauce over meat and serve hot. Makes 6 to 8 servings.

SAUCE

3 cloves garlic
½ teaspoon hot pimento
   powder or sauce

½ teaspoon saffron
1 tomato, peeled and seeded
6 fl. oz. wine

For the sauce, pound garlic, saffron, and pimento powder together in a mortar or on a chopping board. Transfer to saucepan,
and add tomato and wine. Heat till boiling. Season to taste. If
sauce is too thin, thicken with a little flour.

Lamb Stew from Jerez [Calderete de cordero]

'Lamb is food for gentlemen,' the Spaniards say, and this is a lamb
stew I ate in Jerez, where sherry comes from. The sherry makers
of Jerez are most hospitable indeed and happy to show their
cellars to visitors. When I was there, under the auspices of an
English wine merchant, they were even more hospitable. I can't
remember the name of the vintner who lunched us on this stew
and gave us his own driest of all sherries, the likes of which

never can be bought. But should he ever see this book, this is my way of saying thank you for the trouble he took in forwarding this recipe to me in England.

3 lb. young boneless lamb, cut in 2-inch pieces	1 teaspoon powdered cumin
	4 tablespoons oil
Equal parts of water and very dry sherry	2 cloves garlic
	2 onions, sliced
Salt	About 2 tablespoons flour
Pepper	8 fl. oz. very dry sherry, boiling

Marinate lamb pieces for 2 to 3 hours in enough water and sherry to cover. Drain, dry, and sprinkle with salt, pepper, and cumin. Heat oil in casserole and brown garlic cloves in it. Remove garlic and reserve. Brown meat in oil and push to one side of the casserole. Add onions and flour, and brown, stirring constantly. Spread meat around casserole and spoon onions over it. Pour boiling sherry over meat. Mash garlic cloves and add to casserole. Cover, and simmer slowly until lamb is cooked – 1 hour or more, depending on the tenderness of the lamb. If the sauce is too thin, uncover meat and let it cook this way until the sauce is the right consistency. This is served with fried potatoes and a salad of red and green pimentos and black olives. For 2 to 3 people.

Pork à la Laragon [Cerdo a la laragonesa]

2 lb. boneless pork, sliced	2 cloves garlic, chopped
Salt	4 tomatoes, peeled and chopped
Pepper	8 fl. oz. dry white wine
Flour	1 teaspoon cinnamon
Oil	2 hard-boiled eggs, chopped fine
1 onion, sliced	Chopped parsley

Season the pork slices and flour them lightly. Heat oil in skillet and brown pork slices in it. Transfer to casserole. In the same oil, fry onion and garlic golden brown. Add tomatoes, wine, and cinnamon. Cook for 2 to 3 minutes. Pour sauce over meat, cover, and simmer for 1 hour, or until well done. Sprinkle with chopped eggs and parsley and serve very hot in the same dish. Saffron rice or new boiled potatoes might accompany this dish.

Portuguese Roast of Lamb [*Carneiro asado*]

One of the best of all possible ways to cook a well-developed leg of winter lamb. The recipe was given to me by Portuguese friends in Brazil, *Portuguese legitimos*, as they are called by the inhabitants of the old Portuguese colony. My friends said this is the way the shepherds cooked lamb back home in northern Portugal, although there they roasted it on a spit. It is almost as good roasted in the oven, and an unqualified success even with people who don't like aromatic cooking. Since the lamb is cooked for a long time, it will not slice as neatly as normally roasted lamb, but rather comes off in chunks. Saffron rice, a green salad, and a very dry, slightly astringent white wine are what I serve with this *carneiro asado*, which is also very good cold.

There is no hard-and-fast rule as to the amount of stuffing used. I merely give quantities that I have found satisfactory.

1 6- to 8-lb. leg of lamb	Pepper
Salt	About ¾ pint dry white wine

2 *Cups Stuffing*, composed more or less, of:

1 whole bulb garlic, peeled and chopped fine	2 teaspoons cardamom
	Chopped parsley
3 tablespoons rosemary	3 tablespoons oil

Trim lamb most carefully of all fat, gristle, outer and inner skins. This takes some time and patience, but it is essential to the flavour of the dish. The meat will hang partly in loose folds. Mix the garlic, rosemary, cardamom, and parsley, and bind it with the oil. Stuff part of this mixture well into the folds. With a sharp knife, cut deep pockets into meat and stuff with remaining mixture. Rub with salt and pepper. Tie carefully so that meat won't fall apart while cooking. Rub whole surface well with oil. (This can be done well ahead of time – even the day before – and the lamb then stored in the refrigerator.) Preheat the oven to 450° F., gas 8, and sear lamb for about 20 minutes. Lower heat quickly (by opening oven door) to 275° F., gas 1, and roast about 3 hours. Baste frequently with wine. Serves 10 to 12.

*

Leg of Lamb Nelson

5- to 7-lb. leg of lamb	¾ oz. fine dry bread crumbs
Butter	1 oz. grated Parmesan cheese
Purée Soubise Nelson	2 tablespoons (1 oz.) butter

Trim lamb of all fat. Rub surface with butter and sear in a preheated hot (425° F., gas 7) oven for 15 minutes. Reduce heat quickly (by opening oven door) to 300° F., gas 2, and roast lamb, allowing about 20 minutes to the pound.

Fifteen minutes before the lamb has finished roasting, transfer it to a fresh roasting pan or an ovenproof platter that can be brought to the table. Carve the leg in the usual manner, but do not cut the slices off the bone – they must remain attached. Spoon the Purée Soubise thickly between the slices. Tie the leg with string so that the slices won't fall apart. Cover completely with more Purée Soubise. Sprinkle with bread crumbs and Parmesan cheese and dot with butter. Turn oven to hot (425° F., gas 7) and return lamb. Roast until done. Remove string before serving. New potatoes, sprinkled with mint, and a plain green vegetable like buttered peas go well with this.

Note: The amount of Purée Soubise needed depends on the size of the leg of lamb. Roughly speaking, you will need about 1 cup for every 2 lb. meat, plus extra purée for the top. There should be a good amount of purée between the slices and on the top.

PURÉE SOUBISE NELSON

The basic proportions of this purée are 1 cup chopped onion, 1 cup chopped potato, 1 tablespoon butter, ¼ cup thick Béchamel sauce (page 127), 1 egg yolk, 1 tablespoon grated Parmesan cheese, salt, pepper, and a pinch of finely crumbled rosemary. For a 5- to 7-lb. leg of lamb, you'll need about:

3–4 large onions, chopped	3 egg yolks
¾ lb. raw potatoes, peeled and chopped	3 tablespoons grated Parmesan cheese
2 oz. butter	1½ teaspoons salt
¾ cup thick béchamel, made with 3 tablespoons butter, 3 tablespoons flour, 4 fl. oz. double cream and 4 fl. oz. milk	¼ teaspoon white pepper
	1 teaspoon finely crumbled rosemary

Over low heat, cook onion and potatoes in butter in a covered saucepan until very soft. They must remain white. If they show signs of sticking or burning, add a little water – a tablespoon at a time. Strain, or blend in a blender to an absolutely smooth, thick purée. Add remaining ingredients and mix until thoroughly smooth.

Lamb Cutlets Edward VII

An unusual dish that opens vistas into Edwardian life, when meals were not light. It is devastating and very good and men like it.

Very lean, large lamb chops, neatly trimmed	Baked potatoes
Bread crumbs	Iced home-made Herb Mayonnaise (page 256)
Beaten egg	

Dip lamb chops in bread crumbs, beaten egg, and again in bread crumbs. Grill under a very hot grill. Serve chops very hot with potatoes baked in their skins and Herb Mayonnaise. The potatoes must be served on a separate plate without any butter as the mayonnaise takes its place. It is essential that the lamb chops be very hot and the mayonnaise iced.

Two Traditional English Meat Pies

I dedicate these recipes to a Dr Alexander Hunter, who in 1804 wrote a cookbook which he inscribed 'To those Gentlemen who gladly give two guineas for a Turtle dinner at the Tavern, when they might have a more wholesome one at Home for Ten Shillings'.

Veal and Ham Pie

Flaky pastry is best for this. Traditionally, a veal and ham pie is eaten cold with a salad. In this case, it should be baked in a loaf pan lined with pastry dough and covered with a top crust.

1½ lb. veal, trimmed of all fat
   and gristle and cut in ½-inch
   pieces
½ lb. lean ham, cut in strips
2 or 3 hard-boiled eggs, sliced
   not too thin
1 tablespoon minced onion
1 tablespoon chopped parsley

Grated rind of 1 lemon
Salt
Pepper
Strong consommé that will jell
Pastry dough, rolled ⅛ to ¼
   inch thick
1 egg, beaten with ⅛ teaspoon
   salt

Arrange veal, ham, eggs, onion, parsley, and lemon rind in 2–3-
pint greased casserole, seasoning with salt and pepper. The layers
should rise in a slight dome. Proceed as for Steak and Kidney Pie
– see below.

Steak and Kidney Pie

½ lb. beef kidney or 4 lamb
   kidneys
2 lb. good boneless beefsteak in
   1 piece
Salt
Pepper
1 tablespoon chopped parsley
½ teaspoon thyme

1 medium-sized onion, minced
Seasoned flour
Beef bouillon
Pastry dough, rolled ⅛ to ¼ inch
   thick
1 egg, beaten with ⅛ teaspoon
   salt

Soak kidney in cold water for ½ hour, changing water frequently.
This removes the strong taste many people object to. Drain; remove outer membrane. Cut into ¼-inch slices and snip out fat
and tubes with kitchen scissors. Slice the steak in even strips about
3 inches long by 2 inches wide. Flatten them out with the back of
a knife, and season each piece with salt and pepper. Roll slices in
parsley, thyme, and onion. Lay a slice of kidney on each strip of
beef and roll up. Then roll each bundle of meat in flour. Grease
2–3 pint pie-dish and pile meat bundles in it pyramid fashion.
They should rise in a slight dome above the dish. Do not pack too
tightly, or pie will be dry. Fill the pie-dish three quarters full with
beef bouillon. Moisten edges of dish with water.

   Cut ¾-inch-wide strip from pastry dough. Press this strip on
edge of pie-dish, and moisten with water. Arrange pastry dough

over pie-dish. Press down edges firmly with fork and trim. Roll out surplus pastry and cut into diamonds 2 inches long by 1 inch wide. With back of knife, mark diamonds lightly to represent the veins of a leaf.

With a sharp knife, cut a hole in top centre of pie, to allow steam to escape. Arrange pastry diamonds neatly around hole. Brush with beaten egg. Bake in hot (425° F., gas 7) oven for about 25 minutes, or until pastry is well risen and golden. Lay a piece of dampened brown paper over top of pie to avoid excessive browning. Lower heat to 350-75° F., gas 4-5, and bake about 1¼ to 1½ hours, or until meat is tender when tested with a knitting needle, a cake tester, or a fine skewer. If the pie browns too much, dampen paper again. Just before the end of baking time, pour 4 fl. oz. of hot bouillon through a small funnel into the top slit of the pie.

*

Sausages with Onions

The following recipe is more sophisticated than most, since it comes from an English friend who, though fond of the traditional way of combining onion and the flesh of pig, is sufficiently corrupted by continental ways to use wine in the cooking of his sausages.

2 lb. pork sausage	⅛ teaspoon thyme
1 lb. onions, thinly sliced	Salt
12 fl. oz. dry white wine	Pepper

Fry sausages in skillet until golden brown. Remove them and keep hot. Pour off three quarters of fat in skillet. Sauté onions in remaining fat over low heat for about 10 minutes, or until soft. Do not brown. Add wine, thyme, salt, and pepper. Cover, and simmer for about ½ hour. Stir occasionally. Add sausages, cover, and simmer for another 15 minutes, or until the onions have lost their shape and become a creamy sauce. Serve with rich mashed potatoes.

Fillet of Beef
[Filet de Bœuf]

The *filet de bœuf* is recognized on the Continent as the finest cut of beef, though the English may disagree and reserve the place of honour for sirloin. The *filet* is a luxury cut that is usually trimmed at the ends to make a shapely roast, the ends being used for such delicious small steaks as tournedos (a 1-inch-thick slice), filet mignon (1½- to 2-inch-thick slice), and a chateaubriand (2 inches thick and more). There is nothing to beat a first-class *filet de bœuf* for elegance and taste. Its price is high, but the absence of waste is complete, since a fillet has no bone or fat.

Filet de bœuf is a most tender cut, but it is also rather dry and must be either larded and buttered or wrapped in suet to give a juicy roast. It should be cooked rare, about 13 minutes to the pound.

Fillet of Beef with Goose Livers
[Filet de bœuf strasbourgeoise]

5- to 6-lb. fillet of beef	Butter
1 carrot, minced	8 fl. oz. Madeira
2 onions, thinly sliced	8 fl. oz. good dry white wine
⅛ teaspoon dry thyme or 1 sprig fresh thyme	1 lb. foie gras*
1 bay leaf	Flour

Have the butcher trim the *filet* and lard it. If you lard it yourself, use lardoons soaked in brandy. Spread the *filet* generously with butter. Sauté vegetables and herbs in 3 tablespoons butter for 2 to 3 minutes. Do not brown. Put vegetables in the bottom of a well-buttered roasting pan. Stand rack on vegetables and lay *filet*

---

*This is *not* pâté de foie gras but the whole goose liver. Some delicatessens prepare their own, but it can also be bought canned, imported from France.

on rack. Preheat the oven to 450° F., gas 8, and roast meat in it for 20 minutes, turning after 10 minutes to brown other side. Baste each side twice. Add Madeira and white wine and cook 15 minutes longer, basting very frequently. Transfer meat to hot serving dish and keep hot. Strain pan juices and skim off fat. Over high heat, reduce the sauce by boiling to obtain good ½ pint. Keep hot. Slice foie gras, coat slices lightly in flour, and brown quickly in hot butter. Keep hot. Slice meat and insert a slice of foie gras between each 2 slices of meat sandwich fashion. Decorate with watercress. Serve sauce separately. Both meat and sauce should be served very hot. Mushrooms sautéed in butter are a good accompaniment. About 8 servings.

Beef Fillet Minute Steaks

Cut trimmings from beef fillet into very thin steaks. Heat skillet and melt butter in it – they should both be very hot. Brown steaks very quickly – they should not cook more than 2 to 3 minutes altogether. Place on hot serving dish and keep hot. Add a little Madeira or dry white wine and some chopped parsley to pan juices, boil up quickly, and pour over minute steaks. Serve very hot, garnished with Fried Parsley (page 242). Asparagus or artichokes with hollandaise sauce would be good with these little steaks.

*

Bungundian Beef Stew [Bœuf bourguignon]

This must be the best-known and most popular of all French dishes. It is a classic of regional cooking, the region being Burgundy, where some of the world's greatest wines are grown. Like all stews, bœuf bourguignon reflects a cook's individuality. Some cooks add mushrooms, others Madeira, some use butter rather than salt pork, others omit the brandy – though salt pork and brandy, to my mind, make all the difference for the better. What is essential, however, is in the initial process of browning the meat until it is almost black.

4 oz. diced salt pork
2 lb. lean beef, cut in 1½-inch
  cubes
1 tablespoon (½ oz.) butter
3 medium-sized onions, chopped
2 tablespoons flour
About ¾ pint red Burgundy

Salt and pepper
Pinch of ground cloves
Bouquet garni
Water
2 tablespoons brandy
2 fl. oz. Madeira or dry Marsala
  (optional)

Place salt pork in heavy casserole and render. When all the fat
has run out, remove pork pieces. Brown beef in pork fat until
almost black. Pour away excess fat. In a separate frying pan,
heat butter and brown onions in it. Add onions to beef. Stir in
flour, blend thoroughly, and keep free from lumps. Add wine –
enough to cover two thirds of the meat. Season to taste, add
ground cloves and bouquet garni. Add just enough water to cover
the meat. Cover pan and simmer gently for about 3 hours, or until
the meat is tender. Check occasionally – if necessary add a little
more hot water. Half an hour before serving time, remove bouquet
garni. Flame the brandy in a warmed spoon and pour into the
bœuf bourguignon. Add Madeira or Marsala. Cover and simmer
again for half an hour. Buttered noodles or rice or, best of all,
plain boiled new potatoes go well with this dish.

Old-fashioned French Veal Stew
[Blanquette de veau à l'ancienne]

A classic of French cooking and a gentle dish of the cuisine de
famille. It is both excellent and thrifty. In my experience, blan-
quette de veau has been very successful for an informal buffet
when accompanied by a risotto and a tossed green salad and
served with a good dry white wine. Don't omit the nutmeg.

2 lb. shoulder of veal, cut in
  1½-inch pieces
1½ pints cold water
1 teaspoon salt
2 carrots, sliced
1 bouquet garni made from 3
  sprigs parsley, 1 stalk celery,
  1 leek (when in season), 1 bay

leaf, 2 sprigs fresh or ⅛
teaspoon dry thyme, tied
together in a bundle or in
muslin
1 onion, stuck with 2 cloves
12 small white onions (preferably
  pickling onions)
½ lb. whole mushrooms, sliced

5 tablespoons (2½ oz.) butter	2 or 3 egg yolks
2 tablespoons flour	8 fl. oz. cream
Salt and pepper	Juice of ¼ lemon
⅛ teaspoon nutmeg	1 tablespoon chopped parsley

Put veal pieces in deep saucepan, cover with water, add salt, and bring to the boil. Skim thoroughly. Add carrots, onion, and bouquet garni. Simmer covered for 1 hour or until the meat is tender. After ½ hour simmering, add small onions. Remove meat and vegetables from broth, put into a serving dish, and keep warm. Discard clove-studded onion and bouquet garni. Sauté sliced mushrooms in 2 tablespoons butter until golden. Strain, add mushrooms to meat and vegetables, and keep warm. Add mushroom liquid to broth – there should be about 1¼ pints of broth altogether. Keep warm. In another saucepan heat remaining butter, add flour, and cook until smooth and golden, stirring constantly. Add broth slowly to butter–flour mixture, stirring constantly until smooth and thick. Cook over low heat 10 more minutes, stirring occasionally. Add salt, pepper, and nutmeg. Beat egg yolks, cream, and lemon juice together. Add about 6–8 tablespoons of the sauce, stirring constantly. Remove sauce from heat, add egg–cream mixture to it, and cook for about 5 minutes, keeping just below boiling point. The sauce must not boil, or it will curdle. Pour sauce over meat and vegetables and sprinkle with parsley. (This may sound more involved than it is – but since I should like to see this dish served more often, I have explained the cooking step by step.)

Beef Miroton

A pleasant and unpretentious way of using up cold roast or boiled beef. *Petits pois à la crème* (peas dressed in hot cream) go well with it, and so does Fried Parsley (page 242).

3 or 4 onions, minced	¾ pint beef broth, hot
2 tablespoons (1 oz.) butter	Salt and pepper
1 tablespoon flour	1 teaspoon chopped parsley
1 tablespoon vinegar	1½–2 lb. cold beef, sliced
1 tablespoon tomato purée or paste	Bread crumbs

Cook onions in butter until very soft and golden brown. Sprinkle
flour over them and stir in well. Moisten with vinegar and add
broth and tomato purée, blending into a smooth sauce. Season
highly with salt and pepper. Add parsley. Put half of sauce into a
baking dish. Place beef slices in it and cover with rest of the sauce.
Sprinkle lightly with bread crumbs, dot with butter, and brown
in hot (425° F., gas 7) oven.

French Ham with Port [*Jambon au porto*]

A good way of finishing off a ham. Instead of port, a dry Madeira,
Marsala, or sherry could be used. The French prefer port or
Madeira with ham.

6 large slices from a cooked ham	6 fl. oz. port
1 tablespoon (½ oz.) butter	4 fl. oz. double cream
1 tablespoon flour	Salt and pepper
1 teaspoon tomato paste	

Have ham at room temperature. Melt butter, stir in flour and
tomato paste. Add wine and stir over medium heat until the mixture comes to the boil. Slowly add cream and salt and pepper. On
warm ovenproof serving dish, arrange ham slices so that they
overlap slightly. Cover with sauce. Put in moderate (350° F., gas 4)
oven for 10 minutes, or until ham is heated through. Serve with
creamed spinach and Potato Croquettes (page 244).

Ham Mousse [*Mousse au jambon*]

1 lb. minced cooked ham	2 eggs, separated
1 teaspoon prepared mustard	2 fl. oz. dry sherry or Madeira
1 tablespoon gelatine	or port
½ pint chicken bouillon	Continental Radish Salad
4 fl. oz. double cream	(page 48)

Mince ham three times, or blend in electric blender, to have it
absolutely fine and smooth. Stir in mustard. Dissolve gelatine in
a little chicken bouillon. Heat remaining chicken bouillon and
add gelatine to it, stirring until perfectly dissolved. Beat egg yolks
slightly and gradually stir in the warm gelatine–bouillon

mixture. Return to moderate heat, heat until mixture begins to thicken, stirring constantly. Cool.

Whip cream. Blend together the minced ham, the gelatine–bouillon mixture, and the whipped cream. Stir in sherry, Madeira, or port. Beat egg whites and fold in lightly. Oil a 2½-pint ring or other mould with salad oil and pour mousse in it. Chill overnight. Unmould on serving platter by placing hot wet towel on bottom of mould and shaking loose. Fill centre of mould with well-drained Continental Radish Salad. Around the mousse place overlapping slices of unpeeled cucumber (score the cucumber with the tines of a fork lengthwise before slicing). Keep chilled until serving time.

French Sausages with White Wine
[Saucisses au vin blanc]

1½–2 lb. pork sausages	1 tablespoon flour
2 tablespoons (1 oz.) butter	⅛ teaspoon thyme or marjoram
1 shallot, minced, or 2 tablespoons minced onion	1 pint dry white wine

Use large sausages, since the tiny ones are apt to shrink too much in this dish. Prick sausage skins with fork so that they will not burst during cooking. Brown sausages in skillet. When done, drain on absorbent paper and keep warm. Pour off all fat in the skillet. Melt butter and sauté shallot or onion in it until golden. Do not brown. Stir flour into it and cook for about 3 minutes, stirring constantly. Add thyme (or marjoram) and wine. Cover, and simmer sauce for 15 minutes. Return sausages to sauce and simmer until thoroughly heated through. Serve with fried potatoes and a full-bodied vegetable such as brussels sprouts.

Cassoulet

Cassoulet is a regional dish from Toulouse. From there it has spread to other regions, each of which makes the dish with its own favourite ingredients, each, naturally, considering its own version the best. The various cassoulets may include lamb, pork, roast or potted goose, or duck. But what each must have is dried white beans and garlic sausage.

Cassoulet is extremely substantial and one of the best examples of very good peasant cooking. Go light with everything else when you serve cassoulet. Skip the hors-d'œuvre. A tossed salad and a fruit dessert are enough to round out the meal. A chilled, very dry white wine goes best with cassoulet.

1½ lb. haricot beans	1½ lb. lean pork, cubed
Good 3 pints water	1 lb. lamb, cubed
1 tablespoon salt	2 onions, chopped
2 cloves garlic, minced	3 shallots, chopped
2 carrots, quartered	3–4 stalks celery, thinly sliced
2 onions, stuck with cloves	1 6-oz. can tomato sauce
Bouquet garni (parsley, celery, bay leaf, and thyme tied in muslin)	8 fl. oz. dry white wine
	1 garlic or Polish sausage
4 oz. diced salt pork	1 roasted duck removed from the bone and cut into bite-sized pieces (or canned preserved goose)
2 tablespoons duck dripping or cooking oil	

Combine beans, water and salt in a large pan. Let stand overnight, or boil 2 minutes and let soak 1 hour. Add garlic, carrots, onions, bouquet garni, and salt pork. Bring to the boil, then simmer 1 hour. Skim surface. Heat dripping, add pork and lamb, and cook until brown, then add meat to bean mixture.

Cook chopped onions, shallots, and celery in dripping until tender. Add tomato sauce and wine and simmer for 5 minutes, then add to the beans. Add garlic sausage, cover, and simmer until meat and beans are tender (about 1 hour), adding water if necessary to cover beans. Skim off excess fat. Discard bouquet garni.

Transfer mixture to a large earthenware casserole. Add the pieces of roasted duck. Bake for 35 minutes in a medium (350° F., gas 4) oven. Serves 8 to 10.

*

Italian Veal Cookery

Veal is used even more extensively in Italy than in France. It comes from a pale, almost white, fine-fleshed baby calf that has never been fed anything but milk and is slaughtered when only a few weeks old. For the benefit of travellers who might be confused by the terms on menus, veal, in Italian, is called *vitello*. *Vitellone*, on the other hand, is tender young (up to 2 years old) beef which has been grazed but never worked. *Manzo* and *bue* are oxen and, generally, rather tough.

One reason why so much veal is eaten in Italy is that it is cheaper to raise than beef. Another is the comparatively poor flavour of Italian beef. Pasturage is scarce, and animals that grow up to adulthood must work for their living in the fields like the Italian peasants. Even the best grass-fed Italian beef or other meat cannot compare with English or some French beef, since the pasturage in more northern climates is much more succulent.

Veal is a bland meat; therefore it is usually cooked with such flavourings as Marsala, herbs, and cheese, and/or a sauce. Veal does not lend itself to grilling or to plain roasting as good beef does. If roasted, veal should be done with herbs, and basted with wine.

Most of these recipes call for thin slices – scaloppine – and it is best to buy them cut this way from the butcher. If this is not possible, buy a solid chunk of veal in one piece and cut it yourself with a sharp butcher's knife and flatten it out, as thinly as possible, with a meat mallet or an empty bottle.

A great many Italian veal dishes rely for flavour contrast on prosciutto, smoked Italian ham, which is found only in Italian groceries or delicatessens. English cooked ham can be used instead, but since it is also a bland meat, the combination is not nearly as good. As a substitute for prosciutto, I suggest either the German smoked meat called *Rauchfleisch*, or Westphalian ham.

As a final note, never serve veal rare. It should be well done but *not* overcooked.

Saltimbocca

A Roman speciality which means, literally, 'jump into your mouth'.

2 lb. scaloppine, each piece about 5 inches square	3 tablespoons (1½ oz.) butter
	Salt
1 teaspoon sage	Pepper
¼ lb. prosciutto or ham, sliced thin	2 to 3 tablespoons dry white wine

Sprinkle veal slices with sage and place equal-sized slices of ham on them. Pin them together with toothpicks. Melt butter and fry meat in it. Season to taste. Cook, covered, over high heat for 2 to 3 minutes on each side until veal is browned. Place slices of cooked meat on heated platter, ham side up. Keep hot. Add wine to pan and scrape bottom. Boil up once. Pour sauce over meat and serve hot.

Scaloppine al Marsala

This is about the same dish as Saltimbocca, except that no ham is used, and it is made with Marsala instead of white wine.

Bocconcini

Another variation of Saltimbocca. A thin slice of Swiss cheese is substituted for the ham.

Veal Lucullus from Piedmont
[*Vitello Lucullo alla piemontese*]

To be perfectly correct, the cheese used should be Fontina, a semi-soft cheese from Piedmont, but Gruyère is a good substitute. For each person, take:

1 veal chop, cut 1 inch thick	1 thin slice Gruyère or Fontina
Salt	1 slice black or white truffle
Pepper	Butter
1 thin slice prosciutto or ham	Dry white wine

Ask your butcher to cut a pocket in each chop. Sprinkle with salt and pepper. Insert ham, cheese, and truffle in each chop. Fasten tightly with toothpicks. Brown on both sides in butter. Pour off excess butter. Add enough wine to come three quarters of the way to top of chops. Cover pan tightly and simmer about 15 minutes, or until chops are tender. Remove to hot platter and keep hot. Boil up sauce to reduce and pour over chops. Serve very hot, and, if you want to be really Italian, with a French-dressed green salad.

Milanese Braised Shin of Veal [Ossi buchi alla milanese]

A famous dish that shows the typical Italian talent for making do with little meat. It must contain no tomatoes and should be finished off with *gremolata* (a mixture of parsley, garlic, and chopped lemon peel), or it won't be the traditional *ossi buchi alla milanese*. 1 shank feeds 1 person – for more servings, increase proportions accordingly.

2 tablespoons (1 oz.) butter	8 fl. oz. dry white wine
4 veal shanks, 4 inches long and 2 inches thick, with plenty of meat	Hot bouillon
	1 tablespoon minced parsley
	1 clove garlic, minced
2 tablespoons flour	Yellow peel of 1 lemon, minced fine
Salt	
Pepper	

Heat butter in heavy casserole. Roll shanks in flour, season with salt and pepper, and brown thoroughly, turning over several times. Stand shanks upright, so that the marrow in the bones won't fall out as they cook. Pour wine over them and cook uncovered for about 5 minutes. Add 4 fl. oz. hot bouillon, cover pan, and cook for about 1 hour, or until tender. Ten minutes before serving, combine parsley, garlic, and lemon peel, and place over bones. Cook 5 minutes longer. Check sauce. If too thick, add a little more hot bouillon and a little butter and blend well. If too thin, thicken sauce with about 1 tablespoon butter and ½ tablespoon flour kneaded together into a smooth paste. Risotto alla Milanese (page 132) is the traditional accompaniment for *ossi buchi*.

Italian Veal Roll from Parma [*Vitello rolé di Parma*]

Parma is one of the loveliest Italian cities, home of such specialities (the order of preference is individual) as an imposing twelfth-century cathedral, an incredible octagonal baptistery, the sensuous paintings of Correggio, the home of Verdi, Parma violet, Parmesan cheese, ham, butter, and other delicacies, and a sanctuary of such good eating that people make gastronomic pilgrimages to the town. Parma is also one of the most romantic Italian cities, and it is not hard to imagine veiled ladies, Parma violets pinned to their sable muffs, stealing to a lovers' meeting in the Duomo. Parma's great restaurant is the Aurora, where the cooking is both opulent and delicate. The following recipe comes from there.

1½ lb. veal from leg, trimmed free of fat, sinew, and gristle and flattened out as much as possible (ask the butcher to do this)	Pinch of ground cloves
	Enough thin slices of prosciutto ham to cover meat
	2 large or 3 small hard-boiled eggs
Salt	1 tablespoon (½ oz.) butter
Pepper	1 tablespoon oil
Grated rind of 1 lemon	About ¼ pint dry white wine
Pinch of sage	

Season veal with salt, pepper, lemon rind, sage, and cloves. Cover with prosciutto. Place whole eggs on ham. Roll meat up and tie with string. Melt butter and oil and brown meat roll in it. Pour wine over meat and cover pan tightly. Simmer very slowly for about 2 hours. To serve, cut in slices and serve sauce separately. Veal roll is good cold also; in this case, chill sauce separately until the solid layer of fat can be taken off the top.

Note: This is a pretty dish, the colours of the meats and egg making *un'ottima figura* (an excellent appearance). I had it in Parma hot, with a dish of Fennel au Gratin (page 236). Cold, it would be good with a chicory salad and with cut-up new potatoes garnished with truffles – which, in Italy, would be white truffles from Piedmont.

Italian Veal with Tuna Fish [Vitello tonnato]

A summer dish found everywhere in Italy. It's a very refreshing way of eating meat and, with a Rice Salad with Shrimps (page 37), an ideal buffet dish. Vitello tonnato can be made in any quantity – just increase ingredients proportionately.

2 tablespoons olive oil
3½ lb. boneless rolled leg of veal
1 large onion, thinly sliced
1 2-oz. can anchovy fillets
½ pickled cucumber
1 7-oz. can tuna, drained
8 fl. oz. dry white wine
2 cloves garlic, cut in halves
2 stalks celery, thinly sliced

1 carrot, thinly sliced
3 sprigs parsley
½ teaspoon thyme
1 teaspoon salt
¼ teaspoon freshly ground black pepper
4 tablespoons capers
2 tablespoons lemon juice
Mayonnaise

In a deep pot with a tight-fitting cover, heat the oil. Add the meat and brown it very lightly on all sides. Add the onion slices, anchovy fillets, pickled cucumber, tuna, wine, garlic, celery, carrot, parsley, thyme, salt, and pepper. Cover the pot tightly and bring to the boil. Reduce the heat and simmer until the meat is tender, about 2 hours. Remove the meat to a large bowl. Purée the broth over the meat. Place the bowl in the refrigerator and let stand overnight or longer. Just before you are ready to serve it, carve the veal into very thin slices. Arrange the sliced veal on a deep platter. Garnish with capers. Make sauce by blending the marinade (from which fat has been removed) with the lemon juice and enough mayonnaise to give the sauce the consistency of thin cream. Pour sauce over veal slices. Serves 6 to 8.

*

Florentine Pork Roast Arista

A dish that preserves the aromatic flavour of Renaissance cooking. Arista, au fond, is a manner of cooking, and I have used it successfully with other roasting cuts of pork, with leg of veal, boned rump of veal, and with leg of lamb. Traditionally, pork arista is served cold, but it is also good hot.

Loin of pork, about 3–4 lb.	3 whole cloves
3 cloves garlic	Salt
1 tablespoon dried rosemary or 2 tablespoons fresh rosemary leaves	Pepper
	Red or white dry wine

Trim pork of excess fat. Wet garlic and roll in rosemary. Cut pockets in meat by inserting pointed knife and making each hole large enough to hold a garlic clove. Insert garlic cloves and whole cloves into these pockets, and rub meat with salt and pepper. Place on rack in roasting pan with an equal mixture of water and wine, which should be about 2 inches deep. Cook in open pan in slow (300° F., gas 2) oven. Baste occasionally. Allow 45 minutes' roasting time per pound. Cool in its own juice. The meat should be moist. Serve with cold – not chilled – string beans or broccoli dressed with a simple French dressing.

Arista Perugina

Proceed as above, but instead of rosemary use fresh fennel leaves, chopped, or fennel seed. A salad of fresh fennel, sliced thin and dressed with oil, salt, and pepper only, is an excellent accompaniment.

Roman Pork Chops with Artichokes
[Coste di maiale con carciofi alla Romana]

Both pork and artichokes are much used in Rome and, cooked together, they show great affinity. This is a dish of the *cucina di famiglia* (home-style cooking), as cooked in Roman homes or in the small family-run *trattorie*, the wineshop-restaurants in the small side streets of old Rome along the Tiber. Those streets, dating back to the Renaissance, are about the only ones left that look much as they did in *Roma dei Papi*, the Papal Rome that came to an end in 1870.

2 large or 4 medium-sized artichokes, sliced	Pepper
3 to 4 tablespoons olive oil	2 cloves garlic, minced very fine
6 pork chops	½ to 1 teaspoon herbs, such as rosemary, basil, or sage
Salt	1 14-oz. can Italian tomatoes

Slice artichokes according to method given on page 228. Heat olive oil in deep skillet or shallow casserole and fry pork chops until brown. Arrange artichokes around the meat, add the seasonings, and cover with tomatoes. Cover, and simmer for 1 hour, or until meat and artichokes are tender. If sauce is too thin, simmer uncovered until sufficiently reduced.

Note: This is another more-or-less dish. If you like more artichokes, put them in. You can cook as many or as few pork chops as you wish in this manner, adapting the proportions of the ingredients. Frozen artichokes are not suited to this dish because they cook too quickly and disintegrate before the pork chops are ready.

Venetian Liver with Onions [Fegato alla Veneziana]

The best and quickest way to serve liver. But be sure the slices are thin or this dish won't come off, since its trick lies in the quick cooking.

1½ lb. calf's liver	Salt
2 oz. butter	Pepper
2 tablespoons olive oil	Juice of ½ lemon (or less)
4 large onions, finely chopped	Chopped parsley
4 fl. oz. dry white wine	

Wash and dry liver thoroughly. Cut in very thin, 2-inch slices. Heat butter and olive oil together in a frying pan and cook onions until soft and golden. Add wine and season to taste. Cook for 2 to 3 minutes. Add liver and fry quickly until brown on both sides. Add lemon juice. Sprinkle with parsley. Serve immediately on a hot platter, with a salad of watercress and chicory dressed with lemon juice and a little oil.

Swiss Veal with Lemon en Casserole
[Veau à la Rigi Kloesterli]

The Rigi is a Swiss resort mountain, near Zug, where the Swiss go when they want to live well and enjoy a glorious view. Since the Swiss draw a line between themselves and the foreign tourists, the Rigi is not well known to foreigners – entirely their loss, I may add. Unlike most hotel dishes, this one is suited to home cooking, since it can be made any size. Veau à la Rigi Kloesterli is equally delicious hot or cold.

1 solid piece of veal, such as a 4- to 5-lb. boned rump (allow about ¾ lb. per person)	Chopped parsley
Salt	Pinch of cinnamon
Pepper	Pinch of nutmeg
	Lemon juice (juice of about 1 lemon to each pound of veal)

The trick of this dish is to cook it very slowly indeed, in a heavy casserole with an absolutely tight-fitting lid.

Trim veal of all fat, sinew, and gristle. Place it in the casserole, add salt, pepper, a little chopped parsley, and 1 tablespoon water for each pound of meat. Add cinnamon and nutmeg, cover tightly, and cook very slowly. After 1 hour, add lemon juice. Cover and simmer until veal is done, about 2 to 2½ hours.

Note: Celeriac goes well with veal. If veau á la Rigi Kloesterli is served hot, accompany with Celeriac au Gratin (page 234). If served cold, celeriac cut in julienne strips and bound with a well-seasoned mayonnaise and a dish of watercress would make a good ensemble.

Danish Boneless Birds [Benloese Fugle]

Salt pork, cut in strips a little shorter than length of meat	Salt and pepper
Round steak cut into ½-inch-thick slices, 2 for each person	Finely chopped parsley
	Butter
	Boiling water

Soak salt pork in cold water if too salty. Dry well before using. Pound round steaks thin. Season with salt and pepper, but use little salt since the pork will be salty. Place a strip of salt pork and a generous teaspoon of chopped parsley on each slice of beef. Roll up and fasten with toothpicks. Melt butter and fry birds in it until golden. Add enough boiling water to cover. Cover pan and simmer for about 1 hour, or until tender. Place birds on heated serving platter and keep hot. Boil up gravy and thicken with beurre manié (2 parts butter and 1 part flour kneaded together). Pour sauce over birds or serve separately. Garnish platter with tiny boiled potatoes sprinkled with dill, and little mounds of buttered green peas and buttered carrots separated by slices of dill pickle.

Burning Love [Braendende Kaerlighed]

Thrifty, simple, and remarkably popular with men.

Fry as much Danish bacon as you need and keep hot. Pile very rich, hot mashed potatoes on a flat, hot serving dish. Cover potatoes with bacon. Garnish with fried onions and decorate with pickled beetroot. Serve with more pickled beetroot on the side.

Swedish Boiled Lamb with Dill and Dill Sauce
[Kokt Lamm med Dillsäs]

Boiled lamb with dill is a typical Swedish combination and a surprisingly good one, since the pronounced flavour of the dill cuts the blandness of the lamb. Dried dill seeds will not do for this dish – fresh dill is essential.

2 to 3 lb. breast or shoulder of lamb	Boiling water
	3 or 4 white peppercorns
1 tablespoon salt to every quart of water	1 bay leaf
	5 dill sprigs

Trim meat of excess fat and scald quickly in boiling water. Drain, place in pan, and add boiling water to cover. Bring to the boil and skim. Add salt, peppercorns, bay leaf, and dill sprigs. Cover and simmer 1 to 1½ hours, or until meat is tender. Drain and reserve stock. Cut meat in serving pieces. Place on hot platter, garnish with more dill sprigs. Serve with Dill Sauce in a separate dish and with boiled potatoes.

DILL SAUCE

2 tablespoons (1 oz.) butter	1½ tablespoons vinegar
2 tablespoons flour	2 tablespoons sugar
½–¾ pint hot stock from lamb	Salt
2 tablespoons chopped dill	1 egg yolk, beaten

Melt butter, add flour, and stir until well blended. Add stock gradually and blend thoroughly. Simmer 10 minutes, stirring occasionally. Add dill, vinegar, and sugar. Season to taste. Remove from heat and add egg yolk. Do not boil again. Serve hot.

Swedish Meatballs [Köttbullar]

Meatballs with cream gravy is among the best and most famous Swedish dishes. Swedish meatballs must be light. The secret of their lightness is cold, mashed potatoes.

1 tablespoon (½ oz.) butter	1 large cold potato, mashed
2 onions, minced	4 fl. oz. cream
1 lb. freshly and very finely minced beef (round or chuck)	2 fl. oz. water
	1 egg
½ lb. freshly and very finely minced lean pork	Salt
	Pepper
2 tablespoons fine dry bread crumbs	About 4 oz. fat for frying

FOR GRAVY

8 fl. oz. cream	Salt
1 tablespoon flour	Pepper

Heat butter and sauté onion in it until soft and golden. Put in large mixing bowl with meat, potatoes, bread crumbs, cream, water, and egg. Add salt and pepper. Mix until smooth, with a spoon or, more easily, with hands. Shape into balls, which can be as large or as small as desired. Fry meatballs in hot fat until brown, shaking pan often to make them round. Remove each batch from skillet with slotted spoon and keep hot on serving platter. Make gravy by blending flour into cream; stir into pan juices and blend until smooth. Cook gravy over medium heat 5 to 10 minutes, or until thickened, stirring constantly. Add salt and pepper, and pour gravy over meatballs. Serve with cranberries and any starchy dish, such as rice, noodles, or potatoes, which will soak up the gravy.

Swedish Loin of Pork with Prunes
[Plommonspäckad Fläskkaré]

One of the excellent dishes of Scandinavian cooking which reflects the Nordic custom of combining meats and fruit. The ginger is essential, since both the ginger and the prunes cut the fat taste of the meat.

3- to 4-lb. loin of pork	1 to 1½ teaspoons ground ginger
20 large prunes, pitted	Butter
2 to 3 teaspoons salt	¾ pint hot bouillon or water
½ teaspoon pepper	

Trim meat of all fat. Rinse prunes in warm water and halve them. With a sharp pointed knife, cut little pockets deep into meat and insert prunes. This should be done at regular intervals, so that a decorative design results when the meat is sliced. Rub meat with salt, pepper, and ginger and tie with string if necessary. Brown on all sides in butter in a casserole with a close-fitting lid. Add hot bouillon or water and simmer, covered, over low heat 1½ hours, or until meat is tender. Baste occasionally and add more bouillon if needed. To serve, place meat on hot platter, remove string, cut away bone, and slice. Strain and skim the pan juice and serve separately as gravy. A side dish of hot prune purée or hot apple sauce, flavoured with ginger, and fried potatoes go well with this dish.

Whole Roast Pig

Before going to the trouble of ordering and cooking a whole pig, you had better make sure that your guests are not squeamish, preferring pork to whole pig, and that your pans and oven are big enough to take it.

There are many ways to stuff a whole roast pig. I think the Central European fashion of using sauerkraut and apple one of the best, since its tartness tempers the great richness of the meat. A 12-lb. pig will give at least 25 servings.

How to carve a sucking pig. A sucking pig should rest on a platter of sufficient size to give the carver ample room to work. The platter should be placed so that the pig faces away from the carver, at a 45-degree angle with the edge of the table. First, insert the carving fork between the two shoulders, straddling the backbone, and sever the head from the main part of the shoulder. This is done by cutting between either pair of the four middle neck vertebrae. The second step is to remove the front legs in a circular cut. The third step is to remove the two small hams.

Now remove the fork from its original position and place it securely in the left flank at about the centre of the pig. Next, starting at the rear end, split the entire backbone lengthwise, dividing the pig into two long halves, each half consisting of a forequarter and a hindquarter.

After this, each half is divided into the number of chops necessary for service. The chops being small, it is advisable to make each chop double thickness.

This method of carving sucking pigs sounds more difficult than it actually is. Only very young pigs can be served as sucking pigs, and it will be noted, particularly when splitting the backbone, that although accuracy is essential the task is much simplified by the fact that the bones are very soft and can be cut quite readily.

According to the size of the sucking pig, the small hams and front legs can be served whole or carved into two servings by cutting each along the bone and thus dividing it.

In carving a sucking pig, it will soon be noticed how important it is to baste the pig frequently in order to make sure that the skin remains tender.

Roast Sucking Pig

1 sucking pig, weighing about 12 lb. dressed	1 onion, chopped
Salt	4 unpeeled, tart apples, cored and chopped
1 tablespoon caraway seeds	½ lb. bacon in 1 piece
4 oz. butter	½ pint beer
2 lb. sauerkraut	

Wash and dry pig well. Rub inside with salt and caraway seeds. Heat butter and sauté sauerkraut and onion for about 10 minutes. Add apples. Stuff pig loosely with this mixture (too tight a stuffing will make it burst open during the roasting) and fasten with skewers. Lace or sew the opening with heavy kitchen string. Truss hind and fore legs close under the body, facing forward.

Heat oven to 350° F., gas 4. Lay pig on rack in large roasting pan, or use 2 wooden spoons as a rack. Place a wooden plug in its mouth and cover the ears and tail with little envelopes of brown paper, buttered, to prevent scorching. Soak the bacon in the beer and keep warm on stove. Roast the pig for 4 to 5 hours, depending on size, or until it is golden brown. To test for doneness, insert skewer into thickest part of meat. If watery liquid comes out, the meat is still raw; if it spurts fat, the meat is ready.

Now this is important: Baste the meat frequently – every 10 minutes at first, and every 5 minutes for the last hour – by rubbing the beer-soaked bacon over the surface, and by using the pan drippings. Otherwise the skin won't crackle, and a good crackling skin is one of the highlights of roast pig.

When the pig is done, uncover the ears and tail, and replace the plug in its mouth with a red apple. Serve on a bed of watercress and garnish with glazed apples.

Sour Pot Roast [Sauerbraten]

Since so many German restaurants have built their fortunes on the insatiable demands of the citizens for this most famous of all German meat dishes, here is a recipe for it from that renowned Munich beer spa, the Spatenhaus.

8 fl. oz. vinegar	2 oz. flour
8 fl. oz. water	1 oz. lard
2 medium onions, chopped	1 carrot, chopped
2 bay leaves	½ medium parsnip, chopped
12 peppercorns	1–2 stalks celery, chopped
2 cloves	About 2 teaspoons salt
½ teaspoon thyme	Pepper
3 lb. topside of beef	2 fl. oz. red wine

In saucepan, combine vinegar, water, half the chopped onion, bay leaves, peppercorns, cloves, and thyme. Bring to boiling point, then remove from heat. Place meat in earthenware crock or an enamel vessel (*never* in a steel or aluminium pot) and pour marinade over meat. Cover crock, refrigerate, and marinate for any length of time from overnight to 3 days. Drain and reserve marinade. Dry the meat and dredge with half the flour. Heat lard in heavy pan and brown meat in it on all sides. Add remaining onions and vegetables and cook for 5 minutes, stirring constantly. Pour marinade over meat. Cover and simmer until meat is tender, about 3 hours. Mix remaining flour with salt and pepper and blend with a little water into a smooth paste. Stir into sauce and cook until thickened. Place meat on hot platter and keep hot. Strain sauce, add red wine, and boil up once. Pour over meat. Dumplings are a traditional accompaniment to *Sauerbraten*, but plain boiled potatoes serve equally well for soaking up the gravy. Serve red cabbage or some other cabbage dish with it.

Pork Hocks with Sauerkraut
[*Schweinehaxen mit Sauerkraut*]

Germans, especially Bavarians, love this and they always serve plenty of beer with it.

6 fresh pork hocks	6 sprigs green celery tops
2 lb. raw sauerkraut	2 tablespoons caraway seeds
2 large bay leaves	(optional)
6 sprigs parsley	

Wash the hocks thoroughly and, if necessary, scald and scrape to clean them. Place in a large pan, cover with water, and simmer for 1 hour. Remove hocks from water and set them aside. Add the sauerkraut to the water in the pan and add bay leaves, parsley, and celery tied together. Arrange the pork hocks over the top, cover, and simmer 2 hours, or until both meat and sauerkraut are tender. If caraway seeds are used, add them about 30 minutes before the end of cooking time. Drain and arrange pork and sauerkraut neatly on a platter. Serve with boiled potatoes, Erbsenpüree (Purée of Dried Peas) (page 243), and lots of beer.

German Veal Roast Hamburg Fashion
[*Kalbsbraten nach Hamburger Art*]

The great advantage of pot-roasting veal this way – and it is a typical German way – is that you may use small roasts, which would shrink to nothing if oven-roasted. But the *Kalbsbraten* can be equally well made in larger sizes – just increase ingredients accordingly.

2 lb. solid veal, trimmed of fat, sinews, and gristle, and tied if necessary	2 tablespoons (1 oz.) butter
	About ¼ pint dry white wine
	1 medium-sized onion
Salt and pepper	Pinch of thyme
1 tablespoon flour	4 fl. oz. sour cream

Rub veal with salt and pepper and dust with flour. Brown well in butter in heavy casserole. Add about 1½ inches wine. Add onion and thyme. Cover tightly and simmer about 1 hour, or until done. Remove from heat and stir in sour cream. Return to heat but do not allow to boil. Slice meat and arrange on heated platter. Strain sauce over it. Garnish with parsley. Makes 3 to 4 servings. Serve with Kartoffelkroketten (Potato Croquettes) (page 244) and a green salad.

German Ham with Mayonnaise
[Berliner Mayonnaise Schinken]

As served in the pre-war Haus Vaterland, a large restaurant building where each room represented a German region and served its specialities.

1 whole ham	½ teaspoon thyme or marjoram
Dry white or red wine	3 sprigs parsley
2 stalks celery and tops	Jellied Mayonnaise
1 onion, stuck with 4 cloves	Stuffed olives
1 carrot	Green pepper
3 bay leaves	Quick Aspic Jelly

Place ham in a deep pan and cover with wine. Add remaining ingredients. Bring quickly to the boil. Reduce heat so that wine barely simmers but does not bubble. Cover and simmer about 25 minutes to the pound for a medium ham, 30 minutes for a smaller ham, or 20 minutes for a large one. Cool ham in wine. If a processed ham is used, follow wrapper instructions on how to prepare.

Remove all fat and skin from ham, except a portion around the bone. Score this skin into sharp points. Coat whole ham, except skin, with 3 layers of Jellied Mayonnaise, chilling each layer until set before adding another. Smooth on mayonnaise with a spatula or broad knife. Keep mayonnaise icy cold at all times, but do not allow to set.

Decorate last layer of mayonnaise with flower designs made from slices of stuffed olives and leaves and stems cut from green peppers. Coat whole ham, including skin, with 3 layers of clear, very cold Quick Aspic Jelly, chilling each layer until set before adding another. Dribble aspic jelly from a spoon. Keep aspic jelly icy cold at all times, but do not allow to set.

Arrange finished ham on large platter, taking care not to disturb coating. Surround with mounds of chopped aspic, bunches of watercress, and red radish roses. Cover exposed bone with paper frill. Keep ham chilled in refrigerator until the very last moment before serving.

A 10- to 12-pound ham will yield about 22 servings.

JELLIED MAYONNAISE
This basic recipe may be increased or decreased as the dish demands.

1 tablespoon (1 envelope) gelatine	8 fl. oz. mayonnaise
1 tablespoon water	1 tablespoon lemon juice

Soak gelatine in cold water and dissolve it over hot water. Fold into mayonnaise, add lemon juice, and blend thoroughly. Before using for coating, chill until almost set but still soft.

QUICK ASPIC JELLY
This basic recipe may be increased or decreased as the dish demands.

1 tablespoon (1 envelope) gelatine	½ pint clear consommé
	3 fl. oz. dry white wine or port

Soak gelatine in 4 tablespoons of the consommé. Heat remaining consommé to boiling point and dissolve gelatine in it. Add wine. Before using for coating, chill until aspic is almost set but still liquid.

CHOPPED ASPIC

Rinse out bowl in cold water before pouring liquid aspic jelly into it. Chill until set and firm. Turn out on wetted greaseproof paper and chop with a large knife. Avoid touching with your fingers. Work fast, or aspic will melt. Keep in refrigerator until just before using.

Austrian Pot Roast with Mushrooms
[Groedener Jagdbraten mit Schwaemmen]

In my youth I used to climb and ski in the Dolomites – a part of the Austrian Tyrol that became Italian with the signing of the Versailles Treaty. A village in the Groedener Tal, or Val Gardena, its official name, was my headquarters. I used to stay with Frau Obletter, a dragoon of a woman who in her youth had been cook at one of the imperial Austrian hunting lodges. This pot roast was her speciality and it is wonderful, especially when served with Topennudeln (noodles with pot cheese) as she did. The long slow cooking impregnates the whole roast with the flavour of mushrooms. Frau Obletter used wild mushrooms, whose taste is far superior to that of cultivated mushrooms. But even without these the dish is excellent. Its success depends entirely on the correct proportion of mushrooms to meat, which should be 1 to 2. That is, you use 1 lb. mushrooms to every 2 lb. meat. You need a large, heavy casserole with a very tight-fitting lid for this Jagdbraten. Allow 1 lb. meat per person since pot roast shrinks.

4–6 lb. beef, topside or rump	Pinch of cardamom or nutmeg
4 tablespoons (2 oz.) butter	2–3 lb. mushrooms, sliced
Salt and pepper	Sweet or sour cream (optional)

Brown meat in butter in heavy cooking utensil. Season to taste with salt, pepper, and cardamom or nutmeg. Add mushrooms. Cover tightly and simmer very slowly until tender – about 30 minutes per lb. The natural juice of the mushrooms should provide enough liquid for the pot roast and make the gravy. Check occasionally, however, adding a little hot water if needed. Serve mushroom gravy on the side. If you like, stir a little sweet or sour cream into the gravy.

Austrian Veal Goulash à la Richard Strauss

This was, according to his wife, the favourite goulash of the composer. He accompanied it with a chilled Moselle.

1½–2 lb. veal, cut in 1½-inch squares and free of all fat and gristle	1½ tablespoons flour
	Good ¼ pint dry white wine
	4 fl. oz. sour cream
Salt and pepper	2 teaspoons caraway seeds
2 oz. unsalted butter	Paprika
2 medium-sized onions, sliced	Juice of ½ lemon
2 large tomatoes, peeled and quartered	About 4 tablespoons hot beef bouillon

Season veal pieces with salt and pepper. Heat butter to foaming point and brown meat. Add onions and tomatoes, and stir until the juice has been reduced and practically none remains. Dust with flour and brown for 1 minute. Add wine, sour cream, caraway seeds, a sprinkling of paprika, the lemon juice, and bouillon. Cover tightly and simmer until the meat is tender – about ¾ to 1 hour. Check at intervals to see that the meat is not too dry; if it is, add a little more hot bouillon. Before serving, remove the meat and keep hot. Strain the sauce and pour back over meat. Serve with buttered rice, noodles, or a Barley Casserole (page 140).

Hungarian Goulash [*Gulyás*]

Goulash is the national dish of Hungary and should be considered a generic name for a variety of dishes made with either beef, veal, pork, lamb, game, or a combination of meats. These are cooked the *gulyás* way, or, in plain words, stewed. Usually Hungarian goulash contains paprika to the cook's taste. Other seasonings used besides paprika, salt, and pepper are caraway seeds, marjoram, and garlic.

The recipe below is a good basic recipe which can be varied. Dry white wine or bouillon can be used instead of water. 1 lb. cooked sauerkraut can be added about ½ hour before the simmering is completed to make a Transylvanian (Skekely) goulash. Sauerkraut is added and the sour cream omitted to make Szegediner goulash – and in this case the sauce is thickened with flour. Sometimes raw quartered potatoes and/or tomatoes or tomato sauce are simmered with the meat. In any event, goulash must have plenty of onions in it.

1½–2 lb. beef chuck, cut in 1½-inch squares and free of fat	1–1½ lb. onions, sliced
	Paprika
Salt	1 tablespoon flour
Pepper	Hot water
2 oz. unsalted butter	¾ pint sour cream

Season beef pieces with salt and pepper. Heat butter to foaming point and brown meat. Add onions and stir in sufficient paprika to colour the meat and onions a reddish brown. Stir until all the juice generated by the onions has been absorbed. Dust with flour and brown for 1 minute. Add sufficient hot water to cover meat. Cover tightly. Simmer gently for 1 to 1½ hours, until all the onion has been cooked to pulp. Add sour cream. Buttered egg noodles sprinkled with caraway seeds are the classic accompaniment to beef goulash.

Meat Dishes from the Balkans

Moussaka with Potatoes [Mysaka cu Cartofi]

Moussakas are meat–vegetable combinations which are eaten in about every Balkan country wherever a little meat has to go far, and when a change from the everlasting stews is wanted. They can be made with cauliflower, with celery, with aubergine, with noodles – in short, with whatever is at hand – and are typical of the more-or-less kind of family cooking without which no home could exist. What makes moussakas different is that they are usually covered with a white egg sauce and baked in the oven. I give here a Rumanian version, made with potatoes and, like all moussakas, one of the nicer ways of feeding the family differently. Moussakas are also good for simple buffet parties.

3 onions, chopped
3–4 oz. butter
1 lb. beef, veal, or pork, finely
   chopped
1 tablespoon chopped parsley
Pinch of thyme
2 teaspoons fennel seeds
Salt

Pepper
2 tablespoons flour
2 fl. oz. dry white wine
4 eggs
8 fl. oz. cream
2 lb. potatoes, sliced
Bread crumbs

Cook onions in 1 oz. melted butter until soft and golden. Add meat
and cook about 3 minutes longer. Add parsley, thyme, fennel
seeds, salt and pepper to taste, and blend well. Take 1 tablespoon
of the flour and stir it in. Now add the wine and cook about 5
minutes, stirring constantly. Remove from heat, cool, and pass
through the fine blade of the mincer. Separate 2 of the eggs.
Blend the yolks with 2 tablespoons of the cream and incorporate
into meat mixture. Beat the whites until stiff and add to meat.

Fry sliced potatoes in part of the remaining butter until semi-soft
and golden. Butter an ovenproof dish and sprinkle with bread
crumbs. Fill it with alternate layers of potatoes and meat mixture,
ending with potatoes. Dot with butter, and bake in a moderate
(350° F., gas 4) oven for about 20 minutes. Beat remaining cream
and flour into the 2 remaining eggs and pour over moussaka. Bake
for another 10 to 15 minutes, or until brown and bubbly on top.
Serve with a tomato dish, such as a sauce, stewed tomatoes, or a
tomato salad.

Stuffed Vine Leaves [Dolmas]

Dolmas, or stuffed vine leaves, are eaten wherever the Byzan-
tine influence survives – in Turkey, Greece, Bulgaria, Rumania,
and even in Yugoslavia. Yugoslav cooking, though, owing to that
country's past affiliation with the Austro-Hungarian Empire, is
closer to that of Hungary, and even Russia and Poland, as re-
flected in the many dishes made of sweet or sour cabbage, beetroot soups, and mince balls.

In this context, it must be said that the Balkan countries are
not only very different from each other but that the food in each
also varies according to whether the country is more or less West-

ernized, and according to the social class by which it is eaten. Wherever the old Austro-Hungarian Empire cast its shadow, the middle class would tend toward Austrian cooking, rich with cream gravies. In Rumania, where French airs were much admired in more ways than cooking, we find elegant dishes with a French manner. But the peasants kept to their national eating habits. Now, back to *dolmas*.

Dolmas taste very good, even to people not used to them. They furnish one of the not too frequent instances where the necessity of making a little meat go a very long way has produced a dish that is neither heavy nor coarse. They are made with lamb, the national meat of the Balkans, and flavoured according to the taste of the country. The Greeks may use currants and raisins in them, as they do in their rice pilaffs, the Turks pine nuts, the Rumanians and Bulgarians dill and lovage. There are other stuffings, some of them meatless.

The recipe given here is a basic one. To one's liking, 2–4 oz. pine nuts or raisins may be added, or a flavouring of herbs. Tinned vine leaves can be bought at or ordered from any food stores carrying Near Eastern groceries.

1 lb. minced lamb	Juice of ½ lemon
3 medium onions, finely chopped	2½ tablespoons tomato paste
2 oz. long-grain rice	1 lb. vine leaves
3 tablespoons chopped parsley	Chicken broth or water
1 teaspoon salt	2 tablespoons olive oil
Freshly ground pepper to taste	

Preheat oven to 350° F., gas 4. In a large mixing bowl, combine the lamb, onions, rice, parsley, salt, pepper, lemon juice, and tomato paste. Rinse the vine leaves in cold water. Place shiny side of leaves on a flat surface. Place 1 teaspoon of lamb mixture in centre of each leaf and roll fairly tightly, tucking in the ends. If the leaves are torn, use a second leaf for each roll. Place in rows in baking dish. Add enough broth or water to cover and the olive oil. Weight leaves with a plate. Cover the baking dish and bake for 1 hour. Serve hot as a main course or cold, but do not chill or the flavour will be lost. Garnish with lemon slices. Makes about 36 *dolmas*. Enough for about 6 servings.

Two odd but surprisingly tasty Balkan Stews

The wife of a British consul, who had lived in different parts of the Balkans, made these for me in London, saying that in one form or another they turn up in both Bulgaria and Rumania. I like them both for a change. Like eastern European soups, they reflect the regional custom of souring dishes.

Lamb Stew with Parsley

This could not be simpler.

2 lb. lamb, cut into 1½-inch pieces
1 tablespoon cooking fat
5–6 oz. chopped parsley
3 thick lemon slices
Salt and pepper
¾ pint water

Fry lamb pieces in fat until brown. Add parsley, lemon, salt and pepper to taste, and water. Simmer, covered, until the liquid is nearly absorbed and meat tender. Serve with potato salad.

Meat Stew with Quinces

2 lb. beef, veal, or pork, cut into 1½-inch pieces
4 oz. butter or lard
1 tablespoon flour
¾ pint stock or water, hot
Salt and pepper
6 medium-sized quinces
1 tablespoon sugar

Fry meat in half of the fat until brown. Sprinkle with flour, cover with stock, and season to taste. Simmer, covered, until half cooked – the cooking time varies with the kind of meat used. Pare and core the quinces, cut them into quarters, and fry them in remaining fat until golden. Add to meat, with sugar, and cook until both are tender. The quinces should retain their shape; they are apt to get mushy, so do not overcook.

*

Greek Pork with Celeriac and Egg Lemon Sauce
[*Hirino me selino avgolémono*]

Pork and celeriac are very good together, especially when accompanied by the glorious Saltsa Avgolémono.

2 lb. lean pork, cut in 2-inch pieces	About 6 fl. oz. dry white wine
3 tablespoons (1½ oz.) butter	2 tablespoons chopped parsley
3 medium-sized onions, finely chopped	2 lb. celeriac
2 tablespoons flour	Greek Egg and Lemon Sauce (page 252)

In casserole, cook pork in butter until golden brown. Add onions and brown. Stir in flour, wine, and parsley. Cover and simmer until meat is done – about 1¼ to 1½ hours. Meanwhile, peel and wash celeriac. Depending on size, cut into thick slices or quarters. Add to pork, and add a little hot water, if needed, to prevent scorching. Cover and simmer until done. Make Egg and Lemon Sauce, using broth from meat instead of the water. Remove meat from heat, pour sauce over it, and return to heat but do not allow to boil. Serve very hot, with Rice Pilaff (page 129) or new boiled potatoes.

Greek Beef Ragout with Onions [*Stifado*]

One of the most popular Greek dishes, and deliciously spicy and aromatic, especially if made ahead of time and then reheated just before serving. As in all dishes of this kind, the proportions are not terribly important. But – you must use the same weight of onions and meat, and the onions must be the small white ones (the smaller the better), the kind used for pickling.

1 tablespoon (½ oz.) butter	2 cloves garlic
5 tablespoons olive oil	1 2-inch piece whole cinnamon
3 lb. topside of beef, cut into 2-inch pieces	4 whole cloves
8 fl. oz. dry red wine	1 bay leaf
12-oz. can Italian tomatoes	Salt
2 tablespoons tomato paste	Pepper
3 lb. small white onions, whole	Chopped parsley

Heat butter and 2 tablespoons olive oil in heavy casserole and brown meat on all sides. Add half the wine, cover, and simmer for 10 minutes. Add tomatoes and tomato paste and continue to simmer, covered. Heat remaining oil in skillet and very quickly brown onions in it. Add onions to meat, together with garlic, cinnamon, cloves, bay leaf, and remaining wine. Season to taste. Cover pan and simmer extremely slowly for about 3 hours, or until meat is tender and the sauce the consistency of purée. Stir occasionally, and add a little water if needed. Sprinkle with parsley and serve with Rice Pilaff (page 128).

Polish Meat Cookery

Poland is a country with a very fine and distinctive kind of cooking of its own. Were the Polish language as widely known as French, German, or Italian, Polish cooking would have the fame it deserves, for both its quality and its variety. There is a traditional Polish peasant cuisine, of which potatoes, buckwheat, cabbage, and sour milk are mainstays. But there is also an *haute cuisine polonaise*, indulged in by the pre-war Polish aristocracy, a most elegant and internationally-minded group of people who tempered the Slav elements in their cooking (such as the excessive use of sour cream found in Russian cooking) with their own Westernized culture.

Polish cooking, by virtue of the country's historical and geographical location, has many of the elements of Central European, especially Austrian, cooking. But it is much more subtle and refined and chic, as exemplified by the following way of making pot roast, which also reflects the Poles' talent for delicate stuffings or forcemeats.

Polish Sauerkraut Stew [Bigos]

This is probably the most traditional of all Polish dishes, celebrated by poets and novelists, evoker of deep nostalgia and cause of much toast-drinking among all Poles. It is a hunting dish, to warm the chilly hunters. Considering that Poland to this day is a paradise for big and small game, including wild boar, which even the present-day Poles hunt whenever they can, and that *bigos* combines the elements so dear to Slavic cooking, mushrooms and sauerkraut, its continued popularity is scarcely surprising. The best *bigos* is made in large quantities, with many different meats including game, and is better when reheated. This makes it an excellent dish for large outdoor parties, since it can be prepared in advance and is easily transported for reheating over an open fire or whenever a barbecue is too complicated. I have made it on such occasions and the guests loved it. The quantities given below are approximate, and some meats can be left out, of course. But dried imported mushrooms are essential, since cultivated mushrooms are too delicate in flavour. And so are salt pork and Madeira, a wine much used in Poland for cooking. If *bigos* is made from scratch, the meats are better pot-roasted than oven-roasted, though of course any leftovers can be used successfully. There are no vegetables in *bigos*. Lesser *bigos*, for family consumption, can be made by decreasing the ingredients proportionately. By the same token, larger *bigos* can be made by increasing them. It is really a very simple dish to assemble, once you have the ingredients ready.

2 lb. dried mushrooms
1/4 lb. salt pork, diced
4 onions, sliced
1 oz. flour
6–8 lb. sauerkraut
Salt, pepper, and sugar to taste
At least 1/2 pint Madeira

At least 1/2 lb. each of the following pot-roasted or oven-roasted meats, diced in approximately 1-inch pieces: beef, veal, lamb, pork, venison, hare or rabbit, chicken, duck, ham, spicy sausage

Cook mushrooms until tender in enough water to cover. Drain, reserve liquid. Cut mushrooms into thin strips. In a large enough pan to hold the *bigos*, cook salt pork until golden, then fry onions in the fat until soft; blend in flour (or else fry in skillet and then transfer to large pan). Combine ingredients, except Madeira, in the pan, blend thoroughly, and season to taste. Add mushroom liquid, cover tightly, then simmer for about 1 hour. Then add Madeira, taking care that the *bigos* is not too thin. Simmer for another hour. Serve with boiled potatoes sprinkled with dill and a salad, if you must have greens. If served in the open air, fruit and cheese will take the place of salad and will be more than enough. About 20 to 25 servings.

Polish Hussar Roast [*Pieczen Huzarska*]

4 lb. beef rump	1 onion, sliced
4 fl. oz. vodka or vinegar, very hot	4 oz. chopped mushrooms
	1 medium onion, minced
2 tablespoons flour	2 tablespoons bread crumbs
Salt	Pinch of nutmeg
Pepper	1 egg, beaten
2 oz. butter	Double cream
6 fl. oz. bouillon, hot	

Scald meat with hot vodka or vinegar (vodka is better). Season flour with salt and pepper and dredge meat in it. Heat butter and brown meat well. Add bouillon and onion. Cover tightly and simmer about 2½ to 3 hours, or until done. Turn meat occasionally and baste from time to time.

Make stuffing by combining all other ingredients, using just enough cream to bind the mixture.

Remove meat from pan and slice thinly, but do not cut slices completely from the bone, if there is a bone in the meat. Place stuffing between slices. Skewer or tie meat slices so that they won't fall apart. Return to pan, baste with the juices, cover tightly, and simmer for another ½ hour or so. Add more hot stock, if needed. Remove to hot platter and keep hot. Strain gravy, correct seasoning, and thicken with a little *beurre manié* (butter kneaded with flour). Serve with potatoes and a delicate green vegetable such as asparagus, flageolet or baby lima beans, or with hearts of artichoke.

Polish Veal Cutlets Zingara
[*Kotlety cielece à la zingara*]

Slices of beef or veal, cooked in a casserole with vegetables and sometimes ham, turn up frequently in Central European cooking under different names, such as *à la Esterhazy* in Austria. Of all the various versions, I like the Polish one best. The original calls for the famous Polish ham, but cooked ham can be used.

6 loin veal chops, ¾ to 1 inch
  thick, boned and slightly
  pounded
Salt and pepper
6 slices cooked ham, about ¼
  inch thick, and same size as
  veal
2 oz. butter
1 onion, chopped

1 carrot, diced
1 parsley root, diced
1 small celeriac, peeled and diced
1 stalk celery, chopped
2 oz. string beans, sliced
About 8 fl. oz. strong bouillon,
  hot
About 8 fl. oz. dry white wine

This dish is better when the veal is larded with salt pork, but
it is not strictly necessary. Season veal with salt and pepper.
Brown veal and ham in hot melted butter. Remove meat and
keep hot. Brown vegetables in butter. In buttered ovenproof casserole, place alternate layers of vegetables, veal, and ham. Pour
bouillon and wine over layers. Cover tightly and cook in moderate (350° F., gas 4) oven, or simmer on top burner, for about
1 to 1½ hours, or until veal is tender. Correct seasoning.

There are two ways of serving this dish. The vegetables can be
strained or puréed in blender and mixed into a smooth sauce
with the gravy and returned to the casserole. Or they can be left
as cooked. I prefer this latter version, since I think the dish tastes
better, and it saves labour, too. Serve from casserole. Potatoes or
rice croquettes are good side dishes.

*

Beef Stroganoff

This is the classic recipe, beef Stroganoff as it should be. Though
they are tasty, and sometimes even used in Russia, tomatoes
and mushrooms are alien to the true nature of beef Stroganoff.
This is a sure-fire party dish that lends itself to chafing-dish
cookery.

1½–2 lb. fillet of beef, or sirloin
  or tenderloin steak
Salt
Pepper
4 oz. butter
2 small onions, thinly sliced

1 tablespoon flour
1 teaspoon dry mustard
8 fl. oz. bouillon, hot
4 fl. oz. sour cream
1 tablespoon chopped parsley

Trim meat of all fat and gristle. Two hours before needed, cut it into strips about 1 inch long and ¼ inch thick. Sprinkle with salt and pepper and let stand – but do not chill. Melt butter and fry onions in it until golden. Add meat and fry together for 5 minutes, stirring with a fork. Sprinkle with flour and fry for another 2 to 3 minutes. Add mustard and hot bouillon and boil up once. Add salt and pepper. Add sour cream, cover pan, and simmer very gently for 15 minutes – do not allow to boil. Sprinkle with parsley and serve with boiled new potatoes sprinkled with a little fresh dill.

Note: You may have to adjust the proportions a little to get the sauce right – it should be the consistency of thick cream.

Russian Meat Pie
[Coulibiac]

The Russians are very fond of savoury pies, and they make them in a variety of sizes, with all kinds of meat, fish, egg, and vegetable fillings, using yeast or short dough or, most elegantly, puff paste. A coulibiac differs from other Russian pies in its shape, which is narrower and taller, but is no more difficult to make than other pies. A coulibiac should not be made too large or it becomes un-wieldy to handle; therefore, for a buffet, it will be necessary to make several. A handsome coulibiac se présente bien, as the French say, and it could be made the centre of a summer luncheon buffet à la russe which would not be too exotic to frighten guests.

How to fill a coulibiac. Think of the coulibiac as a parcel to be wrapped for mailing. The dough is the paper, the filling the contents of the parcel. The filling must be completely enclosed in the pastry, or it will leak out during baking. And the filling must not be packed in too tightly, or it will burst the coulibiac while it bakes.

Sprinkle a clean kitchen cloth heavily with flour. Put dough on it and roll out in a rectangle. Put filling in the middle in a narrow pile, along the length of the dough. Leave a 4- to 5-inch border free of filling on all sides. Moisten the edges of the dough with water, bring the long sides of the dough together over the centre, and pinch the edges firmly together over the filling. Then fold the two short sides over toward the centre and seal securely. It is most important that the *coulibiac* be well sealed. Butter and flour a baking sheet and put alongside the *coulibiac*. Lift kitchen cloth and carefully roll the *coulibiac* on the baking sheet so that the folded edges will be underneath. Decorate the *coulibiac* with pastry leaves which have been brushed on the underside with white of egg to make them stick. Prick *coulibiac* with fork several times to let steam escape during baking.

If a yeast dough is used for the pastry, let the *coulibiac* rise in a warm place for about 20 minutes before baking. If puff paste or other pastry is used, refrigerate for 30 to 40 minutes. Before baking, brush the *coulibiac* with 1 egg yolk beaten with 1 tablespoon cold water.

Steak Coulibiac

This filling is sufficient for a 12- to 14-inch *coulibiac*, or 4 to 6 servings.

Pastry for Coulibiac	2 tablespoons chopped parsley
4 oz. butter	Salt
2 onions, chopped	Pepper
8 oz. chopped mushrooms	4 oz. cooked cold rice
1½ lb. chopped steak	3 hard-boiled eggs, chopped
2 tablespoons chopped dill	Beef bouillon

Heat 1½ oz. of the butter and sauté onion in it until soft and golden. Add mushrooms, steak, dill, parsley, salt, and pepper, and cook 5 minutes longer over moderate heat. Fill *coulibiac* by making alternate layers of rice, meat, and hard-boiled eggs, beginning with rice. Melt remaining butter and add to filling. If *coulibiac* looks dry, add 1 to 3 tablespoons beef bouillon. Arrange filling in pastry as described above. Bake in hot (400° F., gas 6) oven for 10 minutes. Reduce oven heat quickly to moderate (350° F., gas 4) and bake 20 minutes more, or until golden brown. Test for doneness by pricking pastry with knitting needle or skewer, which should come out dry.

PASTRY FOR COULIBIAC

The most elegant *coulibiacs* are made with puff paste, but any kind of pastry is suitable. Here, however, is a yeast pastry recipe which is characteristic and will suit the filling.

1 yeast cake or 1 envelope granulated yeast	1 egg, beaten
8 fl. oz. lukewarm milk	1 teaspoon salt
2 oz. soft butter	¾ lb. sifted flour

Dissolve yeast in a little milk. Stir in remaining milk, butter, egg, salt, and flour. Knead on slightly floured board to a smooth dough. Place in greased bowl and let rise in a warm place (80–85° F.) until double in bulk. (One good way to obtain this temperature is to stand the bowl of dough in a large pan or in a sink filled with lukewarm water. As the water cools, reheat it by adding hot water. Never keep the dough warm over a hot burner or a pilot flame.) Return dough to floured baking board, punch down, and roll out about ½ inch thick. Add the filling and proceed as indicated above.

Russian Veal with Sour Cherries

Unusual, and very good, especially when made with fresh sour cherries, though I have used the canned variety successfully. The spices are essential, and you need a roasting dish or ovenproof casserole with a cover.

3- to 4-lb. piece of veal from leg or rump	2 teaspoons cardamom
Salt	½ teaspoon cinnamon
Pepper	2 tablespoons flour
½ lb. sour cherries, or about 25 cherries, stoned	8 fl. oz. hot bouillon
	4 fl. oz. juice from fresh or canned cherries
2 tablespoons (1 oz.) butter, melted	4 fl. oz. dry white wine

Rub veal with salt and pepper and with a sharp pointed knife make 25 incisions in the surface. Insert a stoned cherry in each incision. Place veal in roasting dish and brush with melted butter.

Sprinkle with cardamom and cinnamon. Heat oven to 450° F., gas 8, and brown meat well. When brown, sprinkle with flour, cover, return to oven, which has been turned down to 350° F., gas 4. Cook for about 20 minutes, then add bouillon, cherry juice, and wine. Cover, but baste frequently. Cook for about 1½ hours, or until done, allowing about 30 minutes per pound, all-over cooking time. Slice and place on heated platter. Pour unstrained sauce over meat. Garnish with spiced cherries.

Vegetables

The most depressing thing ever said about vegetables is that they are good for one; as if the human race ever abided by the reasonable dictum that one should do, or eat (in this case), what is good for the human frame.

Unless properly cooked – that is, in as little water as possible, and only just enough to take away rawness but preserve crispness – vegetables can be most depressing. On the other hand, vegetables intended as an entity in themselves, and not merely as an accompaniment to worthier foods, are delicious. The French do this, and properly serve their vegetables as a separate course, a practice I think admirable, since in themselves vegetables do not really complement meats or fish, though habit decrees that this is so. There are only three simple rules for vegetable cookery, and here they come :

(1) The freshest vegetables are always the best; young and small ones are better than the larger and older; wilted and bruised vegetables are worthless.

(2) Vegetables should be cooked in a minimum of time and water.

(3) The water in which vegetables are cooked should be saved for soups and gravies.

The noblest vegetable of all is the truffle. Alas, no canned or preserved truffle even remotely presents the ineffable flavour and fragrance of fresh truffles. Yet I still recommend the use of whatever kind of truffles are available to you, for even in their preserved form they add a flavour and an aroma to food that no other ingredient even remotely approximates. To make the best of canned truffles, they should only be finely sliced and gently heated to preserve their fragrance, since they have already been cooked. The dish they are to favour should be prepared first, and the truffles added to it at the last moment.

The literature of truffles is enormous and amusing, and dates back to the ancient Romans. Suffice it here to quote Brillat-Savarin's *Physiology of Taste*: 'The truffle is not a positive aphrodisiac; but on certain occasions, it can make women more tender and men more amiable'; and the Frenchman who said that for a 'true gourmand there exist no blue eyes, white teeth, or rosy lips that may take the place of a black truffle'.

How to Prepare Artichoke Hearts

Many people regard globe artichokes with suspicion in general, and feel that to prepare their hearts or bottoms (the only part that is really worth eating) is simply too difficult even to try. It is not, though it takes a little (not much) practice to achieve the smoothness that characterizes the canned artichoke hearts that can be bought. I am talking of the hollowed-out artichoke discs that are free of all leaves and choke spikes, bearing no resemblance to the original fresh vegetable. The frozen artichoke hearts are a different proposition altogether, since they retain part of their leaves.

Artichokes discolour once they are cut open. As soon as they are prepared, they must be kept until cooking time in water acidulated with wine vinegar or lemon juice (about 3 tablespoons to 1 quart of water). Therefore, have a bowl of this acidulated water handy before preparing the artichokes. A sharp paring knife is also essential for the job.

Slice off and discard the stem at the base of the artichoke, leaving not more than about ¼ inch. Tear off and throw away the large outer leaves. Place artichoke on its side and cut off all leaves, leaving only about ½ inch or less of white leaf on the base. Trim this base with paring knife carefully and neatly to achieve a smooth surface. This is best done in one continuous motion, as when peeling a whole apple.

To remove the choke, use either the paring knife, a grapefruit knife, or a sharp-edged coffee spoon. With a circular motion, scoop out the choke, the way the core of half a grapefruit is scooped out. Drop the heart at once into acidulated water. Cook artichoke hearts in boiling salted water until tender. If a very light heart is desired, add some lemon juice to the water.

This method of preparing the artichoke hearts is necessary for a dish like Artichoke with Goose Liver Pâté, where the vegetable is first parboiled in water and then finished in wine. If the artichoke is to be used in dishes that require only cooking in water as the first step, the following method can be used – it is easier.

After trimming the base to a smooth surface, cook the artichoke until tender, in boiling salted water to which some lemon juice has been added (about 3 tablespoons to 1 quart of water). When done, trim off all the leaves and remove the choke with a paring knife or a spoon. What remains is the artichoke heart, to be used as the recipe dictates.

Baked Artichokes Tuscan Style [Tortino di carciofi]

This Tuscan *tortino di carciofi* is delicious and stands on its own feet as a luncheon or supper entrée. Remember that, like mushrooms, clean and prepared artichokes turn black if exposed to the air; they should be dropped immediately into water to which lemon juice or vinegar has been added. Drain and dry before cooking.

6 small artichokes	6 eggs
Juice of 1 lemon	Salt and pepper
3 tablespoons flour	2 fl. oz. single cream or milk
½ pint olive oil	⅛ teaspoon nutmeg

Remove tips and stems of artichokes and tough outer leaves. Cut into thin slices, removing the choke at the centre. Drop imme-

diately in water and lemon juice. When ready to use, drain, dry
well, and roll in flour. Heat olive oil and fry artichokes until
tender and golden brown. Drain on absorbent paper.

Place fried artichoke slices in shallow buttered baking dish.
Beat together eggs, salt, pepper, cream, and nutmeg. Pour over
artichokes. Bake in moderate (350° F., gas 4) oven 15 to 20
minutes, or until golden and puffy. Serve immediately with a
dish of peas with Ham (page 230), if the *tortino* is to be the main
dish of the meal.

Jerusalem Artichokes [*Topinambours*]

A New World tuber that was first observed in Massachusetts in
the early 1600s, and introduced to France a few years later. It
has now fallen into disgrace in America, whereas to this day it
is beloved in France. The 'artichoke' part of the name is easily
explained, since the tuber's taste bears a faint resemblance to the
globe artichoke, to which, however, it is not at all related, in
either species or appearance; it looks like a knobby little potato.
But the 'Jerusalem' part is unexplained, though apparently it has
nothing to do with the Holy Land. As for the silly French name
– that is owed to the fact that the Jerusalem artichoke arrived in
France at the same time as a captive band of Brazilian Indians,
and so enchanted the Parisian natives that they could not keep
their strange overseas visitors apart.

Though most recipes for Jerusalem artichokes say that before
being prepared in their final form they must be either peeled or
pared, I think it is better to steam them or boil them in just
enough water to cover – well scrubbed, of course. When tender,
the skin can be rubbed off easily. They are then cut into pieces
and either sautéed in butter or cooked au gratin, made into croquettes or fried, the latter method being very good indeed. In
short, they can be prepared like potatoes.

Jerusalem Artichokes Provençale
[*Topinambours provençale*]

In England, Jerusalem artichokes are usually served with a white
sauce, which is all right if the white sauce is really good, rich

and creamy. A few capers help it along in this case, to my mind, though I prefer the following recipe. In any case, do not overcook the vegetable – it should be just tender. Since Jerusalem artichokes vary in size and age, it is impossible to give an accurate cooking time. Steaming, though, takes longer than boiling in water.

Heat equal quantities of butter and olive oil and cook a few peeled and chopped fresh or canned tomatoes in it. When soft, season with salt and pepper to taste, and add a herb of your choice – basil, fennel, or what have you. Toss in the cooked slices of Jerusalem artichokes and heat through thoroughly.

Hungarian Asparagus in Sour Cream [Tejfeles Spárga]

Steam cleaned and trimmed asparagus until almost tender. Drain well. Place in shallow baking dish and dribble a little melted butter over it. Barely cover with sour cream. Sprinkle top with fine dry bread crumbs and dot with butter. Bake in hot (425° F., gas 7) oven 5 to 10 minutes, or until golden brown.

Note: Only the tender parts of the asparagus should be used for this dish.

String Beans, Wax Beans, Fava Beans, Lima Beans, or Peas with Ham [Legumi col prosciutto]

This is a method of cooking vegetables rather than one single recipe, and it makes them more interesting. Prosciutto is used in Italy, of course, because it is more savoury, but if none is available, use any cooked ham.

Cook vegetable in just enough water to prevent scorching, until three quarters done. Drain. For each pound of vegetable, heat together 2 tablespoons butter and 1 tablespoon oil. Sauté 2 teaspoons minced onion and ¼ teaspoon minced garlic. Stir in 2–3 oz. chopped ham and cook 3 to 4 minutes. Add vegetable and season with salt and pepper. If necessary, add a little bouillon to prevent scorching while cooking. Cover and cook until tender, stirring occasionally. Before serving, sprinkle with 1 tablespoon finely chopped parsley.

Broccoli or Cauliflower Roman Style

[Broccoli o cavolfiori alla romana]

1 medium-sized bunch broccoli or 1 medium-sized cauliflower	Salt Pepper
4 tablespoons olive oil	Good ½ pint dry red or white
2 cloves garlic	wine

Trim broccoli or cauliflower and cut into small flowerets. Wash well and drain. Heat olive oil in large skillet and brown garlic. Remove garlic. Add vegetable, salt, and pepper, and cook over medium heat 5 minutes. Add wine, cover skillet, and simmer over low heat 10 to 15 minutes, or until vegetable is tender. Stir occasionally, taking care not to break flowerets.

Note: White wine is a better choice for cauliflower, since it will preserve the vegetable's white colour.

Brussels Sprouts

To cook sprouts, cut off the outer leaves and the coarse part of the stem. Wash them in plenty of cold water. Either cook in plenty of salted water over high heat for 10 to 15 minutes, or until just tender; or simmer them, covered, in a little consommé. The cooked sprouts may then be sautéed in butter or bacon fat; combined with sautéed ham or crumbled cooked bacon, with boiled and peeled chestnuts (half the volume of the sprouts); served Au Gratin or with Greek Egg and Lemon Sauce (page 252) or hollandaise or white sauce. In any case, they must be served extremely hot.

Brussels Sprouts au Gratin

Sauté cooked brussels sprouts in hot butter and season with salt, pepper, and a touch of nutmeg. Place sprouts in a shallow buttered baking dish and sprinkle with grated Swiss cheese. Moisten with a little thick cream and brown under grill.

Danish Red Cabbage [Roedkaal]

3 lb. red cabbage	4–5 oz. red-currant jelly
3 tablespoons (1½ oz.) butter	2 peeled and cored apples,
1 tablespoon sugar	chopped
1 tablespoon vinegar	Salt
¼ pint water	Pepper

Remove tough outer leaves from cabbage and shred. In heavy
saucepan, heat butter and melt sugar in it. Do not brown. Add
cabbage, cook 3 minutes, and add vinegar and water. Simmer,
covered, for 2 to 3 hours, or until very tender. Stir occasionally
and add more water – hot – to prevent scorching. Half an hour
before cabbage is done, add red-currant jelly, apples, salt, and
pepper. Taste – the cabbage should be quite sweet-sour. Add a
little more vinegar and sugar if needed.

Red cabbage is best if made the day before it is to be used,
and reheated.

Cardoons [Cardi]

Like the globe artichoke, cardoons belong to the thistle family,
and they can grow as tall as a child. Cardoons are bunched, like
celery, and, like celery, they have tough skins and strings that
must be removed.

The ancient Romans favoured cardoons, and their popularity
is great to this day in Italy. The Spaniards love them too, and
sometimes use the dried flowers (which are never eaten) instead
of rennet for curdling cheese.

Only the stalks, and the inner stalks at that, of cardoons are
eaten. The outer stalks, however perfect-looking, are much too
tough. The prickles of the inner stalks are pared off, and the
skin and strings peeled, as when preparing tough celery stalks.
The stalks are then cut into 3- to 4-inch lengths, and boiled in
salt water for 10 to 15 minutes, or until just tender. After being
drained, they are finished off like celery – that is, with butter, or
creamed, or braised for a short time, or au gratin, or sautéed. Or
best of all, they are served with a Greek Lemon and Egg Sauce
(page 252).

Flemish Carrots [Carottes à la flamande]

This dish is characteristic of Belgian cooking, which is very rich.
In Belgium the carrots used are tiny babies, and simply delicious.
If you have to use bigger carrots, cut them into sticks about half
the size of a little finger. Or you can use the imported canned
French carrots, which are small. In this case, the carrots do not
have to be cooked first – they need merely be heated before adding
the sauce.

6 to 8 carrots, cut into small sticks	3 egg yolks
4 tablespoons water	4–5 fl. oz. double cream
4 oz. butter	2 tablespoons melted butter
Salt	2 teaspoons lemon juice
Sugar	2 tablespoons minced parsley

Blanch carrots in boiling water for 3 minutes. Drain. Place carrots
in buttered casserole. Add water, butter, and salt, and sugar to
taste. Cover casserole and bring to boiling point. Reduce heat and
cook over low heat until carrots are tender. (The cooking time of
carrots varies, depending on their age.) Shake casserole every 3 or
4 minutes to prevent sticking. Beat together egg yolks, cream,
and melted butter. Remove carrots from heat and stir in sauce
and lemon juice. Sprinkle with parsley and serve immediately.

Celeriac [Céleri Rave]

A cousin of celery cultivated for its root, which looks like a
knobby turnip, and a winter mainstay, especially in France,
where it is eaten in hors-d'œuvres and as a vegetable covered
with melted butter, hollandaise, or au gratin. As a salad, celeriac
is especially good when mixed with chicory; puréed, it serves as a
standby for potato purée. The taste is robust, and much appre-
ciated by men, in my experience.

Small roots are best; the bigger ones are often woody or hollow.
Celeriac must be boiled in water until soft yet firm to the touch
before it can be prepared in other ways. Whether it is peeled
before or after boiling is a matter of personal preference. However,

it must not be overcooked. The cooked and peeled root is then cut either in julienne strips or in rounds. I like it best with a Greek Lemon and Egg Sauce (page 252), but the following two recipes are also excellent ways of preparing this vegetable, which is now quite common in our markets.

Celeriac au Gratin

Place the cooked rounds or julienne strips in a shallow buttered baking dish. Pour a good cream sauce over them. Cover with bread crumbs and a layer of grated Swiss cheese. Dot with a little butter and bake in a moderate to hot (375° F., gas 5) oven about 10 to 15 minutes, or until cheese is melted and golden.

Sautéed Celeriac

Sauté cooked rounds or julienne strips in unsalted butter until golden brown. Season well and sprinkle with plenty of chopped parsley.

Celery Amandine

For reasons that I have never been able to fathom, celery was considered to have aphrodisiac qualities, and for all I know, it may still have that reputation. Whether this is a deserved reputation is for the reader to decide. However, all the tomes devoted to *la cuisine amoureuse* have many celery recipes, and the German army under the Kaisers marched to a famous march whose spurious words began with : 'Be glad, Fritzchen, today we'll have celery salad.'

Celery amandine is a sort of universal recipe, and a very good one.

1 medium head celery, cut in pieces	1 tablespoon chopped onions
Salt	2 teaspoons flour
Pepper	4 fl. oz. single cream
3 tablespoons (1½ oz.) butter	2 fl. oz. chicken bouillon
	4 oz. shredded toasted almonds

Cook celery, salt and pepper to taste, butter, and onion over low heat 15 minutes. The saucepan must be tightly covered. Stir occasionally. The celery should be dry, but if it shows signs of scorching, add a little water. Sprinkle with flour and mix well. Add cream and bouillon. Cook over medium heat until sauce is thickened, stirring constantly. Stir in almonds. This is especially good with roast pork.

Braised Chicory [Endives braisées]

In this country chicory is almost always eaten as a salad. But in Belgium and France it is just as popular cooked. Like cooked celery – and both vegetables can be prepared the same ways – chicory goes well with the heavier roasted meats, such as pork and beef.

8 large chicory heads	About ¼ pint bouillon or water
1 medium-sized onion, sliced	Salt
2 tablespoons chopped parsley	Pepper
2½ oz. butter	

Place chicory in saucepan and top with onion slices and chopped parsley. Dot with butter and cover with bouillon. Add salt and pepper to taste. Simmer, tightly covered, over low heat about 30 minutes, or until chicory is tender and liquid absorbed.

Italian Marinated Courgettes [Zucchine in insalata]

This is a dish from Giannino, one of Milan's finest restaurants. It can also be made with yellow squash, or even aubergine, and will keep for at least 3 days in the refrigerator. Serve well chilled.

6 courgettes	6 chopped fresh basil leaves or
Olive oil for frying	1 tablespoon dry basil
8 fl. oz. mild vinegar	Salt
4 fl. oz. olive oil	Pepper
½ teaspoon garlic powder	2 tablespoons chopped parsley

Trim courgettes, scrape lightly (to remove waxy coating), and cut into 1½-inch sticks – the size of a little finger. Fry slowly in olive oil until golden. Drain on absorbent paper. Combine vinegar, olive oil, garlic powder, basil, and salt and pepper to taste, and simmer 5 minutes. Arrange courgettes in layers in glass or china dish; do not use metal. Pour hot marinade over and sprinkle with parsley. Cover, and chill at least overnight. Drain before serving with roast or grilled meat or poultry.

Note: Do not overfry the courgettes; they should have body and not be mushy.

Dutch Stewed Cucumbers with Caper Sauce
[Gestoofde Komkommers]

A pleasant little side dish. Sometimes the capers are omitted and vinegar to taste substituted. It should be rather mild.

Cucumbers	Salt
Salted water	Pepper
2 tablespoons (1 oz.) butter	1 tablespoon chopped parsley
2 tablespoons flour	1 tablespoon capers
8 fl. oz. chicken bouillon	

Peel cucumbers and cut into 3- to 4-inch strips. Cook in salted water 5 to 10 minutes, or until tender. They should be soft but not mushy. Drain and keep hot. Melt butter and stir in flour. Cook over medium heat 2 to 3 minutes, stirring constantly. Stir in chicken bouillon. Season with salt and pepper. Cook 5 to 8 minutes, or until thickened and smooth, stirring occasionally. Add parsley and capers and mix in cucumbers. Heat through thoroughly and serve with meats.

Italian or French Fennel au Gratin
[Finocchio or fenouil au gratin]

Fennel is now more easily found in England and deserves popularity cooked as well as a salad vegetable. It has a faint flavour of anise and goes very well with fish.

Fennel was known to mankind long before the Christian Era. It was credited with helping toward a clearer vision and cultivated as a medicinal herb in the earliest monks' gardens. Before that, the Romans crowned their heroes with fennel, just as the Greeks decorated theirs with crowns of dill.

Especially around the Mediterranean, fennel is much beloved, both raw and cooked.

4 large fennel heads, trimmed of green tops	Pepper
Salt	5 oz. butter, melted
	3 oz. grated Parmesan cheese

Trim off tough outer stalks. Cut off hard base. Cut fennel into slices, cutting with the grain, not crosswise. Cook in boiling salt water to cover 5 to 10 minutes, or until tender. Drain well. Butter shallow baking dish and place half the fennel slices on it. Season with salt and pepper. Pour half of the melted butter and sprinkle half of the cheese over fennel. Repeat process with remaining fennel, butter, and cheese.

Bake in hot (425° F., gas 7) oven 10 minutes, or until cheese is golden brown. Or grill at least 6 inches from heat until cheese is brown. Serve immediately.

Leeks

Leeks are a very good vegetable, which can be served in any of the ways asparagus and celery are served. To cook leeks, cut off the coarse outer leaves and the greater part of the green tops. Leave about 1 inch of the green tops on if they are tender; if not, cut green tops off completely and use white part of leek only. Cut into 3- to 4-inch pieces. Wash leeks extremely carefully, because the soil in which they grow has a habit of seeping under the leaves. Cook in rapidly boiling water until just tender. Leeks fall apart easily, so do not overcook.

Leeks Mornay

Boiled leeks are extremely good served with Mornay Sauce (page 255) or with any rich cheese sauce. They are even better when baked in a hot (400° F., gas 6) oven in the sauce, with a little extra cheese sprinkled on top.

Purée of Lentils [Linsenpüree]

This is popular in Germany, and made like Erbsenpüree (page 243). Both purées are very worth-while ways of using two cheap legumes, and a change from the everlasting soups into which both peas and lentils are usually made. Leftovers can be diluted with stock and used as a soup, with fried croutons.

Florentine Mushrooms [Funghi trifolati]

A classic Italian way of cooking sliced mushrooms.

1 lb. mushrooms	1 tablespoon (½ oz.) butter
3 tablespoons olive oil	4 anchovy fillets, chopped
1 clove garlic	2 tablespoons chopped parsley
Salt	Juice of ½ lemon
Pepper	

Slice mushrooms thinly. Heat olive oil in large skillet and brown garlic. Remove garlic. Add mushrooms, salt, and pepper and cook over high heat until all the mushroom liquid has evaporated. Add butter, anchovy fillets, and parsley, and cook over medium heat 5 minutes longer. Remove from fire, add lemon juice, and serve very hot.

Polish Baked Mushrooms [Pieczarski w muszelkach]

Czechoslovakia, Poland, Russia, Scandinavia – these are the mushroom countries where many varieties grow wild and where many people pick them. Delicate as cultivated mushrooms are, the flavour of wild mushrooms is so superior that words fail me when I try to describe their taste and the subtle characteristics of the many varieties. The following recipe makes a very agreeable side dish for any plain meat or fish, and it serves also as a meatless entrée.

½ lb. mushrooms	2 tablespoons grated Parmesan
Lemon juice	cheese
1 tablespoon minced onion	8 fl. oz. double cream
2 tablespoons (1 oz.) butter	2 egg yolks, lightly beaten
Salt	2 tablespoons fine white bread
Pepper	crumbs
1 tablespoon flour	Butter

Cut bottoms off mushroom stems and slice thinly. Sprinkle with lemon juice to keep white. Simmer, tightly covered, with onion and butter. Season with salt and pepper and stir in flour and Parmesan cheese. Cook about 3 minutes. Place in buttered baking dish or individual ramekins. Mix cream and egg yolks together. Pour over mushrooms. Sprinkle with bread crumbs and dot with butter. Bake in hot (450° F., gas 7) oven 10 minutes, or until golden brown.

Rumanian Wine Mushroom Stew [*Ciuperci cu vin*]

This should be served warm or cool, but not chilled.

1 lb. mushrooms	Juice of 1 small lemon
4 tablespoons olive oil	Salt
1 tablespoon chopped chives	Pepper
1 teaspoon fennel seeds	4 fl. oz. dry white wine
2 tablespoons parsley	

Trim mushrooms and slice. Fry in warm olive oil with chives, fennel seeds, and parsley for about 6 to 8 minutes. Sprinkle lemon juice over mushrooms and season with salt and pepper. Cook 3 minutes longer. Add wine, cover, and cook over low heat 5 minutes. Serve with roast meat.

Spanish Grilled Onions

These bring back memories of southern Spain, where I ate them for lunch in a little country inn, with crusty bread and a sharp red wine. Outside, the sun scorched the earth, but the one-room inn was cool and dark.

4 to 6 large onions	4 tablespoons olive oil
2 tablespoons parsley	Salt
2 teaspoons fresh chopped basil or ½ to 1 teaspoon dried basil	Pepper

Peel onions and boil in water to cover 10 minutes. They should be not quite tender. Drain and cut into halves crosswise. Place in grill pan and sprinkle with parsley, basil, olive oil, salt, and pepper. Grill well away from the source of heat 10 to 15 minutes, or until tender. Before serving, sprinkle with a little more oil and a touch of lemon juice, if desired. Excellent with any grilled meat.

Sweet-sour Onions

This way of cooking onions – and one of the best – turns up in so many countries that it would be hard to pin it on one single cuisine. Small white onions, preferably the pickling variety, should be used.

About 25 small white onions	1 to 2 teaspoons sugar
3 tablespoons (1½ oz.) butter	Salt
1 tablespoon flour	Pepper
8 fl. oz. bouillon or onion broth	1 tablespoon chopped parsley
1 tablespoon vinegar	

Boil onions in salt water to cover until not quite tender. Drain, and reserve 8 fl. oz. of the broth. Heat 2 tablespoons of the butter and cook onions over low heat 3 to 4 minutes, or until just golden. Remove onions and keep hot. Add remaining 1 tablespoon butter to skillet butter. Heat until golden, not brown. Stir in flour and bouillon or onion broth. Cook over low heat until thickened and smooth, stirirng constantly. Add vinegar, sugar, salt, and pepper. Put onions back into sauce and simmer, covered, for 5 minutes. Sprinkle with parsley before serving.

Sicilian Baked Onions [Cipolle al forno]

Baked onions, by whatever means they are cooked, are absolutely delicious. Hot, they are eaten with butter, salt, and pepper, just liked baked potatoes; cold, with salt and pepper, a little olive oil and a squeeze of lemon dribbled over them.

The onions must be unpeeled. Put medium-sized or large onions into a roasting pan and bake as you would potatoes, for about 1 to 1½ hours. The skins then come off, and the onions are full of flavour.

Salsify [*Salsifis*]

One of the very best of winter vegetables, a tapering white root with a faint flavour of globe artichoke hearts. Salsify must be scraped before being boiled until just tender, drained, and finished in very hot butter or fried in deep fat either by itself or in fritters. But as each root is scraped, it must be plunged at once into a little lemon or vinegar and water or it will turn black. The proportions are about 3 tablespoons lemon juice or vinegar to each quart of water. The roots are then cut in 2- to 3-inch pieces, and kept in the vinegar-and-water bath until cooking time.

The young leaves of the plant are eaten as a delicious little spring salad. Incidentally, the Italian *scorza nera* ('black skin') is often confused with salsify, though it belongs to a different botanical variety. Its flavour, too, is excellent, and it is prepared like salsify.

Salsify Fritters [*Beignets de salsifis*]

Boil salsify until just tender, drain, and dry with a kitchen towel. Roll pieces of chopped parsley and sprinkle with a little lemon juice. Let stand for 15 minutes. Dry salsify pieces again if necessary and dip in French Fritter Batter. Fry in deep hot (375° F.) fat until golden brown. Drain on absorbent paper, season with salt, surround with Fried Parsley, and serve in a napkin.

FRENCH FRITTER BATTER

This batter is much lighter than most, thanks to the beer and extra egg white. There is no taste of beer in the finished product.

2 oz. flour	1 egg, well beaten
¼ teaspoon salt	4 fl. oz. beer
1 tablespoon butter, melted	1 egg white, stiffly beaten

Sift together flour and salt. Blend together butter and whole egg. Add to flour. Stir in beer gradually, stirring only until mixture is smooth. Stand in warm place for 1 hour to let batter become light and foamy. When ready to use, fold in beaten egg white. Makes about 1 cup batter.

FRIED PARSLEY

Wash parsley and dry well. Drop sprigs into hot (390° F.) deep fat and fry for a few seconds. Drain fried parsley sprigs on absorbent paper. Sprinkle with a little salt and serve at once.

Spinach Roman Style [Spinaci alla Romana]

Spinach is excellent when cooked in no more water than clings to its leaves after washing, and for no more than 3 minutes or so until barely softened. It should be cooked over fairly high heat. The following recipe should be made with bacon fat or lard, and not oil, since the first two are very characteristic of Roman cooking.

2 lb. washed spinach	2 tablespoons pine nuts
3 tablespoons (1½ oz.) bacon fat or lard	1 tablespoon raisins, soaked in water to soften
1 medium-sized onion, finely chopped	Salt and pepper
	⅛ teaspoon nutmeg

The spinach for this dish must be coarsely chopped. This can be done either before or after cooking. I find it easier to do it before, snipping the spinach with kitchen scissors.

Cook spinach until barely tender. Drain thoroughly. Heat bacon fat in large skillet and sauté onion in it 3 to 4 minutes, or until soft. Stir in pine nuts and raisins and cook 1 minute longer. Add chopped spinach, season with salt, pepper, and nutmeg. Cover and cook together 5 minutes, stirring occasionally.

Spanish Sautéed Chick-peas [Garbanzos fritos]

Chick-peas, which look like little yellow bullets, are much eaten in the Mediterranean region. They are sold in the streets in barrels, to be eaten out of hand, they are put in soups and stews, and combined with meats and macaroni. Chick-peas come dry and can be prepared like any other dried beans – that is, soaked in water, then boiled in salt water until soft. Or the little yellow bullet-like peas can be bought canned in salt water. I see no virtue in preparing my own chick-peas when the canned ones are inexpensive and just as good. Only, when using canned chick-peas, wash off their liquid under running water and drain well.

Chick-peas ought to be better known as a substitute for the eternal potatoes. The following recipe goes well with fish, especially with Spanish Sherry-baked Brook Trout (page 71), which the nut-like flavour of the chick-peas seems to complement.

1 lb. cooked chick-peas	Pepper
Olive oil	Chopped parsley
Salt	

Sauté chick-peas lightly in hot olive oil until they are thoroughly heated through. Season with salt and pepper and sprinkle with chopped parsely. Serve as you would potatoes.

German Purée of Dried Green Peas [Erbsenpüree]

Erbsenpüree is a very popular dish in Germany, where it is eaten with pork and Salzkartoffeln (plain boiled potatoes).

1 lb. dried green peas	Salt
2 tablespoons pork fat (rendered salt pork, lard, bacon, or pork drippings)	Pepper
	Dash of allspice
	Onion Butter (page 248)
2 tablespoons flour	

Soak peas according to package directions. Drain and cook until tender. Put through sieve or blend in blender – the peas must be absolutely smooth. This can be done in advance and the pea purée stored in the refrigerator. Before serving, melt the pork fat, stir in the flour, and cook until brown, stirring constantly. Add to pea purée. Add salt, pepper, and allspice. Heat slowly, taking care not to burn. If purée is too thick, add a little hot water. Serve with Onion Butter poured over purée.

Swiss Potato Cake [Roesti]

The national way of cooking potatoes. In the country, it is often the mainstay of the evening meal, served with café au lait. Roesti is really a version of fried potatoes, and certainly the best.

6 large potatoes	1 large onion, minced (optional)
2 oz. lard or butter	Salt and pepper

Boil potatoes in their skins. Peel immediately and cut into very thin slices or dice. Heat lard, add potatoes, and onion. Season with salt and pepper. Fry potatoes over medium heat until browned. Lower heat, and fry about 10 minutes or until a golden crust has formed at the bottom. Turn by sliding potatoes on a plate and sliding them back into the pan. Fry again until the bottom has a golden-brown crust. Serve very hot, with any meat.

Swiss Potatoes Parmesan [*Pommes fondues au Parmesan*]

4 large potatoes, peeled and cut into small dice	3 tablespoons (1½ oz.) butter
	Salt
1 teaspoon meat glaze or meat extract, blended with 1 tablespoon water	Pepper
	3 tablespoons butter, melted
	1 oz. grated Parmesan cheese

The potatoes must be washed and carefully dried. Cook potatoes, covered, in butter for 6 to 8 minutes, or until tender, stirring occasionally. Add meat glaze. Place in buttered baking dish. Season with salt and pepper and sprinkle with melted butter and cheese. Bake in hot (425° F., gas 7) oven 10 minutes, or until cheese is melted and golden brown.

Potato Croquettes [*Kartoffelkroketten*]

4 large or 5 medium-sized mealy potatoes	Pepper
	Nutmeg
3 tablespoons butter, melted	Flour
2 eggs	3 oz. bread crumbs
Salt	Fat

Boil potatoes, peel while hot, and mash smooth and free of all lumps. Separate one of the eggs. Add melted butter, 1 whole egg and 1 yolk, and seasonings to the potatoes and blend thoroughly. Cool. Shape mixture into croquettes. Since the mealiness of potatoes varies, it may be necessary to add a little flour to hold the croquettes together – add it 1 tablespoon at a time, and no more than necessary, to keep croquettes light. Beat remaining egg white, dip croquettes into it, then dip in bread crumbs. Chill thoroughly before frying in deep hot fat (390° F. on frying thermometer, or sufficiently hot so that a bread cube dropped into it will brown in 1 minute). Drain on absorbent paper and serve hot.

German Creamed Vegetables [*Leipziger Allerlei*]

The German name of this dish means, literally, a 'little of everything from Leipzig'. It is representative of the way Germans, Swiss, and other Teutonic people serve their vegetables with a thickened gravy.

½ lb. asparagus tips	2½ oz. butter
2–3 carrots, cut in ½-inch pieces	¼ lb. mushrooms, sliced
1 small cauliflower, divided into small flowerets	2 tablespoons flour
	Salt
1 turnip, diced	Pepper

Cook all vegetables but mushrooms separately in salted water to cover. Drain and reserve liquid. Sauté vegetables together in hot butter 2 to 3 minutes. Remove and keep hot. Sauté mushrooms in the same butter, remove, and add to other vegetables. Keep hot. Stir flour into remaining butter. Measure about ¾ pint vegetable liquid and stir into flour. Cook over low heat about 5 minutes, or until thickened and smooth. Season with salt and pepper. Arrange vegetables on hot platter, keeping cauliflowerets on top. Pour sauce over vegetables and serve with any meat.

Vegetable Stews

These are an integral part of southern European cooking, substantial, and eaten as the main dish of a meal, as real food, not merely as an accompaniment to meat.

The beauty of a vegetable market has best been described by D. H. Lawrence in his *Sea and Sardinia*: 'The near end of the street was rather dark and had mostly vegetable shops. Abundance of vegetables – piles of white and green fennel, like celery, and great sheaves of young, purplish, sea-dust-coloured artichokes, nodding their buds, piles of big radishes, scarlet and bluey purple, carrots, long strings of dried figs, mountains of big oranges, scarlet large peppers, a last slice of pumpkin, a great mass of colours and vegetable freshnesses.' Any traveller who has seen the orderly rows of French or Swiss vegetable markets, or browsed around the vegetable stalls of Greece and Italy, cannot help being touched by the beauty of the earth's bounty.

A big stew of vegetables – stewed, not boiled or fried, in olive oil – is one of God's gifts for summer. For luncheons, for picnics, to which it can be carried in its own casserole, there is almost nothing better.

Rumanian Vegetable Stew [Ghiveciu cu zarzavaturi]

Stews of this kind are highly characteristic of the Balkan countries; sometimes a little minced or other meat is added, though, to my mind, the stew is better without it. The Greeks call it *youvetsi*, the Bulgarians *gyovech*, the Yugoslavs *djuvec*. If it is to be made more nourishing, eggs beaten with lemon juice and a little flour are poured over the stew in last 5 minutes of baking.

As with all truly popular – or people's – dishes of this kind, measurements matter little. You put in what you have, and the olive oil blends the vegetables into a harmonious whole. The following recipe will feed 8 or 10 people.

4 large carrots, sliced
4 large potatoes, peeled and diced
1 medium-sized aubergine, diced
6 oz. green peas
6 oz. string beans, sliced
2 green peppers, seeded and sliced
6 oz. fresh lima beans
1 turnip, diced
1 small head cabbage, chopped
1 small head cauliflower, separated into flowerets
1 green or yellow marrow, sliced

2 leeks, sliced
1 cup okra, sliced
8 tomatoes, peeled and chopped
2–3 oz. chopped parsley
About 1 oz. chopped mixed fresh herbs, or fresh or dried herbs to taste
4 cloves garlic, chopped (or more or less, to taste)
5 large onions, sliced
½ pint olive oil
¾ pint meat or vegetable bouillon
Salt and pepper

Combine all vegetables except onions and place in large baking dish. Fry onions in ¼ pint of the olive oil until soft and golden. Heat remaining oil with bouillon. Season the vegetables with salt and pepper. Pour fried onions and bouillon with oil over the vegetables. Stir until mixed. Cover and bake in moderate (350° F., gas 4) oven until the vegetables are cooked and the liquid absorbed. This takes about 30 to 45 minutes and depends on the vegetables. If the stew appears too liquid, bake uncovered. If there is danger of scorching, add a little hot bouillon. Stir occasionally.

Ratatouille

This is the vegetable stew of Provence, to be eaten hot or cold. The vegetables should be simmered in the oil, not fried. The ingredients listed below are the classic ones but I sometimes add, with good effect, a handful of sliced okra, and even a little fresh corn cut from the cob.

1 medium-sized aubergine
4 fl. oz. olive oil
2 large onions, sliced
2 red or green sweet peppers, diced
4 large tomatoes, peeled and chopped
1 clove garlic, minced
2 courgettes, sliced
Salt and pepper
2 tablespoons chopped parsley
¼ teaspoon marjoram
¼ teaspoon basil or thyme

Peel aubergine and cut into ½-inch-thick slices. To drain off the excess liquid in it, salt the slices lightly and place in colander. Weight down with a plate placed on top of the aubergine. Heat olive oil in large skillet over low heat. The oil must not be very hot. Cook – but do not fry – onions, garlic, and peppers in it until soft. Add tomatoes, courgettes, and the aubergine slices, which have been drained and diced. Season with salt and pepper and add parsley, marjoram, and basil or thyme. Simmer, covered, over low heat for about 30 minutes. Uncover and simmer 10 minutes longer, or until liquid is absorbed.

*

Onion Butter

Good for purée of dried peas or lentils, for boiled potatoes, and for boiled fish.

1 large onion, finely chopped   2 oz. butter

Cook onion in melted butter until soft and golden, not brown.

Sauces

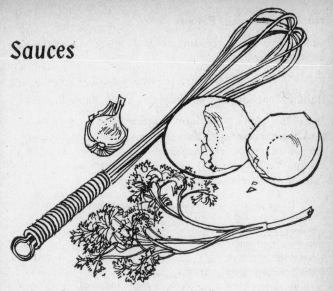

Many cookbooks have excellent chapters on sauces, and so it would be redundant to list again such famous sauces as mayonnaise, hollandaise, and béarnaise, to cite a few from a long and distinguished list.

At the risk of sounding heretical, I should like to say that the importance of sauces has been overemphasized to a sorry degree. True, a fine sauce is often essential, especially in France, where the *saucier* (the sauce cook) occupies an important position. To many home cooks, sauces have become a mystical experience, approached like the Holy Grail, with an awe and trepidation that are pitiful to behold. The skill of making sauces can be learned like any other skill, and practice makes perfect. But it should always be borne in mind that the most elegant sauce will never hide a poorly cooked dish. It is far better to cook well and not to make sauces than to do things the other way round.

Sauces should never be too thick. Nor should they be overly spicy. The flavouring of sauces, in the last analysis, depends on personal taste. Even classic sauces can differ in taste, depending on the cook, just as two pianists can interpret the same piece differently.

As for the tricks and basic rules of sauce making, I refer the reader to his or her standard cookbook, whose information can seldom be improved on.

Italian Meat Sauce from Bologna [*Ragù alla bolognese*]

One of the world's great sauces, which bears no more resemblance to ordinary tomato sauce than the swan to the goose. In Bologna, the Italian capital of gastronomy, this sauce is served with Lasagne Verde (page 123), but it is excellent with any kind of pasta or with a risotto. This recipe will serve 6.

¼ lb. Italian prosciutto or bacon, minced	1 tablespoon tomato paste
1 tablespoon (½ oz.) butter	4 fl. oz. dry white wine
1 medium-sized onion, minced	8 fl. oz. beef bouillon
1 carrot, minced	Salt and pepper
1 small piece of celery, minced	⅛ teaspoon nutmeg
½ lb. lean minced beef	1 teaspoon grated lemon rind
¼ lb. chicken livers, minced	2 cloves (optional)
	8 fl. oz. double cream

In heavy saucepan, cook ham or bacon in butter until soft and golden. Add onion, carrot, and celery. Cook over low heat until browned. Add beef and brown evenly. Add chicken livers and cook for 2 to 3 minutes. Stir in tomato paste and wine and cook for another 2 minutes. Add beef bouillon, salt and pepper to taste, nutmeg, lemon rind, and cloves. Cover, and simmer over low heat 40 minutes. Before serving, heat cream but do not boil. Stir into *ragù*.

Note: Cream or butter, stirred into tomato sauce at serving time, does wonders for the sauce, since it removes the acid taste of all tomato sauces.

Neapolitan Pizzaiola Sauce

For this sauce the tomatoes are cooked just long enough to soften, but they must not be reduced to pulp, or the sauce will lose its very fresh taste. Pizzaiola sauce is usually served on steaks, but it is excellent on the lighter pasta, such as spaghetti, linguine, or thin noodles.

4 tablespoons olive oil
1½–2 lb. fresh tomatoes, peeled,
   seeded, and chopped
2 cloves garlic, minced
Salt

Pepper
1 teaspoon dried oregano or 1
   tablespoon chopped fresh basil
   or 2 tablespoons chopped
   parsley

Heat olive oil in heavy saucepan. Add tomatoes, garlic, salt and
pepper to taste, and herb. Cook over high heat about 10 to 15
minutes, or until tomatoes are just soft.

Three Great Garlic Sauces

For garlic lovers only, since they cannot be made less garlicky and
still be worth eating.

Italian Bagna Cauda

A sauce from the Piedmont, whose name means, literally, a 'hot
bath'. Good for raw or plain boiled vegetables, boiled fish and
meat. A small sliced truffle improves the sauce greatly.

4 oz. butter
4 tablespoons olive oil
6 cloves garlic, sliced paper-thin

2 2-oz. cans anchovy fillets,
   minced

Over lowest possible heat (you may have to use an asbestos mat)
cook together butter, olive oil, and garlic for 15 minutes. Do not
let boil. Stir in anchovy fillets and simmer until they dissolve.
Keep the sauce hot over a candle or alcohol plate warmer. *The
sauce must never boil or brown.*

Italian Basil Sauce [*Pesto alla genovese*]

For pasta, and heavenly. In Genoa this sauce is made with a
pungent Sardinian ewe's-milk cheese, but Romano cheese can
be used for it, or Romano and Parmesan cheeses mixed, which
makes a milder *pesto*. The basil *must* be fresh.

3 to 5 cloves garlic, minced
1–2 oz. fresh basil leaves,
   minced
1 tablespoon chopped pine nuts

1 oz. grated Romano and
   Parmesan cheese, mixed
6 tablespoons olive oil

In a mortar, pound all ingredients except the olive oil into a smooth paste. Or blend in blender. Gradually add olive oil to this paste, a few drops at a time, stirring constantly until the sauce is smooth and thick.

Note: Pesto can be stored in the refrigerator in a jar, covered with olive oil. When adding it to cooked pasta, add a lump of butter at the same time.

Greek Garlic Sauce [Skordaliá]

This very popular Greek sauce is wonderful with fish and vegetables.

6 medium-sized potatoes
4 to 6 cloves garlic, minced
1 teaspoon salt

6–8 fl. oz. olive oil
4 tablespoons lemon juice

Boil potatoes in their skins. In a mortar, pound garlic and salt to a smooth paste. Or blend in blender. Peel potatoes and, while hot, add them to the garlic mixture, blending everything to a smooth paste. Gradually add olive oil, a few drops at a time, alternating with lemon juice. The sauce should be very smooth and the consistency of thick cream.

Note: The olive oil may have to be adjusted, since different kinds of potatoes absorb olive oil differently. Mealy potatoes are best for this sauce.

Greek Egg and Lemon Sauce [Saltsa avgolémono]

This is the national sauce of Greece, and one of the best in the world, good with meat, fish, and vegetable dishes. And it is so simple and easy to make! There are various ways of making it, but they do not differ greatly. The trick is not to boil the sauce while adding the hot broth, or it will curdle.

3 egg yolks
1 egg

4 tablespoons lemon juice
8 fl. oz. hot stock

Beat egg yolks and egg until light. Add lemon juice gradually, beating constantly. Add hot stock, a little at a time, beating constantly.

German Bacon–Onion Sauce [*Specksauce*]

This is eaten with fried fish, vegetable soufflés, or meat.

6 slices bacon, diced	1 tablespoon vinegar
2 tablespoons (1 oz.) butter	1 teaspoon meat glaze
1 large onion, thinly sliced	Salt
3 tablespoons flour	Pepper
¾ pint beef bouillon	2 tablespoons dry white wine

Over low heat, sauté bacon in butter until limp and transparent. Add onion and cook until soft and golden, stirring frequently. Sprinkle with flour and cook over medium heat until flour is browned. Gradually add beef bouillon, vinegar, meat glaze, salt, and pepper and bring to the boil. Simmer 10 minutes, stirring frequently. Before serving, add wine. Serve very hot.

White Butter from Normandy [*Beurre blanc normand*]

In Normandy this sauce is made by the bucketful, yet it is difficult to pin down the exact ingredient quantities: people are so familiar with this sauce that they don't bother to write it down. It is used on fish.

8 fl. oz. strained Court Bouillon for Fish (page 89)	½ lb. butter, cut in pieces
	Salt
2 tablespoons white vinegar	Pepper

Over very low heat, simmer Court Bouillon and vinegar together for 10 minutes, or until liquid is reduced to a good ¼ pint. Add butter, one piece at a time, stirring constantly in the same direction. Add salt and pepper to taste. Pour into heated sauceboat as soon as butter is melted.

Cumberland Sauce

An excellent sauce, named after the Duke of Cumberland, King of Hanover. Serve it cold with either hot or cold meat.

10 oz. red-currant jelly
8 fl. oz. port
Juice of ½ lemon
Juice of ½ orange
2 teaspoons grated lemon rind
2 teaspoons grated orange rind

2 teaspoons English mustard
Salt
Pepper
¼ teaspoon cayenne pepper
¼ teaspoon ground ginger

Melt currant jelly. Stir in port and lemon and orange juice; cool. Blend in all other ingredients.

Note: This sauce improves if kept a day or two. There are other, blander versions of this sauce, but I think the spicier sauce is better. In any case, the spices and mustard can be decreased according to taste.

French, Dutch, and Belgian White Butter Sauce
[Beurre blanc]

This is very good with grilled meat or fish. The trick of making it consists of using very low heat. The thermostat, if your stove has one, should read about 180° F. If the heat of the stove cannot be easily controlled, place one or two asbestos plates over the heat, to tame it.

½ lb. butter
3 shallots, minced, or 1
    tablespoon minced onion
    (shallots are much better)

1 teaspoon vinegar
½ teaspoon salt
¼ teaspoon pepper

Melt butter over lowest possible heat and stir in all other ingredients. Stir constantly with a wooden spoon in the same direction. As soon as the butter is melted pour into heated sauceboat.

Vinaigrette Sauce

According to the Larousse Gastronomique, the final authority on at least classic French cooking, a sauce vinaigrette is what we call a French dressing. The classic French proportions are 1 scant part vinegar to 3 parts of oil, with salt and pepper to taste. Other ingredients can be added to it. The most usual are chopped parsley, chopped spring onions or chives, chopped tarragon, and minced capers, in whatever combination you prefer. One that I like is 1 cup of *vinaigrette* with 1 tablespoon each of chopped parsley, chopped spring onions or chives, and 1 teaspoon of minced capers. A little prepared mustard may be added as well – about ½ to 1 teaspoonful, depending on taste.

Mornay Sauce

A rich cheese sauce for eggs, fish, vegetables, and white meats. It can be made with any kind of cooking cheese, but I think that a mixture of Parmesan and Swiss cheese gives the best flavour.

3 tablespoons (1½ oz.) butter	6 fl. oz. hot cream
3 tablespoons flour	1 small onion, stuck with 1 clove
½ teaspoon salt	2 oz. grated Parmesan cheese
¼ teaspoon white pepper	2 oz. grated Swiss cheese
6 fl. oz. hot chicken bouillon	

Melt butter. Remove from heat. Blend in flour and seasonings. Gradually add hot bouillon and cream, stirring constantly until smooth. Add onion. Cook over low heat, stirring constantly, until thick and very smooth. Continue cooking 5 minutes longer. Remove onion. Add cheese and stir until well blended. Yields about ½–¾ pint sauce.

Rémoulade Sauce

A piquant sauce much used in France, Germany, and the Scandinavian countries on fish and sea food, cold meats, and vegetable salads.

1 teaspoon English mustard	1 tablespoon minced capers
1 teaspoon paprika	2 tablespoons minced scallions
¼ teaspoon salt	2 tablespoons minced celery
¼ teaspoon pepper	3 tablespoons vinegar (wine
¼ teaspoon cayenne pepper	vinegar is best)
2 teaspoons horseradish	¼ pint olive oil
4 anchovies, minced	

Combine all ingredients and beat until thoroughly mixed and blended. Yields about ½ pint sauce.

Herb Mayonnaise

This is nothing but a home-made or bought mayonnaise to which finely chopped herbs have been added. It should be quite green. As to the herbs, your own taste – as well as what herbs are handy – should guide you. Fresh herbs, of course, are infinitely best for this mayonnaise, but, *faute de mieux*, some dried ones can be smuggled in, provided that they have been soaked in a little cold water and squeezed dry, to remove their initial stiffness. The amount of herbs, and their proportion too, is a matter of personal preference; the recipe below is a guide.

The consistency of mayonnaise is another matter of opinion. Used as a dunk, I like mine stiff; but when the mayonnaise is to serve as a salad dressing I dilute it with fresh lemon juice to the consistency of a good French dressing, so that the salad will absorb it smoothly and properly. If a less tart thin mayonnaise is wanted, the lemon juice can be mixed with a little water. The herbs are added after the dilution.

½ pint mayonnaise
1 tablespoon chopped chives
2 tablespoons fresh or 1 teaspoon dried tarragon
2 tablespoons chopped parsley
1 teaspoon chopped chervil (optional)
1 teaspoon chopped dill (optional)

Combine all ingredients and blend thoroughly. Let stand for at least 1 hour before serving.

Gooseberry Sauce

This excellent gooseberry sauce goes extremely well with boiled or fried fish and other fried foods, as well as rich fowl, such as duck or goose.

1 pint gooseberries
8 fl. oz. water
Handful of spinach or sorrel leaves, chopped (optional)
1 tablespoon (½ oz.) butter
⅛ teaspoon grated nutmeg
Sugar to taste

Cook gooseberries and water together until berries are soft. Add spinach leaves and cook 3 minutes longer. Drain and reserve juice.

Rub berries and spinach through a food mill or a fine sieve. Return to saucepan and combine with juice. (The purée should be the consistency of a thin batter.) If too liquid, boil over high heat until right consistency is achieved by evaporation. Add butter, nutmeg, and sugar to taste. Simmer 2 to 3 minutes, stirring constantly. (If no spinach is used, add a few drops of green food colouring for right colour.)

Caucasian Plum Sauce [Tkemali]

Very good for roast chicken or other fowl and for shashlik.

½ lb. blue plums, stoned
2 to 3 cloves garlic, minced
Salt
Pepper
1 tablespoon minced parsley

Cook plums in water to cover. Drain, and reserve liquid. Rub plums through a sieve or purée in a blender. Stir sufficient plum liquid into the purée to achieve the consistency of cream. Add garlic, salt and pepper to taste, and parsley. Bring to the boil. Reduce heat and simmer 5 minutes.

Truffled Madeira Sauce from Périgord
[Sauce périgueux]

Some of the richest cooking in France comes from the Périgord, where the goose, the pig, and the truffle are highly esteemed and utilized in a delightful manner. This sauce is just one example – it is served with roast meat or chicken. It won't be as fragrant with canned truffles, but the sauce is still extremely worth while.

2 tablespoons (1 oz.) bacon fat
4 shallots chopped, or 1 small onion, minced
6 fl. oz. dry white wine
4 tablespoons Madeira
1 to 2 tablespoons flour
About 2 tablespoons bouillon
Pan juices of roast meat or chicken, or 1 teaspoon meat glaze
2 truffles, minced

Heat bacon fat and brown shallots or onions in it. Heat together with wine and Madeira but do not boil. Sprinkle flour on shallots or onion. Cook until browned, stirring constantly. Moisten with bouillon and add wines. Cover, and simmer over lowest possible heat 15 minutes, stirring frequently. Strain sauce and heat again. Add pan juices from meat, or stir in meat glaze until dissolved. The sauce should be dark brown. Add truffles and cook 3 minutes. Serve very hot.

Polish Juniper Berry Sauce [Sos jalowcowy]

This sauce goes well with a pâté or with ham or game birds.

2 tablespoons (1 oz.) butter	Pepper
2 tablespoons flour	Salt
8 fl. oz. bouillon or brown stock	1 to 2 teaspoons ground juniper
4 fl. oz. Madeira	berries

Heat butter until brown. Stir in flour and cook over low heat 5 minutes, stirring constantly. The mixture should be medium brown. Add bouillon or brown stock, and simmer 15 to 20 minutes, stirring occasionally. Add Madeira, salt and pepper to taste, and ground juniper berries. Simmer another 10 minutes. If the sauce is too thick, dilute with a little more hot bouillon.

Note: Juniper berries can be ground in a nut grinder, or pounded in a mortar, or put between two sheets of wax paper and crushed with a rolling pin.

Desserts

Northern Europeans go in heavily for desserts, and southern Europeans don't, preferring fruits and cheese. Except for special occasions, northern European desserts, which turn up at every meal, are much simpler than those fancied by the southern Europeans when they do trouble to make them. Desserts, in the countries of the Mediterranean, are very sweet and rich morsels, far more usually bought at a pastry shop than made at home. In Italy, for instance, no hostess would dream of making her own cakes or desserts for a dinner party – and quite rightly so, because nothing equals the splendour of a rum cake or a St-Honoré cake made by a good confectioner. In central Europe, however, it is a lady's prerogative to produce stupendous cakes and *Torten*, and in Scandinavia desserts of all kinds are considered part of a cook's achievements.

All along in this book, I have suffered from the *embarras de choix* – what recipes to put in and what to leave out. The choice is at its most embarrassing when it comes to desserts, for there are so many wonderful ones, all worth eating. Unless a dessert is really great, it is a waste of time to make it and a waste of figure to eat it. A great dessert does not necessarily have to be rich and complicated. Some made with fruit, for instance, are very simple. So, once more, I beg my readers' pardon for the omission of any particularly delicious creation that may linger in their memories.

In praise of Fruit Compotes

Next to fresh fruit, fruit compotes are far the best dessert for everyday meals, and are served as such throughout Europe. The basic rules for stewing fruit are the same for all fruit, but the timing and the amount of sugar used vary according to the different kinds of fruit, their sweetness, and their ripeness. The main thing to bear in mind is never, but never, to overcook the fruit, or it will be mushy.

The flavourings and seasonings of fruit compotes depend on individual tastes. The French use vanilla for their apples, pears, peaches, and apricots, the Italians favour lemon rind. Spices such as mace, ginger, cloves, cinnamon, coriander, and nutmeg are other excellent flavourings, and so are wine and liqueurs.

Fruit compotes can consist of either one fruit or a combination. When combinations are used, it is better to cook each fruit separately. The drained fruits are combined in the serving dish, and their syrups boiled together until thickened by evaporation. Then they are poured over the fruits.

Basic method. For each pound or quart of fruit, use – generally speaking – ¼ lb. sugar, ½ pint water plus the flavouring of your choice. Make a syrup by boiling sugar, water, and flavouring in covered saucepan for 5 to 10 minutes. Add washed fruit, a few pieces at a time, and poach over medium heat until done. Remove with slotted spoon and repeat process until all fruit is used. If syrup is too thin, boil rapidly until the right consistency is achieved. Pour over fruit and serve hot or chilled, with or without fresh cream.

SOME GOOD FRUIT COMBINATIONS

Apples and blackberries (also good in pies)

Apricots, peaches, and plums

Apricots and strawberries

Bilberries and peaches

Pears and bananas

Raspberries and pineapple

Strawberries and rhubarb

Cherries are best stewed by themselves.

Improved fruit compotes. Fruit compotes are often vastly improved if a little liqueur is added to the syrup before it is poured over the fruit. Brandy, kirsch, and rum are good flavourings, but whisky is not.

French Pear Compote with Red Wine
[Poires au vin rouge]

Standard, and very good, especially since pears that are not really worth eating otherwise can be used to advantage.

8 pears	1 stick cinnamon
5 oz. sugar	4 fl. oz. red wine
8 fl. oz. water	

Peel the pears but leave the stems on. Place peeled pears in cold water mixed with a little lemon juice or white vinegar to prevent them from turning brown. Boil together sugar, water, and cinnamon for 5 minutes. Simmer pears in syrup until tender. Do not overcook. A few minutes before the pears are done, add the wine. Remove pears with slotted spoon and stand upright in serving dish. Boil down the syrup until thick, and pour over pears. Serve hot or cold.

Note: Peaches can be cooked in the same manner. Peel raw peaches by dropping in boiling water; the skin will then come off easily. The peaches should be ripe but still quite firm.

Rumanian Sultana Compote

10 oz. sultanas	Grated rind of 1 lemon
8 fl. oz. water	2 oz. pine nuts or almonds
10 oz. honey	

Soak sultanas in water to cover for 1 hour; drain. Boil together water and honey for 2 to 3 minutes. Add sultanas and lemon rind; simmer for 10 minutes over low heat. Skim with slotted spoon as needed. Add pine nuts to sultanas. Chill thoroughly before serving.

*

Greek Oranges from France [*Oranges à la grecque*]

Very pretty to look at and so perfectly delicious that they're more
than worth the trouble.

6 large oranges	A few drops of red food
1½ lb. sugar	colouring or grenadine syrup
1½ pints water	

Remove the yellow part of the skin from the oranges with a sharp
knife or a potato peeler – the yellow part only. Cut this into tiny
strips with a pair of kitchen scissors. Plunge strips into plenty of
boiling water and boil 2 minutes. Drain. Repeat process twice,
changing water. This is to remove the bitterness from the peel.
Reserve peel.

Peel off all the white pith from the oranges so that none remains. Use a very sharp knife, and hold oranges over the glass
dish in which they will be served, to save juice. Cut 5 of the
oranges in half through their middle, and remove pips carefully.
Separate the other orange into sections and cover the bottom of a
glass serving dish with these sections. Put the orange halves on
the sections, round side up.

Boil sugar and water together for 10 minutes. Add enough food
colouring or grenadine syrup to give syrup a clear, red colour.
Pour the hot syrup over the oranges and let stand 15 minutes.
Drain off syrup and boil again for 15 minutes. Add peel to the
oranges and pour hot syrup over them. Cool, then chill in refrigerator 8 hours, or overnight.

Swiss Pineapple au Kirsch

Fresh pineapple, one of the best desserts in the world, is a luxury
when served doused with kirsch, the colourless and potent brandy
made from cherry stones that is Switzerland's beloved and much-
consumed drink. Kirsch is good on all fruit, and most invigorating
when poured into black coffee, Swiss fashion.

An average 2-lb. pineapple will serve 4 persons, and a very
large one 6 to 8.

Pineapple	Kirsch
Sugar	

Cut off top and bottom of pineapple. Cut into quarters (or eighths, if pineapple is large). Peel with sharp knife, removing all eyes. Remove hard core. Cut into neat, even pieces. Add sugar and kirsch to taste. Chill thoroughly.

Italian Sliced Oranges and Apples with Marsala [Mele e arance al Marsala]

Slice the oranges into thin, round slices, taking care to remove all white skin and pips. Core but do not peel the apples and slice into rounds. Sprinkle with powdered sugar and add a generous amount of Marsala. Chill for several hours before serving, so that the wine has a chance to penetrate the fruit.

Italian Baked Peaches [Pesche ripiene]

A classic Italian dessert. The peaches must be large and ripe but still firm.

4 large peaches	2 tablespoons mixed glacé fruit,
4 tablespoons almond	shredded fine
macaroon crumbs	Marsala or white wine
8 blanched almonds	

Halve peaches. Remove stones and enlarge hollow slightly with a spoon. Mash this extra pulp and combine it with macaroon crumbs and glacé fruit. Fill peach hollows with this mixture. Butter a deep baking dish. Place peaches in dish. Top each peach half with 1 almond. Sprinkle with Marsala or white wine. Bake in moderate (350° F., gas 4) oven for 15 to 20 minutes, or until just tender. Check for dryness – if necessary, add a little Marsala diluted with water, or some wine. Serve hot or cold.

   Note: A refinement which I don't really think necessary is to bind the macaroon-fruit mixture with the yolk of 1 egg and 1 tablespoon melted butter.

Italian Strawberries with Marsala [Fragole al Marsala]

The best Italian strawberries are the tiny wild ones whose perfume fills a room and is even more enchanting than their taste.

But even the *fragolini*, the big strawberries, are far more fragrant than our own. Since water destroys a good part of a strawberry's aroma, the Italians usually wash theirs in wine.

Strawberries are sprinkled with sugar and Marsala (or white or red wine) and kept in a cool place several hours before serving, since chilling (at least excessive chilling) is detrimental to their flavour. Another good way of serving them is to sprinkle them with sugar and with either lemon or orange juice.

Apple Charlotte [*Charlotte aux pommes*]

A French dessert of the *cuisine ménagère* that deserves the widest popularity. A good charlotte (made from tart apples only, or it is not worth eating) is an outstanding finale to a light meal. It also gives a great deal of cachet to a cook because, like a cheese soufflé, it looks far more difficult than it is. The secret is to line the mould absolutely tightly so that no apple sauce can escape during the baking. And the apple sauce must be very thick.

12 to 14 green cooking apples	Sugar
Grated rind of 1 lemon	Bread
3 tablespoons (1½ oz.) butter	Butter

Peel, core, and slice the apples. Cook apples with lemon rind and butter over low heat until soft and very thick, stirring frequently. Add sugar to taste and cook until sugar is dissolved, stirring constantly. The apple sauce must be extremely stiff. Trim crusts off slices of stale white bread that is firm in texture. Cut into fingers to fit sides of a deep round mould or cake tin (about 8 inches in diameter) and into triangles to fit the top and bottom of the mould tightly. Fry bread in hot but not brown butter until golden, but on one side only. Line the mould with bread fingers and triangles, buttered side next to mould, overlapping each other. The mould must be completely lined. Fill it with apple sauce, and cover with more of the bread fried on one side. Keep buttered side on top. Bake in a moderate to hot (400° F., gas 6) oven about 30 minutes, or until golden brown. The bread lining should have become firm. Cool for 5 minutes before unmoulding on a hot serving dish. Serve with hot Apricot Sauce.

APRICOT SAUCE

Melt some apricot jam with a little water until it is the right consistency. Stir in brandy or kirsch to taste.

Swiss Fruit Croûtes [Croûtes aux fruits]

Cut slices of crustless, stale bread into triangles. Fry them in butter until golden brown. Cover the bread with any kind of sweetened, fresh fruit, such as strawberries, sliced peaches, stoned cherries, or raspberries, and top with a little whipped cream. This is an excellent sweet, but the bread must be very hot and the fruit very cold.

Italian Chestnuts with Marsala and Wine
[Castagne al Marsala]

Chestnuts, both wild and cultivated, are a common food in Italy. Flour made from them is used in tarts and cakes. They are candied as marrons glacés and packed with candied violets. They are eaten roasted or boiled, either plain or with milk, as nourishment rather than a dessert. The following recipe makes a very good and interesting dessert, which can be eaten either hot or cold.

1 lb. chestnuts	8 fl. oz. red wine
4 oz. sugar	8 fl. oz. Marsala

Score chestnuts across rounded side with a sharp knife. Place in boiling water and simmer for 15 minutes. Drain, but keep warm. Slip off both skins. The skins should come off quite easily, provided the chestnuts are warm. Work carefully, since chestnuts break very easily.

Combine sugar, red wine, and Marsala and cook, covered, over low heat, for 5 minutes. Carefully place chestnuts in pan and simmer until tender. Shake pan occasionally so that chestnuts won't stick. Lift chestnuts with a slotted spoon and place in glass or silver serving dish. Reduce syrup and pour over chestnuts. Serve with plain double cream and thin, crisp biscuits.

Mont Blanc of Chestnuts

One of the world's greatest desserts. To be at its peak, it ought to be made only a short time before serving.

Score chestnuts across rounded side with a sharp knife. Place in boiling water and simmer for 15 minutes. Drain, but keep warm. Slip off both skins. Return to pan, cover with boiling water, and simmer for about 45 minutes, or until perfectly tender. Drain and mash with a little salt and with sugar to taste. Over a large serving dish (preferably silver) force chestnuts through a coarse sieve or a food mill with fairly large holes, into the shape of a mound. The chestnuts must be very light and fluffy.

Whip some cream and flavour with a little sugar and vanilla. Smooth cream over chestnut mound. Do not press down, or the Mont Blanc will lose its fluffiness. Chill for a short time and serve.

Note: Some Mont Blanc recipes suggest simmering the chestnuts in a light sugar syrup. I have found this to impair the essential fluffiness of the dessert.

Italian Flamed Chestnuts [*Castagne alla fiamma*]

Simply delicious with wine, the way they are served in country inns in the Abruzzi.

Place roasted and peeled chestnuts on a platter and sprinkle sugar over them. Pour rum or Marsala over chestnuts and blaze.

Dutch Lemon Cream [*Citroenvla*]

This cream can be prepared in advance, provided the egg whites are added just before serving time.

4 eggs, separated	Juice of 2 large lemons
4 oz. sugar	4 fl. oz. dry white wine
Grated rind of 1 large lemon	

Beat egg yolks and sugar until thick in top of double boiler. Add lemon rind. Stir in lemon juice and wine. Cook mixture over hot (not boiling) water, beating constantly with rotary beater, until thick and stiff. Cool. Beat egg whites until very stiff and fold gently into cream. Chill. Serve in sherbet glasses with small biscuits.

Fruit Fritters

Fruit fritters are a favourite sweet the length and breadth of Europe, and they are easy to make. The procedure is always the same: the fruit is stoned, sprinkled with sugar and any desired spices such as cinnamon, cloves, ginger, etc., and let stand for about 30 minutes. Then it is drained and dried between paper towels. The drying is a very important step, for if the fruit is not well dried the batter will not cling to it and the fruit will ooze out when frying. Next the fruit is dipped in the batter and the excess shaken off. It is then fried, a few fritters at a time, in deep fat heated to 365° F. for 2 to 3 minutes, or until golden brown. The fritters are drained on absorbent paper, sprinkled with sugar, and served immediately. Canned fruit is treated in the same manner.

To my taste, the best fritters are made with plums, cherries, apricots, oranges, apples, peaches, bananas, and pineapple, in that order.

FRENCH FRITTER BATTER FOR FRUITS

This is a very light and airy batter, thanks to the beer and the extra egg white. There is no taste of beer whatsoever in the finished fritter.

2 oz. flour	1 egg, well beaten
¼ teaspoon salt	4 fl. oz. beer
1 tablespoon melted butter	1 egg white, stiffly beaten

Sift together flour and salt. Blend butter and egg and add to flour. Stir in beer gradually, stirring only until mixture is smooth.

Stand in warm place for 1 to 2 hours, until batter is light and foamy. When ready to use fold in beaten egg white. Yields about 1 cup batter.

Central European Fruit Dumplings [Obst Knoedel]

Austria, Hungary, Czechoslovakia, and Poland are the countries where the dumpling, sweet or savoury, reigns supreme. This passion for dumplings is seldom shared by outsiders, but I feel that for accuracy's sake I should present my readers with the recipe for the most famous dumpling dessert.

6 medium-sized potatoes	Blue plums, stoned
½ lb. flour	Butter
¼ teaspoon salt	Bread crumbs
1 egg	Sugar

Boil potatoes in their skins. Peel immediately and sieve, while still hot, on to a pastry board. Add flour sifted with salt and mix lightly. Make a well in the dough and break egg into it. Work the ingredients quickly into a soft, light dough. Do not over-work, or dough will be tough. Roll out dough ¼ inch thick. Cut into 3-inch squares. Place a plum in the middle of each square and fold dough over it, covering it completely. Smooth into a perfect round. Cook dumplings in simmering (not boiling) water for about 15 minutes, or until they keep on floating on top of the water. Remove them with a slotted spoon and keep hot.

In a frying pan, heat butter and sauté bread crumbs in it until golden. Over low heat, sauté dumplings in this mixture for 1 to 2 minutes, or until thoroughly coated. Sprinkle with sugar and serve immediately.

Note: These are the famous Plum Dumplings, or Zwetsch-kenknoedel. The equally famous Apricot or Cherry Dumplings (Marillen or Kirschen Knoedel) are made by substituting either a stoned apricot or 3 black cherries for each plum.

German Plum Cake [*Pflaumenkuchen*]

The Germans are extremely fond of open fruit tarts, which take the place of our fruit pies, but in a more festive manner. All sorts of fruits are used, such as apples, pears, gooseberries. peaches, apricots, cherries, plums, the latter two being the favourites. The recipe that follows can be adapted to all of these fruits, though of course the sugar has to be adjusted, depending on the tartness of the fruit.

4 oz. plain flour	5 tablespoons milk
2 teaspoons baking powder	2 egg yolks
½ teaspoon salt	5 fl. oz. double cream
1 tablespoon sugar	2½ oz. sugar
3 tablespoons (1½ oz.) butter	3 oz. blanched chopped almonds
1–1½ lb. plums, stoned and halved	¼ teaspoon nutmeg

Sift together flour, baking powder, salt, and sugar. With a pastry blender or two knives, cut in butter until the mixture resembles oatmeal. Add milk and mix just long enough to combine the ingredients.

Butter an 8- or 9-inch shallow cake tin, preferably one with a removable bottom. Spread dough in bottom and on sides of tin. Crimp sides with the tines of a fork. Arrange plum halves, skin side down, over dough in circles. The plum halves should overlap slightly. Bake in medium hot (400° F., gas 6) oven for 10 to 15 minutes.

Combine egg yolks, cream, sugar, almonds, and nutmeg. Pour mixture over cake and continue baking for 10 to 15 minutes, or until done. The topping should be set and golden brown.

Note : A less elaborate cake is made by omitting the egg–cream mixture and substituting the following topping :

2 oz. sugar	½ teaspoon cinnamon
¼ teaspoon nutmeg	1 tablespoon (½ oz.) butter

French Fried Cream [Crème frite]

This recipe makes 3 to 4 servings.

3 egg yolks, beaten	3 tablespoons milk
1 tablespoon dark rum, brandy, or kirsch	¾ pint double cream
⅛ teaspoon salt	4 tablespoons fine, dry cracker crumbs
2 oz. sugar	1 egg, lightly beaten
⅛ teaspoon nutmeg, mace, or cardamom	3 tablespoons finely ground almonds or filberts
3 tablespoons cornflour	

Combine beaten egg yolks with liquor, salt, sugar, and spice. Blend cornflour with the milk and add to egg-yolk mixture. Scald cream and stir into custard. Cook in top of double boiler over boiling water until thick and smooth, stirring constantly. Pour cream into buttered shallow pan about ¾ inch deep and cool. When cold, cut into diamonds. Roll diamonds in cracker crumbs. Dip in beaten egg and roll in ground nuts. Shake off excess crumbs, egg, or nuts. Chill for about 30 minutes or longer. Fry in deep hot (300° F.) fat for about 2 minutes, or until golden brown.

Drain on absorbent paper. Place on heated serving dish. Pour a little additional rum (or whichever liquor was used in the cream) over the *crème frite* and carry flaming to the table.

The Empress's Rice Pudding [*Riz à l'impératrice*]

The French are very fond of serving rice as a dessert, with apples or other fruit, with custards, or in a rather solid cake. This rice dessert, named after the elegant and frivolous Empress Eugénie, wife of Napoleon III, can only be described as the rice pudding to end all rice puddings with éclat, the way a tableau ends a display of fireworks.

1½ tablespoons chopped citron	1½ tablespoons chopped candied
1½ tablespoons chopped candied	orange peel
lemon peel	4 fl. oz. kirsch

Combine fruits and marinate, covered, in kirsch, for several hours or overnight.

4 fl. oz. water	¾ pint milk
4 oz. sugar	1 2-inch piece vanilla bean or 1
6 oz. rice	tablespoon vanilla essence

Combine water and sugar and bring to the boil. Wash the rice and cook in the boiling syrup 5 minutes, stirring constantly. Drain and reserve syrup. In top of double boiler, heat milk and vanilla. Add rice and mix thoroughly. Cover. Cook over boiling water for about 1 hour, or until almost all the milk is absorbed, stirring occasionally. The rice should be creamy but not liquid.

2 tablespoons (2 envelopes)	1 pint double cream
gelatine	Red-currant jelly
4 fl. oz. cold water	

Soften gelatine in water for 3 minutes, stirring occasionally. Add to hot rice. Blend thoroughly and cool the mixture. Whip cream until stiff and blend with fruits and kirsch. Add mixture to rice pudding. Rinse a 3-pint mould with cold water. Line it thinly with red-currant jelly. Pack rice into mould and let stand overnight. Unmould on a deep platter and serve with both a Raspberry Sauce and an egg custard sauce. For 10 people.

Note: One version of riz à l'impératrice adds egg custard to the cooked rice before the gelatine is added to it. This makes for a creamier pudding. Personally, I prefer to serve the custard, which *does* belong to the riz à l'impératrice, separately.

RASPBERRY SAUCE

Simmer together ½ lb. frozen raspberries with 4 oz. sugar until raspberries are very soft. Strain through a sieve or blend in electric blender. Add 4 fl. oz. kirsch. Chill before serving.

French Chocolate Mousse [Mousse au chocolat]

The simplest and most elegant of all chocolate desserts.

½ lb. plain chocolate	5 eggs, separated
5 tablespoons cold water or coffee	1 tablespoon rum, brandy, or kirsch

Combine chocolate and cold water or coffee and melt over hot water, or over very low heat, stirring constantly. Cool slightly. Add egg yolks, one at a time, stirring until completely blended with chocolate. Stir in liquor. Beat egg whites until stiff but not dry. Fold carefully into chocolate mixture until just blended. Pile into small white soufflé dishes, pots de crème dishes, or sherbet glasses. Chill overnight or at least 8 hours. The mousse must be thoroughly chilled and ripened to acquire the characteristic spongy consistency. This amount will fill 5 to 8 cups, depending on size.

Note: The mousse can also be made with semi-sweet or baking chocolate. In both cases, the chocolate must be melted with sugar to taste, about 1 teaspoon for semi-sweet chocolate and up to 1 tablespoon for baking chocolate. The sugar must be thoroughly dissolved. Also, the mousse should not be too sweet.

French Rum Cake [Baba au rhum]

The true, classic baba is made in France with a yeast dough. The following recipe uses baking powder, and the effect is so similar to the classic formula that it is not worth while to fuss with the yeast.

2 eggs   3 oz. sifted flour
1 teaspoon sugar   1 teaspoon baking powder
2 tablespoons melted butter

Beat the eggs with sugar until light. Beat in the milk and melted
butter. Sift the flour and baking powder together and beat into
the batter. Butter and flour a ring mould or a deep 6-inch pan
and pour in dough. Bake in a hot (450° F., gas 8) oven about 30
minutes, or until golden. Unmould on a deep serving dish. Let
cool, and douse with Rum Sauce.

Note: To be strictly accurate, the above-mentioned dish is a
savarin rather than a baba. What makes a baba a baba is the
addition of 2½ oz. currants, plumped in water and then dried.

RUM SAUCE

This sauce should not be all rum, if for no better reason than
that the baba would not taste very good. But there is no reason
why more or less rum should not be added to the water–sugar
syrup, depending on taste.

Simmer, in covered saucepan, 12 fl. oz. water and 4 oz. sugar
for 10 minutes. Add 4 fl. oz. rum. Pour hot sauce over baba and
serve warm, with whipped cream on the side.

Note: The baba dough can be prepared beforehand and the
cake baked at the last minute. The same goes for the sauce, which,
however, must be reheated before being poured over the baba.

Blackberry Cream

Wild blackberries have been a favourite English berry for centuries, and cottage cookery concerns itself with them to a large
extent, as one of the foods free for the gathering. Blackberry
wine, blackberry amber and custards – these are but a few of
the old English bramble sweets that deserve to be better known.
Among the best of them is the following recipe for a luscious,
refreshing summer dessert.

2 lb. fresh blackberries   4 fl. oz. milk
4 oz. sugar (or more, to taste) 1 tablespoon brandy or kirsch
4 tablespoons water   ½ pint double cream
1 tablespoon (1 envelope) gelatine

Combine blackberries, sugar, and water. Cook over low heat until soft. Strain through sieve; there should be about 2 cups pulp and liquid. Soften gelatine in milk; dissolve over hot water. Blend blackberries and gelatine thoroughly. Stir in brandy or kirsch. Whip cream until stiff. Fold into blackberry mixture. Chill thoroughly before serving.

Note: This cream looks best in a white serving dish or white individual soufflé dishes – the kind used for French vanilla pots de crème.

Trifle

Split ladyfingers (langues de chat), spread with raspberry jam, and put together again. Place in deep glass serving dish – the dish should be about two-thirds full. Pour enough medium sweet or sweet sherry or Madeira over ladyfingers to soak them thoroughly. Make a custard sauce – the proportions are 3 egg yolks to 2 oz. sugar and ¾ pint milk – and flavour it with vanilla. Pour hot custard over ladyfingers. Cool thoroughly. When cold, thickly stud the custard with split blanched almonds. Chill, preferably overnight. At serving time, cover trifle with thickly whipped double cream. Decorate with whole (if small; halves if large) almond macaroons, glacé cherries, and angelica. Sprinkle evenly with hundreds and thousands. Serve immediately.

Note: The amount of custard needed depends on whether the trifle dish is deep and narrow or large and shallow. It should cover the ladyfingers completely and fill the cracks between them.

Devonshire Cream

Devonshire cream can be made only with non-homogenized, very fresh milk, which in some places can be obtained from a farm or dairy.

Take 6 pints of the richest, freshest milk, and mix, for a bigger yield, with a pint of double cream. Pour it into a large, shallow pan. Put pan over the very lowest heat of your stove. Just warm the milk – never let it even come close to being hot or boiling. When the top looks as if it were covered with a shiny, crinkly yellowish skin, remove the milk from heat and cool it overnight in the refrigerator. Next day, skim off the cream, which is too thick to pour, and serve it with fresh fruit.

Summer Pudding

This is very simple to make, and extraordinarily good. Any berries can be used for summer pudding, but the following are best: raspberries (either plain or mixed with a quarter of their weight in red currants), blackberries, or bilberries.

Butter a deep baking dish and line it with overlapping slices of stale bread from which the crusts have been trimmed. The dish must be completely lined on the bottom and the sides, leaving no space through which fruit can escape. Cook berries in sugar to taste until soft. Fill baking dish with berries. Cover the fruit with another layer of bread. Fit a plate or a saucer on top of the dish to press down the fruit. Put a weight on it – canned goods do nicely. Chill overnight. At serving time, unmould the pudding on a deep serving plate. Serve with plenty of cream and sugar on the side.

Water Pudding

This is a very light and delicate soufflé, and easily made.

10 tablespoons cold water	Grated rind of 1 large lemon
4 oz. sugar	Juice of large lemon
1 tablespoon melted butter	4 eggs, separated

Combine all ingredients except the eggs. Beat yolks until light and stir into mixture. Beat whites until stiff but not dry and fold carefully into batter. Butter a 1½-pint baking dish and pour in pudding. Bake in slow (325° F., gas 3) oven about 1 hour, or until firm. Serve with sweetened fresh strawberries or raspberries.

Lemon Cheese

A favourite filling for small tarts. A simple fruit salad of peeled orange rounds and apples, sprinkled with a little sugar and sherry, becomes a handsome dessert when it is served in a crystal or silver bowl with a dish of very small lemon tarts. Lemon cheese is also good on toast.

6 medium-sized lemons	2 lb. sugar
4 oz. butter	6 eggs, well beaten

Grate the rind of 4 of the lemons, and squeeze the juice of all of them. Combine rind and juice and let stand for 15 minutes. Melt butter in top of double boiler. Stir in lemon juice and sugar. When sugar is dissolved, add eggs. Cook over simmering (not boiling) water until mixture is as thick as honey, stirring frequently. Cool and pour into jars. Cover tightly and store in the refrigerator.

Stone Cream

Said to be one of Queen Victoria's favourites, and very famous among old English creams. The following very good recipe is taken verbatim from an old English cookbook.

'One pot of preserved apricots or plums (*jam*), half an ounce of isinglass (*1 envelope of gelatine*), one pint of cream (*double cream*), one lemon, two teaspoonfuls of crushed white sugar.

'Take a glass dish and line it at the bottom about an inch thick with preserved apricots or plums, dissolve half an ounce of isinglass in a little water (*dissolve the gelatine, that is*), add to it a pint of thick cream, the peel of the lemon grated, enough sugar to make pleasant to your taste. Let it boil one minute, then put it into a jug that has a spout. When it is *nearly* cold, but not quite set, squeeze into it the juice of the lemon (*or rather, squeeze the lemon in a cup and add it to the cream, lest a pip should fall into the jug*). Pour it into the dish (*from a jug with a spout*) over the sweetmeat, and let it stand all night. Place on the top a few ratafias (*small almond macaroons*).'

Gooseberry Fool

Gooseberries are among the most popular berries for cooked desserts, and gooseberry fool one of the most popular desserts. The tart gooseberries and the bland cream are an absolutely delicious combination.

1 lb. gooseberries	1 tablespoon brandy (optional)
8 oz. sugar	Green food colouring (optional)
8 fl. oz. water	¾ pint double cream

Remove the stem and blossom end of the berries. Wash them. Combine berries, sugar, and water. Cook over low heat until tender, stirring occasionally. Taste for sweetness – if the berries are very tart, add a little more sugar. Strain berries through a fine sieve. Stir in brandy and a few drops of green food colouring. Cool mixture. Whip cream until stiff. Fold into gooseberry sauce. Chill thoroughly before serving with plain, crisp biscuits.

Boodle's Orange Fool

Juice of 4 oranges	2 tablespoons honey (preferably
Juice of 2 large lemons	heather honey)
Grated rind of 2 oranges	1 pint double cream
Grated rind of 1 lemon	18 ladyfingers

Combine fruit juices, rinds, honey, and cream. Beat together until thickened and frothy. Line glass serving dish with ladyfingers. Pour fruit-cream mixture over them. Chill for at least 4 hours before serving.

Athol Brose

This is really a drink, if you can call anything as thick as an eggnog a drink. It is Highland Scotch, and at Hogmanay – that is, New Year's Eve – toasts were drunk in it. The original version is said to have contained oatmeal, but now there are about as many ways of making it as there are of making eggnog. I consider the following recipe a superb, alcoholic, and most successful dessert.

½ pint Scotch whisky	½ pint heather honey
½ pint double cream	

Combine ingredients and beat until frothy and stiffened. Chill thoroughly. Serve in sherbet or champagne glasses.

Russian Honey Mousse

A sweet that turns up in France, Belgium, and Switzerland as well. The flavour of the honey will determine the flavour of the dessert.

4 large eggs, separated	1 teaspoon grated lemon or
10 oz. honey	orange rind

Combine egg yolks and honey and beat together until thoroughly blended and light. Stir in lemon or orange rind. Whip egg whites until very stiff. Fold carefully into the egg–honey mixture. Fill individual sherbet glasses and chill before serving.

Kissel

The best known of Russian and Polish fruit desserts, of which there are many, made especially with the abundant berries of these countries. Kissel is a fruit purée thickened with potato flour or cornflour, but it can also be made with milk or chocolate. The consistency of kissel varies, depending on taste. It is seldom really stiff the way a gelatine dessert is, but more like a cream or porridge.

This form of fruit cream is not exclusive to the Slav countries. It is also popular in Scandinavia and northern Germany, illustrating again the interweaving of European cooking.

The most typical – and, to my mind, best – kissel is made from cranberries. Canned whole cranberries may also be used, but they need not be sweetened.

Kissel is an excellent, simple dessert for any time of the year.

Cook any ripe berries with sugar to taste, and water to cover, until the fruit is tender. Force through a strainer and measure the purée. Allow 2 to 3 teaspoons potato flour or cornflour to each ½ pint of thin purée. Heat fruit; stir in potato flour or cornflour which has been blended into a smooth paste with a little water. Cook over medium heat until thickened and clear, stirring constantly. Pour into glass serving dish and chill thoroughly. Serve with thick cream.

Russian Sour Cream Soufflé

¾ pint sour cream	2 oz. sugar
2 tablespoons flour	Grated rind of 1 lemon
4 eggs, separated	Bread crumbs

Cook together sour cream and flour until mixture is slightly thickened. Cool. Beat in egg yolks, one at a time. Add sugar and lemon rind. Beat the egg whites until stiff but not dry and fold into batter. Butter a 2½- to 3-pint baking dish and sprinkle with bread crumbs. Fill with batter and bake in moderate (350° F., gas 4) oven for about 20 minutes, or until set. Serve immediately with Red Wine Sauce.

RUSSIAN RED WINE SAUCE

¾ pint red wine	¼ teaspoon cinnamon
3 tablespoons sugar	⅛ teaspoon cloves

Combine all ingredients and simmer for 5 minutes.

Portuguese Egg Pudding
[Pudim d'ovos a moda de Coimbra]

Rich, sweet egg puddings are a Portuguese speciality, representative of that country's high esteem for the egg. In Portugal eggs are used in most sauces, puddings, pastries, and desserts. This egg pudding has been obviously influenced by Moorish cooking – small wonder, since the Moors occupied Portugal during the Middle Ages, leaving traces of their considerable culture which are evident in the country to this day.

¾ lb. sugar	1 teaspoon ground cinnamon
8 tablespoons water	¼ teaspoon powdered cumin or
9 eggs	cloves
2 tablespoons port	

In a heavy saucepan, boil sugar and water until thick. Beat in eggs one at a time. Stir in port, cinnamon, and cumin or cloves. Butter a 3-pint mould and fill with the batter. Cover with a sheet of buttered brown paper for about 10 minutes of total cooking time. Set mould in pan filled with simmering (not boiling) water and cook until pudding is set. Chill and serve with fresh orange slices soaked in port and sprinkled with a little sugar.

Spanish or Portuguese Quince Paste
[*Dulce de membrillo*]

The Spaniards and Portuguese usually eat fruit for dessert, though they also like *flan* (a custard that can be flavoured with oranges, coffee, chocolate, or caramel) and a few jellies. But they are not really dessert lovers. On the other hand, little cakes and biscuits are eaten throughout the day. All these sweets are extremely sugary for our taste. Possibly this Iberian sweet tooth is a legacy from the Moors, with their taste for excessive sweetness.

Quince paste, more a sweetmeat than a dessert in our interpretation of the word, is the very frequent finish to a meal. Often it is eaten with fresh white goat or other plain fresh cheese, in place of bread, and the combination is surprisingly good.

Wash quinces and cook with a little water until tender. Check water frequently, and add more if necessary. Cool, peel and cut in quarters, and mash or grind through the finest blade of the meat mincer. Measure quince pulp and add an equal amount of sugar. Let stand several hours or overnight. Cook over low heat until mixture is very stiff. Stir constantly and vigorously, since quinces burn extremely easily. Turn into bread or cake pan and cool. Unmould on baking sheet. Dry in the sun for 2 days to prevent mould growing. Or dry in cool (200° F., gas ½) oven for 1 to 2 hours. Wrap in aluminium foil and store in refrigerator or a cool dry place.

Spanish Milk Pudding [*Dulce de leche*]

This must be of Moorish origin, since it is both very sweet and very spicy. A heavy saucepan is absolutely essential for the success of this dessert.

1½ pints milk	2 tablespoons ground almonds
1 lb. granulated sugar	1 stick cinnamon

Combine all ingredients in heavy saucepan. Cook over medium
heat until mixture thickens to consistency of a custard, stirring
constantly. Pour into individual bowls. Chill thoroughly before
serving with crisp biscuits.

Italian Ricotta with Coffee [*Ricotta al caffè*]

Ricotta is one of several Italian soft cheeses, somewhere between
cream cheese and cottage cheese, but with a flavour all of its
own, thanks to its preparation. In Italy the true ricotta is made
from sheep's milk by the shepherds.

Ricotta is used much as we use cottage cheese, in main dishes,
puddings, cheesecakes, and as a dessert. With coffee, as in the
following recipe, it makes an original and sophisticated dessert.
Ricotta is sold in all Italian grocery stores and a few supermarkets.

1 lb. ricotta	4 oz. sugar
2 tablespoons freshly roasted, finely ground coffee	4 tablespoons rum

Beat ricotta until fluffy, or press through a fine sieve. Combine
with all other ingredients and blend thoroughly. Chill for at least
3 hours before serving with plain double cream and plain wafers
or crisp biscuits.

Italian Water Ices
[*Granite*]

Roman gourmets knew about iced wine and iced fruit juices,
and how to preserve ice for summer. But the water ices, the true
sherbets, came from the East – from the Arabs and the Persians,
and possibly the Chinese. However, in Europe it was certainly
the Italians who perfected the art of making ices, introducing
them in France to the court of Catherine de' Medici in 1533, and
in England to the court of Charles I. To this day the Italians
excel at making fruit or cream ices that are light and refreshing,
and an ideal end to a rich meal.

Most refreshing on a hot day, granite differ from gelati (cream ices) in that they are made with water and flavourings. They are admirably suited to being made in the refrigerator, since they do not have to be stirred as often as cream ices to avoid the formation of ice crystals. These crystals are part of a granita, which is frozen as you would freeze ice cubes. The freezing time, though, will be longer, because of the sugar in the granita.

Strawberry or Raspberry Ice
[Granita di fragole o di lamponi]

2 lb. fresh strawberries or raspberries	8 fl. oz. water
8 oz. sugar	Juice of 1 small lemon

Strain berries through a fine sieve or purée in a blender. Boil sugar and water together for 5 minutes. Cool. Combine with berry purée and stir in lemon juice. Freeze, stirring occasionally.

Lemon Ice [Granita di limone]

½ pint lemon juice (or more, if a tarter ice is wanted)	1¼ pints water
Grated rind of 1 lemon	5 oz. sugar

Combine lemon juice and rind. Boil water and sugar together for 5 minutes. Cool, then stir in lemon juice. Freeze, stirring occasionally.

Coffee Ice with Cream [Granita di caffè con panna]

6 oz. ground coffee	2 pints boiling water
3 oz. sugar	

Combine coffee, sugar, and water in top of double boiler. Steep, over simmering water, 30 minutes. Cool. Strain through a strainer lined with a triple thickness of muslin. Freeze in ice tray at regular freezing temperature. Stir occasionally. Serve in tall glasses, topped with sweetened whipped cream.

*

Italian Chocolate Dessert [Dolce Torino]

Turin, the capital of Piedmont in the region of Savoy, is a very
elegant city in the French manner – even the local dialect is
Frenchified. It is a city renowned for its eighteenth-century archi-
tecture, for the Fiat industry, for the fashions, and for wonderful
eating, under the sign of the truffle and chocolate. This famous
Turin dessert has its French counterparts, called St Emilion au
Chocolat and Queen Bona's Dessert, and a Hungarian version
as well, which only goes to show the universal appeal of a really
rich and devastating chocolate confection.

24 ladyfingers
8 fl. oz. brandy or rum
½ teaspoon vanilla
½ lb. semi-sweet chocolate
3–4 tablespoons single cream

½ lb. unsalted butter (it must
  be unsalted butter)
2½ oz. sugar
2 egg yolks, slightly beaten

Split ladyfingers and place on platter. Pour brandy or rum over
them and let soak for at least 2 hours. They should be well
drenched with liquor but still retain their shape. Combine vanilla,
chocolate, and cream in top of double boiler. Melt over hot water.
Cream together butter and sugar until light and thoroughly
blended. The sugar should no longer be grainy. Gradually add
egg yolks, mixing well. Add chocolate mixture to butter mixture,
a little at a time, blending thoroughly, until the whole is soft
and creamy. Do not undermix.

On a glass or, preferably, a silver serving dish, arrange a layer
of ladyfingers in the form of a square. Cover with a thin layer of
chocolate cream. Repeat process, finishing with a layer of chocolate. Reserve a little chocolate cream to coat sides. Smooth
chocolate surface with a wet knife. Decorate top with blanched
almond halves and glacé cherries cut in halves. Let ripen in a cool
place for at least 12 hours. At serving time, pipe whipped cream
around the border of the cake.

Note: The reason for keeping the dolce Torino in a cool place
rather than in the refrigerator is that too cold a temperature con-
geals the butter. However, if it must be kept in the refrigerator,
let stand at room temperature at least 30 minutes before serving.

Zabaglione

This is one of the world's great desserts. The combination of eggs, sugar, and spirits occurs in other countries besides Italy, but nowhere else is the formula so happy. At a pinch, sherry can be used instead of Marsala, but the genuine zabaglione must have Marsala. The following recipe is for 3.

4 egg yolks	6 fl. oz. Marsala
5 oz. sugar	

Combine ingredients in the top of a double boiler. Cook over simmering, but not boiling, water, beating constantly with a wire whip or an egg beater, for about 10 minutes, or until very thick. Serve immediately in glasses or small coffee cups.

Cold Zabaglione

Proceed as above. Set pan in a basin filled with cracked ice. Beat zabaglione until thoroughly cold. Pour into glasses or cups and keep refrigerated.

Note: Unless the zabaglione is beaten until thoroughly cold, it will not remain frothy but will collapse and separate.

Rose-Water Cookery

Cooking with rose water is an ancient art in the Middle East, whence it has spread to Turkey and the Balkans, where roses are grown commercially for their basic oil.

Rose flavouring is used in puddings, main dishes, cakes, jams, and preserves – rose jam and preserves are widely made and much beloved. A drop or two of rose water is also used to flavour drinking water in Turkey and Egypt.

European cooking made extensive use of rose water throughout the Middle Ages and the Renaissance, when very heavily spiced and perfumed foods were the order of the day. Old English recipes, down to Victorian times, call for rose water (and orange water as well). The French use it to this day, and they also make excellent rose-petal jam and candy.

Turkish Rose-water Milk Jelly [*Mahallebi*]

The Turks are very fond of extremely sweet, rose-flavoured milk puddings, which are put into little bowls and sold in shops and stalls. The following recipe is simple but rather exotic. People either love it or hate it.

¾ pint milk	2 tablespoons water
2½ oz. sugar	Rose water
1 tablespoon (1 envelope) gelatine	Sugar

Combine milk and sugar and heat almost to boiling point. Do not boil. Soften gelatine in water and stir into hot milk until completely dissolved. Add 4 tablespoons rose water. Pour into glass serving dish or individual dishes. Chill until set. Sprinkle more sugar and rose water over jelly.

Scandinavian Desserts

Scandinavians have a sweet tooth and are extremely fond of all sorts of creams and gelatine sweets, as well as puddings and pancakes. Fruit soups and milk desserts are also popular. Rum, almond, and lemon are favourite flavourings. Jam is much used in puddings and cakes, which are usually served with cream or with a sauce – preferably vanilla. Unlike English puddings, Scandinavian ones are usually cold and of a creamy consistency, unless they are stiffened with gelatine. In summer the luscious Scandinavian berries are extremely popular, either eaten fresh with cream and sugar or made into all sorts of puddings.

Swedish Uncooked Vanilla Sauce

All the Scandinavians are very fond of vanilla sauce, which they serve with cake, fruit, and other desserts. Cooked vanilla sauce is a rich custard made with cream in the standard manner, but here is a rich and delicious uncooked variety which is quickly made.

| 8 fl. oz. double cream | 2½ oz. sifted icing sugar |
| 3 egg yolks | ¾ teaspoon vanilla |

Whip cream until stiff. Beat egg yolks with icing sugar and vanilla until light and foamy. Fold in whipped cream. Chill thoroughly before serving.

Swedish Apple Cake with Vanilla Sauce
[Äpplekaka med vanijsås]

One of the most popular and best Swedish desserts.

6 tart apples, peeled and cubed	4 oz. butter
4 tablespoons water	8 oz. zwieback or rusk crumbs
4 oz. sugar	1½ teaspoons cinnamon
Grated rind of 1 lemon	2 tablespoons (1 oz.) butter
Juice of ½ lemon	Icing sugar

Over low heat, simmer apples, water, sugar, lemon rind and juice until apples are tender. Strain – there should be about 2½ cups thick apple sauce. Melt butter in pan. Add crumbs and cinnamon and cook, stirring constantly, over low heat until crumbs are evenly browned. Butter a deep 8-inch cake tin. Arrange alternate layers of crumbs and apple sauce, ending with a layer of crumbs. Dot with butter. Bake in moderate (350° F., gas 4) oven for 30 minutes. Cool. Unmould on serving plate. Sprinkle top with sifted icing sugar, placing a paper doily over the surface of the cake to make a lacy pattern. Serve chilled, with Swedish Uncooked Vanilla Sauce (see previous recipe).

Rum Cream [Rom fromage]

Fromages are puddings that resemble bavarois and are very popular throughout the Scandinavian countries. In Denmark, rum-flavoured sweets are great favourites, dating back to the days when the Danes had a rum-producing colony in the Virgin Islands.

2 eggs, separated	3 tablespoons cold water
4 oz. sugar	¾ pint double cream
1½ tablespoons (1½ envelopes)	3 tablespoons rum
gelatine	

In top of double boiler, over hot but not boiling water, beat egg yolks and sugar until thick. Soften gelatine in cold water and heat over boiling water. Add gelatine to egg mixture and blend thoroughly. Whip cream until stiff. Whip egg whites until stiff. Combine all ingredients and blend thoroughly. Stir in rum. Rinse a 1½-pint mould with cold water and fill with cream. Or pour cream into glass serving dish. Chill until firm; and, if a mould has been used, turn out on a deep plate. Decorate with fresh strawberries, raspberries, or other fruit, or serve plain with a fruit sauce.

Danish Veiled Country Lass [Bondepige med slør]

This dessert, one of Denmark's most popular, may seem strange at first. It is surprisingly good and a variation of the Swedish Apple Cake. It must be made with very dark rye bread or pumpernickel.

1 tablespoon (½ oz.) butter	Apple sauce
12 oz. finely grated rye bread crumbs	Raspberry jam
2–3 tablespoons sugar	Whipped cream

Melt butter in frying pan. Add crumbs and sugar and cook over low heat until crumbs are crisp, stirring frequently to prevent lumping. Cool crumbs. Line the bottom of a glass or other serving dish with a layer of crumbs. Cover with a layer of apple sauce. Top with more crumbs and a layer of raspberry jam. Cover jam with more crumbs, more apple sauce, and finish with remaining bread crumbs. Cover the top with a thick layer of whipped cream and chill before serving.

Danish Fruit Junket (Rødgrød)

This is another Danish dessert that has been adapted by the other Scandinavian countries. Fruit juices, or puréed fruit, stiffened to a semi-solid consistency with potato starch or cornflour, are extremely popular in northern Europe, Scandinavia, and Russia. They are served with thick cream and eaten in little bowls or sherbet glasses.

2 10-oz. packages frozen
  raspberries
1¼ pints water
1 stick cinnamon
Grated rind of ½ lemon

8 tablespoons cornflour
4 oz. sugar (or more or less,
  according to taste)
8 tablespoons water
Blanched almonds, cut in strips

Boil together raspberries, water, cinnamon, and lemon rind for
5 minutes. Strain and return fruit to saucepan. Blend cornflour,
sugar, and water into a smooth paste. Stir into fruit, avoiding
lumps. Return to heat and bring to boiling point, stirring constantly. Cook for 1 to 2 minutes, or until mixture is smooth and
clear. Pour into glass serving dish and chill, stirring occasionally.
At serving time, stick almond strips upright into the top of the
rødgrød to look like a porcupine.

Finnish Parsonage Standby [Pappilan hätävara]

An efficiency dessert, and a good one. In glass serving dish or in
individual dishes place alternate layers of plain, crisp vanilla
biscuits, lingonberry preserve (or whole cranberry sauce), and
thick whipped cream, ending with a layer of cream. Serve thoroughly chilled. If desired, the biscuits may first be dipped in milk
or any red fruit juice.

Cakes and Biscuits

Italian Fruit Bread from Siena [*Panforte di Siena*]

This hard and rich fruit bread dates back to the Middle Ages, just like the beautiful city it comes from. It is usually bought ready-made, and some delicatessens carry the flat cakes, but I thought it worth while to include the recipe in this book for the readers who might not have access to such a shop. *Panforte* is really excellent and will keep for weeks.

4 oz. blanched almonds
3 oz. hazelnuts, lightly toasted
3 tablespoons cocoa
1½ teaspoons cinnamon
¼ teaspoon allspice
2 oz. sifted plain flour
6 tablespoons candied orange peel, shredded
6 tablespoons candied lemon peel, shredded
6 tablespoons candied citron peel, shredded
8 oz. honey
6 oz. granulated sugar
Icing sugar mixed with cinnamon

Combine all ingredients except honey, granulated sugar, and icing sugar. Blend well. Cook honey and granulated sugar over low heat until a little of the syrup dropped into cold water forms a soft ball, or a sugar thermometer registers 238° F. Stir constantly. Add to fruits and mix thoroughly. Line a buttered 9-inch spring-form tin with well-buttered brown paper. Pour in dough and smooth out with a wet knife blade. Bake in slow (300° F., gas 2) oven about 30 minutes. When cool, sprinkle top with icing sugar and cinnamon.

Simnel Cake

I'll to thee a Simnel bring
'Gainst thou go'st a-mothering;
So that, when she blesseth thee,
Half that blessing thou'lt give me.

Thus sang Robert Herrick in 1648 in his *Hesperides*. The simnel
is a wonderfully rich cake with a layer of almond paste baked into
the dough – a cake that is eminently worth eating. It used to be
baked for Mothering Sunday – that is, the fourth Sunday in Lent,
the day when the children who lived away from home visited
their parents, bringing presents to their mothers.

There are many varieties of simnel cake, depending on the part
of England they were baked in. The Shropshire simnels are black
inside a saffron-coloured crust, whereas those of Lancashire are
decorated with sugar flowers and fruits. Some simnels are first
boiled, then baked; others, like this one, are only baked.

ALMOND PASTE

Combine 4 oz. finely ground almonds with 4 oz. sugar, 1 small egg,
and a few drops of yellow vegetable colouring. Mix thoroughly
and knead into a smooth paste. Set aside. (Or use ready-prepared
almond paste.)

CAKE DOUGH

6 oz. butter
¾ lb. sugar
4 large eggs
8 oz. sifted plain flour

1 teaspoon baking powder
5 oz. currants
6 tablespoons shredded mixed
    candied fruit peel

Cream butter and sugar until fluffy. Add eggs one at a time,
beating well after each addition. Sift together flour and baking
powder. Dredge fruit with half the flour. (This is done to prevent
fruit from sinking to the bottom of the cake during baking.) Stir
remaining flour into batter. Add fruit and mix thoroughly.

Line a buttered deep 8-inch spring-form tin with buttered
brown paper. Pour in half of the cake dough. Roll out almond
paste the size of the cake tin. Place circle of almond paste on cake
dough. Top with remaining dough. (If preferred, the cake may be

divided into 3 layers and the almond paste into 2 layers.) Bake in slow (300° F., gas 2) oven about 2½ hours, or until cake tests clean.

Ice with Almond Butter Icing piped through a pastry tube to form rosettes and decorate with glacé cherries, and strips of candied angelica, citron, and orange peel.

ALMOND BUTTER ICING

4 oz. soft butter
1 lb. sifted icing sugar

2 teaspoons almond flavouring

Beat all ingredients until smooth and of right spreading consistency. Part of the icing may be coloured with food colouring for special decorative effects, such as coloured roses, leaves, flutings, etc.

Basque Cherry Jam Cake [Gâteau basque]

I have had this in both the French and Spanish sections of the Basque country. The cake is best if the dough is made the day before baking.

6 oz. sifted plain flour
1½ teaspoons baking powder
4 oz. sugar
6 oz. unsalted butter, softened and cut in pieces

2 egg yolks
3 tablespoons brandy
Grated rind of 1 lemon
Cherry jam

Sift flour with baking powder. Put into large mixing bowl and make a well in it. Pour all other ingredients except the jam into well. Mix with a wooden spoon. Knead dough with hands until it no longer sticks to the fingers. Wrap in waxed paper and store overnight, but do not chill.

Divide dough into 2 equal parts. Between two sheets of waxed paper, roll out dough into 2 rounds about 1½ inches larger than an 8-inch cake tin. Grease and flour tin. Place one round of dough in the tin and make a border with the excess dough. Spread cherry jam almost to the edges of the tin. Cover with remaining round of dough. Seal edges by pinching dough with fingers. Brush top with a little milk, if a deep brown is wanted. Bake cake in moderate (350° F., gas 4) oven 20 to 25 minutes, or until cake tests clean.

Turkish or Greek Yoghurt Cake [*Maourtini*]

Yoghurt or sour cream cakes and puddings turn up in eastern Mediterranean cooking as well as in Russia. The Turks and Greeks pour syrup over their versions, but if a less sweet cake is wanted, this may be omitted.

3 eggs	1 teaspoon baking powder
8 oz. sugar	1 tablespoon grated lemon rind
8 oz. yoghurt	Whipped cream
4 oz. sifted plain flour	Chopped pistachio nuts

Beat eggs with sugar until thick and lemon-coloured. Add yoghurt and flour sifted with baking powder. Stir in lemon rind and beat mixture until smooth. Pour into buttered and floured 8-inch-square baking tin. Bake in preheated hot (400° F., gas 6) oven 20 to 30 minutes, or until cake tests clean. Cut into diamonds while pastry is still warm and in the tin. Immediately pour Syrup over cake. Cover tin and set aside until all the syrup has been absorbed. Transfer to a plate and chill. Before serving, decorate with rosettes of whipped cream and chopped pistachio nuts.

SYRUP

Mix together 1¼ pints water and 1¼ lb. sugar. Over low heat, boil gently about 15 minutes, or until syrup has boiled down to a bare ½ pint. Stir in 1 tablespoon lemon juice or 1 tablespoon rose water. Pour hot syrup over warm pastry.

Victoria Sponge Sandwich

The classic of the tea table. The true sponge cake contains no butter – butter being a Victorian addition, and a good one.

3 eggs, their weight in butter, sugar, and self-raising flour	Jam
	Icing sugar

Cream the butter until it looks like whipped cream. Add sugar and beat until white. Sift flour. Add eggs to butter mixture one at a time, following each egg with a spoonful of sifted flour. Beat thoroughly after each addition. Butter thoroughly 2 8-inch cake tins. Coat well with flour, leaving no bare spots. Turn batter into tins and bake in moderate (350° F., gas 4) oven 20 to 30 minutes, or until the cake tests clean. Cool in the tins. Before serving, spread one cake with any good jam and top with the other, sandwich fashion. Sprinkle sifted icing sugar over top.

French Walnut Cake [Gâteau aux noix]

This walnut cake, which is inexpensive compared to the lavish Central European nut *Torten*, is a very good one, and better the day after it is made. If an elaborate cake is needed, cut it into slices before serving. Spread slices with apricot jam or red-currant jelly, and place them on top of each other until the cake is assembled again. Cover the whole cake with whipped cream.

5 eggs, separated
6 oz. sugar
Grated rind of 1 lemon
¼ teaspoon mace

6 oz. walnuts, grated or finely chopped
4 tablespoons fine dry bread crumbs

Beat egg yolks with sugar until very thick and lemon-coloured. Add remaining ingredients one by one, stirring well after each addition. Beat egg whites until stiff but not dry. Fold into batter. Pour into well-buttered and floured 8-inch spring-form tin or loaf tin. Bake in preheated slow (300° F., gas 2) oven 1 to 1¼ hours, or until cake tests clean. Cool before filling and covering with cream.

German Hazelnut Torte [Haselnuss Torte]

This is a fine example of the rich nut *Torten* so beloved of Germans, Austrians, and other Central Europeans. It contains no flour and is all the better for it. Walnuts can be used instead of hazelnuts, but the *Torte*, an ample, splendid creation, is much more delicate with hazelnuts, and also more typical.

7 eggs, separated
7 additional egg whites
10 oz. sugar

1½ lb. hazelnuts finely grated
8 fl. oz. double cream

Beat egg yolks and 9 oz. sugar until very thick and lemon-coloured. Add all but 2 oz. hazelnuts. Beat all 14 egg whites until stiff but

not dry. Fold lightly into mixture. Pour into well buttered and
floured 10-inch spring-form tin. Bake in preheated moderate
(350° F., gas 4) oven 40 to 45 minutes, or until cake tests clean.
Turn off heat and leave cake in oven with open door for 10 more
minutes. Cool.

Beat double cream with remaining 1 oz. sugar until stiff. Fold
in remaining grated nuts. Cut cake in half and spread with
filling.

ICING

½ lb. sifted icing sugar
1 tablespoon grated lemon rind
2 teaspoons soft unsalted butter

2 teaspoons warm water
1 stiffly beaten egg white

Combine sugar, lemon rind, butter, and warm water into a smooth
paste. (It may be necessary to add a little warm water, but add
½ teaspoon at a time.) Fold into beaten egg white. Ice cake and
decorate with additional hazelnuts cut in halves. Chill cake in
refrigerator for 3 hours before serving.

Italian Rum Cake [Dolce al rum]

3 eggs
8 oz. sugar
3 tablespoons cold water

2 teaspoons vanilla
4 oz. sifted plain flour
2 teaspoons baking powder

Beat eggs until light. Gradually beat in the sugar and continue
beating until mixture is thick and pale in colour. Use an electric
beater for this, if possible, and beat on high speed 6 minutes.
Stir in the water and vanilla. Sift flour with baking powder three
times and fold into batter. Pour into buttered and floured 9-inch
spring-form tin and bake in preheated moderate (350° F., gas 4)
oven 30 minutes, or until cake tests clean. Cool in tin while
making the topping.

TOPPING

1 tablespoon (1 envelope)
  gelatine
4 tablespoons cold water
¾ pint hot milk
6 oz. sugar

4 egg yolks, lightly beaten
6 tablespoons dark rum
1 large orange
8 fl. oz. double cream

Soften gelatine in cold water for a few minutes. Stir in hot milk and sugar and cook over low heat until mixture is hot. It must not boil. Gradually pour over egg yolks, stirring constantly. Add rum. Set pan in bowl of cracked ice and stir constantly until cool and beginning to set. Peel orange free of all yellow and white peel and skin and separate into segments. Fold orange segments and cream into custard. Pour over cooled cake in the tin and chill until serving time. To serve, remove cake from tin and garnish with orange slices, glacé cherries, and rosettes of whipped cream.

Swedish Mazarin Cake [Mazarintärta]

A nut and jam cake, along the lines of the better-known Austrian *Linzer Torte*, but not quite as heavy, and therefore preferable, to my mind. It keeps well in the refrigerator or in an airtight tin.

6½ oz. sifted flour	4 oz. unsalted butter
1 teaspoon baking powder	1 small egg

Sift flour and baking powder. Add butter and egg and mix and work until smooth. (It is best to do this with the hands.)

FILLING

4 oz. icing sugar	4 oz. blanched almonds, finely
4 oz. unsalted butter	ground
2 eggs	Raspberry jam

Work sugar, butter, and almonds into a smooth paste. Add eggs one at a time and blend thoroughly. Line a buttered 8-inch cake tin with dough. Spread with raspberry jam. Top with filling. Bake in cool to moderate (325° F., gas 3) oven about 40 minutes, or until cake tester inserted in the middle of the cake comes out clean.

Sand Cake [Sand Torte]

This German cake has a fine, grainy quality, and it keeps indefinitely in a tightly closed tin. The cornflour is an essential ingredient. Since this cake has to be beaten a good deal, like an old-fashioned pound cake, an electric mixer will be useful.

8 oz. butter
8 oz. sugar
Grated rind of 2 lemons
2 tablespoons lemon juice or 2
tablespoons brandy or rum

6 eggs, separated
4 oz. sifted flour
4 oz. sifted cornflour
1½ teaspoons baking powder
½ teaspoon salt

Beat butter until soft and creamy. Add sugar to it, a little at a time, beating well after each addition. Stir in lemon rind. Beat egg yolks until light. Add to butter mixture, beating well. Beat in lemon juice, brandy, or rum. Sift flour and cornflour before measuring. Combine and sift again with baking powder and salt. Stir the sifted ingredients into the batter. Beat for at least 15 minutes by hand, or 10 with electric mixer.

Beat egg whites until stiff but not dry. Fold into batter. Grease and flour 9-inch tube pan, and bake cake in it on centre shelf in moderate (350° F., gas 4) oven for about 45 minutes, or until done.

This cake is not usually iced, but if an icing is wanted, use a simple Lemon, Rum, or Brandy Icing.

AUSTRIAN LEMON, RUM, OR BRANDY ICING
[Einfache Zucker Glasur]

Sift icing sugar into a bowl. For each ½ lb., add gradually about 2 tablespoons lemon juice, rum, or brandy. Beat thoroughly to make a smooth-spreading paste, adding more sugar or liquid as needed.

Almond and Brandy Cake

3 eggs
8 oz. sugar
1 teaspoon mace
Grated rind of 2 lemons

3 oz. fine dry bread crumbs
8 fl. oz. good brandy
8 oz. blanched almonds, finely
ground

Beat eggs and sugar until light. Add mace and lemon rind. Stir in bread crumbs and brandy alternately. Add almonds, and mix well. Pour into greased 8-inch cake tin. Bake in moderate (350° F., gas 4) oven for 30 to 35 minutes, or until cake tester shows that the cake is baked through. When cool, ice with Austrian Lemon Icing (see previous recipe) and decorate with toasted halves of almonds.

French Chocolate Cake [Gâteau au chocolat]

This delicious cake differs from the usual chocolate cakes by being rather flat and moist – therefore, do not overbake. In the continental fashion, the layers are put together with a tart jam or jelly such as apricot jam or red-currant jelly. More jam or jelly is spread on the top of the cake, which is then iced with Italian Chocolate Icing and prettily decorated. Candied violets or rose petals look very fetching on it.

4 oz. unsweetened chocolate
4 tablespoons water
4 oz. butter, cut in pieces
4 oz. sugar
3 large or 4 medium eggs, separated

1½ oz. ground or finely chopped nuts
1 teaspoon vanilla or 2 teaspoons rum or brandy
1½ oz. flour
Apricot jam or red-currant jelly

Melt chocolate in water over low heat, stirring constantly. Add butter and stir until completely melted. Remove from heat and blend in sugar. Cool. Add egg yolks, beating well after each addition. Blend in nuts and flavouring. Stir in flour and blend thoroughly. Fold in stiffly beaten egg whites. Grease and flour two round 8-inch cake tins. Bake in medium (325–50° F., gas 3–4) oven for about 25 minutes, or until done. When cool, put halves together with tart jam or jelly. Spread top with more jam or jelly and ice with Chocolate Icing.

ITALIAN CHOCOLATE ICING [Glassatura alla cioccolata]

¾ lb. sugar
12 fl. oz. hot water
2 oz. unsweetened chocolate
1½ oz. cornflour

4 fl. oz. cold water
1 teaspoon vanilla or other flavouring

Mix sugar, hot water, and chocolate in saucepan over fire. Bring to the boil and cook 5 minutes, stirring constantly. Dissolve cornflour in cold water to a smooth paste. Slowly stir cornflour into chocolate mixture and cook 3 to 4 minutes, beating well to avoid lumps. Remove from heat, blend in flavouring, and beat until cool enough to spread.

Spanish and Portuguese Biscuits

In Spain and Portugal biscuits and cakes resemble sweetmeats by our standards, rather than what we call cakes. A Moorish air hangs over most of them, as they are very sweet and very rich, for such is the Arab taste in sweets. Each town and district has its sweet specialities, and many were the inventions of the nuns in their baroque convents that dot the land. Sacheverell Sitwell, in his *Sacred and Profane Love* (Faber & Faber, London, 1940), has described most charmingly a Portuguese convent's annual picnic:
'... the doces de ovo, sweets made with eggs; the ovos moles, especial to Aveiro, and packed in little wooden barrels; toucinho do céu, trouxas and lampreias de ovos from Portalegre and Caldas da Rainha; fios de ovos, aletria from Abrantes; doces de amendoa, doce podre of Evora, morgado and dom rodrigo of Algarve: tijelinhas of Santo Tirso: pasteis de nata, sweet cakes of Tentugal: pães de ló, gingerbreads of Fafe, Ovar, Figuiero, Alfeizerâo: cavacas of Caldas, Felguieras, Resende: the morcela of Arouca: marzipan of Portalegre: arrufadas of Coimbra: fig or almond cakes of Freixo de Espada or Moncorvo: and how many more! ... This is a sweet tooth feasting; and they drink, not wine, but chocolate. Or draughts of lime or orange, orgeat or pomegranate with pounded barley. And sweet ices in great plenty.'

Spanish Fondant Cookies [Yemas]

Yema means yolk, and there are many variations of these cookies, which are always formed into little balls.

1 lb. potatoes
3 eggs
¾ lb. blanched almonds, finely ground

1 lb. sugar
1 tablespoon orange water or rose water or grated rind of 1 lemon

Cook potatoes, peel, and strain through a sieve. Beat eggs with sugar until thick and lemon-coloured. Combine egg mixture, potatoes, almonds, and flavouring and knead until smooth. Pinch off pieces of dough and roll into little balls. Coat with icing sugar.

Place on baking sheets and store in dry place for 24 hours, or until *yemas* are dried.

Madrid Biscuits [*Galletas de Madrid*]

½ lb. sifted plain flour
½ teaspoon salt
4 eggs
1 lb. sugar
1 egg yolk, beaten with 1
  teaspoon water

6 oz. butter
Grated rind of 1 lemon or 1
  teaspoon cinnamon or 1
  tablespoon brandy or anise
  cordial

Sift flour and salt together. Beat 4 eggs with ½ lb. sugar until thick and lemon-coloured. Cream butter with remaining sugar. Add to egg–sugar mixture and stir in flavouring. Gradually stir flour into butter and beat until smooth. With floured hands, pinch off pieces of dough and roll each into strips about ¼ inch thick and 3 inches long. Keep palms floured to prevent dough from sticking. Form into twists by winding 2 strips around each other. Butter and flour baking sheets. Place twists on sheet and brush with egg yolk beaten with water. Bake in moderate (350° F., gas 4) oven about 15 minutes, or until golden.

Note: In an airtight tin, the *galletas* will keep fresh several weeks.

Portuguese Bridal Biscuits [*Casados*]

These biscuits, in various forms, turn up also in Spain, Mexico and Brazil. They will keep for weeks in an airtight tin.

4 oz. butter
1 tablespoon brandy or rose
  water or orange water

Icing sugar
5 oz. sifted plain flour
Blanched almonds

Cream butter. Add 2 tablespoons of the sugar and the flavouring and mix thoroughly. Add flour and knead until dough is light. Pinch off a small piece of dough (about 1 heaped tablespoonful) and press out flat on the palm of the left hand. Place an almond in the middle of the dough. Roll dough around almond, encasing it completely to make a little loaf. Place on baking sheet and bake in moderate (350° F., gas 4) oven about 20 minutes, or until the biscuits just begin to turn brown at the bottom. Do not overbrown. Remove from sheet, cool 2 to 3 minutes, and roll in icing sugar. Cool completely, and roll again in sugar.

*

Serbian Biscuits [Belgrader Brot]

This biscuit, which contains no shortening, is spicy and hard. The dough keeps for at least a week in the refrigerator before baking, and the baked biscuits for weeks when stored in airtight tins.

2 eggs	2 tablespoons blanched almonds,
8 oz. sugar	cut into strips
6½ oz. flour	2 tablespoons finely chopped
1 teaspoon cinnamon	candied lemon peel
2 tablespoons finely ground	1 tablespoon lemon juice
hazelnuts	

Beat eggs and sugar until thick. Sift flour with cinnamon. Add to egg mixture a little at a time. Add all other ingredients and knead until smooth. Let stand overnight but do not chill. On floured baking board, roll out dough ¼ inch thick. Cut into strips ½ inch wide and 2 to 3 inches long. Bake on buttered and floured baking sheet in moderate (350° F., gas 4) oven about 30 minutes, or until golden brown. While warm, ice with thin Lemon Icing (page 295).

Russian Biscuits [Mazurki]

There are many varieties of *mazurki*, among which I prefer the one listed below.

1 cup each : currants, seedless	1 cup thick raspberry or
chopped raisins, chopped	strawberry jam, or thick
blanched almonds, chopped	cranberry preserve
walnuts, and chopped dried	Grated rind of 1 lemon
apricots	½ lb. sifted plain flour
2 eggs	

Combine all ingredients except flour. Sprinkle flour over fruit and mix thoroughly. Spread dough in buttered shallow baking dish about ½ inch deep. Bake in slow (300° F., gas 2) oven about 35 minutes. Cut *mazurki* into diamond shapes while still in tin. Return tin to oven for 5 more minutes to dry out biscuits.

Scandinavian Cardamom Biscuits

The cardamom is native to India, but its use is widespread in Spain and Spanish America. It is sold whole, in which case it must be crushed, or in powdered form. Ground cardamom is a great favourite in the Scandinavian countries, where it is used to flavour pastries and biscuits.

The following recipe makes rich, bland biscuits which are not too sweet.

6 oz. unsalted butter	¾ teaspoon baking powder
8 oz. sugar	1–1½ tablespoons ground
1 egg yolk	cardamom
3½ fl. oz. double cream	6 oz. blanched almonds, finely
1 lb. sifted plain flour	ground

Cream butter and sugar until light. Beat in egg yolk and cream. Sift flour with baking powder and cardamom. Gradually add to batter, stirring until smooth. Add almonds and knead to form a smooth dough. Shape into rolls, wrap in wax paper, and chill overnight in refrigerator. When ready to bake, slice off biscuits about ¼ inch thick. Bake in moderate (350° F., gas 4) oven about 10 to 12 minutes, or until biscuits start turning golden brown. Store in airtight tins – they will keep for weeks.

Almond Macaroons

Almond macaroons are particularly good when served with fruit compotes or, with a glass of sweet wine, as an elegant little snack.

¾ lb. blanched almonds, ground fine and very dry	2 egg whites, beaten stiff
½ lb. sugar	1 teaspoon almond extract

Combine all ingredients and blend together gently but thoroughly. Grease and flour baking sheets thoroughly. Drop batter on baking sheet by teaspoonfuls, leaving a space of 2 inches between macaroons. Sprinkle with icing sugar. Let stand 2 hours to dry. Bake in slow (325° F., gas 3) oven about 15 minutes, or until golden. Cool on baking sheet for 1 to 2 minutes, then remove.

Note: The macaroons may be decorated with half a glacé cherry or a whole almond, pressed in the centre of each one while still hot.

Austrian Anise Biscuits [Anis Kräpfchen]

3 eggs
8 oz. sugar
8 oz. sifted plain flour
½ teaspoon baking powder
1–2 tablespoons anise seeds

Beat eggs and sugar until thick and fluffy. Sift flour and baking powder together and gradually add to egg mixture. Stir in anise seeds. Drop batter by teaspoonfuls on greased, floured baking sheets. Bake in moderate (350° F., gas 4) oven about 10 to 12 minutes, or until golden brown. Serve with fresh fruit or compotes.

German Vanilla Pretzels [Vanillen Bretzeln]

A very rich German Christmas biscuit. The dough can also be shaped into fingers or rings.

5 egg yolks
9 oz. sugar
2 teaspoons vanilla
8 oz. unsalted butter
1 lb. sifted plain flour

Beat egg yolks with sugar until thick and lemon-coloured. Stir in vanilla. Cut butter into flour. Add egg mixture and blend with wooden spoon. With hands, knead until dough is smooth. Pinch off pieces of dough and, with floured hands, roll into strips about ½ inch thick and 6 to 7 inches long. Place on ungreased baking sheet and form into pretzels. Bake in preheated moderate (350° F., gas 4) oven about 10 to 12 minutes, or until pretzels turn brown at the edges. While still warm, glaze with thin Vanilla Icing.

VANILLA ICING

Blend together 4 oz. sifted icing sugar, 1 teaspoon vanilla, and 1 teaspoon (or more) water until the icing reaches the consistency of thick cream.

Scandinavian Spice Cookies [*Pepparkakor*]

With slight variations, these are made in all Scandinavian countries. At Christmas they are decorated and hung on the tree. The *pepparkakors* can be cut into any desired shape with a biscuit cutter, or rolled into a roll, sliced, and baked. They are very pretty if iced in the colourful Scandinavian manner, but equally good when covered with a thin, tart Lemon Icing.

6 oz. butter	1 teaspoon ground cardamom
4 oz. sugar	1 teaspoon cinnamon
5 oz. treacle	1 teaspoon cloves
2 tablespoons brandy	2 teaspoons ground ginger
¾ lb. sifted plain flour	3 oz. blanched almonds, finely
1 teaspoon salt	ground
1 teaspoon pepper	1 tablespoon grated lemon rind

Cream butter and sugar until fluffy; stir in treacle and brandy. Sift flour with salt, pepper, and spices. Add to egg mixture gradually, with almond and lemon rind. Work with hands into a smooth dough. The dough should be stiff. Chill overnight. Roll out as thinly as possible between two sheets of wax paper. Bake on ungreased baking sheet in moderate (350° F., gas 4) oven for about 8 minutes. Cool, and glaze with thin Lemon Icing (page 295).

Viennese Crescents [*Nuss Kipferln*]

Rich butter and almond biscuits are favourites throughout Europe, and the number of excellent recipes for them is legion. But I think this one tops them all. I am indebted – and so are my friends – to the *New York Times* for the following recipe.

1-inch piece vanilla bean
4 oz. sifted icing sugar
6 oz. shelled walnuts, finely
  ground

8 oz. unsalted butter, softened
6 oz. sugar
10 oz. sifted flour

Cut vanilla bean into small pieces. Place in covered jar with icing sugar. Let stand overnight.

With hands or wooden spoon, mix together walnuts, butter, sugar, and flour and work into a smooth dough. Chill several hours. Pinch off pieces of dough and shape into small crescents, about 1½ inches in diameter. Bake on ungreased baking sheet in moderate (350° F., gas 4) oven about 15 minutes, or until golden brown. Cool 2 to 3 minutes. Roll biscuits in vanilla sugar.

Greek Sesame Turnovers [Cretekia patoutha]

The Balkans and Greece abound in very sweet and sticky pastries, filled with nuts and drenched with syrup. They are eaten in between meals, rather than as dessert – dessert consists of fruit. These pastries seem odd at first taste, but they grow upon one. Since I like a bit of something very sweet to finish off a meal, I often serve these turnovers for dessert.

6 fl. oz. olive oil
4 fl. oz. water
Juice of 1 lemon
½ teaspoon salt

2 oz. sugar
6 oz. flour
½ teaspoon baking powder

Mix together oil, water, lemon juice, salt, and sugar. Sift flour and baking powder. Blend ingredients and work into a smooth dough. Roll out on floured baking board to ¼-inch thickness. Cut into 2-inch squares.

FILLING
6 oz. ground pistachios or
  walnuts
6 oz. ground almonds

4 oz. sesame seeds
10 oz. honey

Thoroughly mix together all ingredients.

Place a little of the filling on each pastry square. Moisten the edges and fold over filling. Press together and pinch firmly to close. Brush with beaten egg. Bake in slow (300° F., gas 2) oven 15 minutes, or until just golden.

DIP

Rose water   Icing sugar

While turnovers are still warm, dip in rose water and sprinkle with sugar. Arrange on large platter and scatter candied rose leaves over turnovers.

Herbs and Spices

There are store cupboards for food necessities and there are others for the niceties of eating. It is of the latter that I shall speak briefly.

On the Continent food is seasoned more highly and more imaginatively than ours is. Since almost all standard cookbooks have excellent charts on the use of herbs and spices, I shall not repeat this information here, but merely draw the reader's attention to some of the less familiar seasonings. It must also be remembered that dried herbs and spices lose their freshness and go stale upon long storage, and that it is better to buy small quantities at one time and replace them often – or the whole purpose of cooking with these herbs and spices is lost.

Basil is much loved by all Mediterranean people, and used in stews, sauces (especially tomato sauces), and vegetables.

Borage, with its cucumber-like flavour, is excellent for salads and vegetables. So is *burnet*.

Cardamom (if the whole seed is bought, it must be crushed) gives an intriguing flavour to breads, rolls, biscuits, fruit salads, and jellies.

Coriander, mentioned in the Old Testament as manna (Numbers 11:7), has a delicious flavour of both lemon peel and sage, adding greatly to meats, soups, poultry dishes, as well as fruit salads and compotes.

Cumin, much used by the cooks of Spain and the eastern Mediterranean, does well with eggs, cheese, fish, poultry, and game.

Dill, when fresh, is a basic ingredient of Scandinavian and Russian-Polish cooking, especially for fish and lamb dishes. The seed does well in vegetables, soups, gravies, and creamed foods.

Juniper berries are excellent for duck, geese, wild fowl, game, and venison.

Parsley should be used in far greater quantities than it usually is. Parsley root, when cooked, reminds one of celery, and is invaluable in the flavouring of soups, stews, and slow-cooking dishes.

Poppy seed is a favourite of Central European cooking, where it is used for pastry and for noodles. It has a walnut-like taste, and before being added to a food it should be slightly toasted or sautéed in butter to bring out its full flavour.

Rosemary is essential in much Italian cooking, particularly for veal, lamb, and pork dishes.

Saffron not only colours foods a handsome yellow, but has a delicate, distinctive flavour characteristic of Spanish dishes and Risotto alla Milanese. It is good for fish and shellfish dishes as well.

Sesame has a rich, nutty flavour and is much used in Greek and eastern Mediterranean cakes and biscuits, and confections like halva.

Shallots have a much more delicate flavour than any of the onion family and are used instead of onions in elegant French cooking. It is extremely worth while to keep a supply at hand.

Tarragon is an essential for French poultry cooking, for fish, shellfish, sauces, and vinegars.

Though certain herbs and flavourings are typical of one or other cuisine, there is no hard or fast rule as to their uses. The reader should experiment and decide for himself whether he and his guests really like the flavour of one of these seasonings or not, and omit or substitute accordingly.

Wine Chart

Food	Wine	How	Some Names to Remember
Hors-d'œuvres, snacks	Dry sherry or Marsala, Madeira, light dry wine, rosé, champagne	Chilled	Fino, Sherry, Sercial Madeira, Spanish Montilla, Alsatian Riesling, Chablis, Muscadet, Italian Soave, Dry Vermouth
Soup	Medium sherry, Madeira, light white wines	Room Temp. Chilled	Amontillado Sherry or Dry Oloroso. Verdelho or Rainwater Madeira, Quincy, Graves, Med. White Burgundy, Rhine wines
Oysters, shellfish, all fish, white meat, poultry	Dry white wines, rosé, and for white meat and poultry also some light red wines, such as Beaujolais, Red Rioja, Bardolino	Chilled Room Temp.	Neufchâtel, Moselle, Graves, Chablis, Pouilly Fuissé, Montrachet, Muscadet, Meursault, Rheingau, Steinwein, Soave. Dry Orvieto, Traminer, Dry White Chianti, Rosé. (Choose full-bodied wines according to dish)
Pork, ham, and veal	Champagne, dry white wines, rosé	Chilled	Most of the wines in the previous section

Food	Wine	How	Some Names to Remember
Red meats, stews, poultry, turkey, duck	Claret and other light red wines	Room Temp.	Bordeaux regional and château-bottled wines. Beaujolais, Rioja, Bardolino, Chianti
Game, venison, and all full-flavoured meats	Full-bodied red wines, medium red wines		Burgundy, Rhône reds, Beaujolais, Barolo, Valpolicella
Dessert, ices, sweet fruits, and compotes	Sweet white wines, dessert wines, Champagne	Chilled	Sweet Orvieto, Sauternes, Barsac, Sweet Rheingau, Sweet Tokay
Cheese, nuts, raisins and dried dessert fruits	Sweet sherry, big red wines, port, sweet fortified wines	Room Temp.	Port, vintage or blended, Malmsey Madeira. Sweet Oloroso Brown or Cream Sherry. Burgundy, Châteauneuf-du-Pape, Malaga, Marsala, Aleatico
Coffee	Brandy, liqueurs		Your preference

Index

More about Penguins

Penguinews, which appears every month, contains
details of all the new books issued by
Penguins as they are published. From time to time it is
supplemented by *Penguins in Print* – a complete
list of all our available titles.
(There are well over three thousand of these.)

A specimen copy of *Penguinews* will be sent to you free
on request, and you can become a subscriber for the price
of the postage – 4s for a year's issues (including
the complete lists).
Just write to Dept EP, Penguin Books Ltd,
Harmondsworth, Middlesex, enclosing a cheque or postal
order, and your name will be added to the mailing list.

Some other books published by Penguins are
described on the following pages.

Note: *Penguinews* and *Penguins in Print* are not
available in the U.S.A. or Canada.

Italian Food*

Elizabeth David

Exploding once and for all the myth that Italians
live entirely on minestrone, spaghetti and veal escalopes,
this exciting book demonstrates the enormous and
colourful variety of Italy's regional cooking.
Listing well over four hundred dishes, clearly described
and helpfully classified, the author of
Mediterranean Food and *French Country Cooking*
also enumerates the various herbs and spices
required in many of them, sensibly explaining where
they may be bought, and there are useful
chapters on Italian wines and cheeses. The result
is an extremely readable guide to eating out in Italy which
is also a practical text-book for reproducing the best of
Italian food in your own kitchen.

'I do not remember any other cookery book which has so
impressed me' – Margaret Lane in the *New Statesman*

'Certainly the best book we know dealing not
only with the food but with the wines of Italy' –
Wine and Food

'Will delight anyone who has the art of cooking and
good living at heart' – *Guardian*

Also available
French Country Cooking
French Provincial Cooking*
Mediterranean Food
Summer Cooking

*Not for sale in the U.S.A.

Danish Cooking

Nika Standen Hazelton

Nowhere in the world is good food better prepared than in
Denmark, where the practical spirit of modern
Scandinavian cooking blends with the exotic *haute cuisine*
of France's golden age. Danish layer-cakes, cheeses and
pastries are justly famous here, and smorrebrod is now
almost an English word – but few English cooks even
dream of such delicious dishes as Gypsy Cheese Salad
and Veiled Country-Lass Dessert. Here is your
chance to make them, and over three hundred
other intriguing recipes from country-cottage to corden-bleu
standard. The book also includes chapters on Danish
customs and hospitality and the delights of
Danish restaurants.